The Pied Piper of South Shore

The Pied Piper of South Shore

Toys and Tragedy in Chicago

Caryn Lazar Amster

11/04

Caryn Lazar Amster

CMA Publishing
Medinah, Illinois

Caryn Amster is owner and CEO of a marketing, planning, and consulting firm in Chicago. She has more than thirty years of experience in marketing, public relations, and advertising. She is a professional speaker and trainer and former columnist for the Star Newspapers in suburban Chicago. *The Pied Piper of South Shore* is her first book.

CMA Publishing, Medinah, Illinois
© 2005 by Caryn Amster
All rights reserved. Published 2005
First edition
Printed in the United States of America

ISBN: 0-9758928-0-0

The cover illustration and the line drawings in this edition are by Mitchell A. Markovitz and are reproduced by permission.

Library of Congress Control Number: 2004108342

To Mom and Dad,
for everything

Contents

Foreword

MR. LAZAR WAS THE GREATEST. He was Santa all year round. My best friend, Artie Goldberg, and I spent every free minute riding over to Wee Folks on our bikes just to hang out. Most of the time we had no money to spend, but rarely did Mr. and Mrs. Lazar let us leave empty-handed. We'd hang out at the chemistry display just to the right as you walked past the checkout counter. All we wanted to do was make things that would explode. Mr. Lazar would always guide us toward some spectacular (but safe) possibilities.

He had the paddleballs, the Whiffle balls, the Schwinn bikes. He had the best selection of Revell model planes you could ever want, and plenty of good old-fashioned airplane glue. (I want to take this moment to send a special thanks to Mr. Lazar for all that airplane glue.) He had Lionel trains, old-fashioned pink balls to throw against the stoop, and Duncan Yo-Yos. And there was always Silly Putty at the checkout counter.

But most important, Mr. Lazar had Mrs. Lazar. They were a symbol of everything good that a kid wants to see in an adult relationship. They danced through that store with the greatest of ease as they danced through our lives. They made you believe that one day you could find a dancing partner. I'm certain they're still dancing. They had each other and we had them. And we will forever have the memories of a safe and friendly oasis—from home, from school, from anything and everything in the world that a kid had trouble handling.

Mr. Lazar made you feel loved and safe, and he wasn't even related. Maybe that's the best kind of friend: he just loved you for who you were. Oh, Mr. Lazar, we miss you. We want to introduce our kids and our grandkids to you. I bet you're watching them every second. In fact, when they are reading the assembly directions for a new toy, I'm sure you're the one guiding them through it.

Mr. Lazar, you will live in my mind and my heart forever. I am a better man for having known you and the Mrs. Thank you, thank you, thank you for a place to get away and for a place to dream. But most of all, thank you for your humanity and for not making a kid feel like a second-class citizen. You were my friend. What more can you ask?

Mandy Patinkin
New York, November 2003

Preface

I STARTED WRITING THIS BOOK to tell my parents' story. I meant to talk about how they opened a little Chicago toy store called Wee Folks and lived the American dream. I wanted to show the impact they had on a community. At some point, I realized that I wanted to add details about how idyllic our South Shore neighborhood was in the 1940s and 1950s, and to explain how and why 79th Street evolved. Ultimately, I also realized that I needed to tell the story of Dad's murder. Many people had moved from South Shore before Dad was killed in 1970 and they didn't know what had happened to him or to my family. Writing that part of the story was personally difficult, but it gave hundreds of customers the chance to say "Thank you, Mr. and Mrs. Wee Folks." I believe it gives closure to devoted Wee Folks customers, to friends and neighbors, and to me.

My journey started in 1999, when my son's friend gave me a photography book titled *Chicago's South Shore* by Charles Celander. I knew Charles's father, Hugh, the photographer on 79th Street, for many years. I soon discovered, by accident, that the bookstore manager who sold the book to my son's friend was once the little boy I walked to school in South Shore for twenty-five cents a week. Coincidence? Maybe. But over the past five years, dozens of such coincidences solidified my determination to tell my parents' story. Whenever I was unsure about where to find the answers, the answers came. While never a proponent of divine intervention, I soon became a believer. In Yiddish we call that *bashert,* meaning it was fated or predestined. The whole writing experience has been *bashert* for me.

As a first-time author, I knew nothing about publishing. So, once the book was substantially started, I thought I needed to find an agent. I made inquiries and learned that having my book accepted by a publisher wouldn't be easy. It might take a long time and might never happen. It was discouraging. A friend told me about the MegaBook Marketing Seminar in California. We attended together and there I learned about self-publishing. I decided I would publish my book myself. Much later, I also decided to create a companion Web site (www.chicagospiedpiper. com).

When I started writing, I believed I already knew the whole story. I didn't know how much research would be involved to tell the story well. If you look at the bibliography and notes, you'll see the extent to which I read books, articles, and reports—in print and online—just to write what started out as a simple family history. Now that the project is complete, I realize how much I've learned.

To the best of my ability, I have taken care to ensure that all of my work in this book is both accurate and original. If I have inadvertently included errors, or if I have presented the work of others without giving them due credit, I sincerely apologize. They are the honest mistakes of a very green writer.

One more caveat: While this story is true, I have changed some names, dates, and other details throughout the book. I changed the names of innocent people to protect them, particularly witnesses as well as police officers, lawyers, and judges who arrested and tried the killer and who may still be practicing law or in law enforcement. I also changed the names of the killer and his associates so as not to honor or celebrate the criminal and his crime.

Along the way, I encountered many helpful people. I started chatting online and subscribed to Classmates. Through these and other venues I met Mitch Markovitz, a professional fine artist-illustrator who lived in South Shore in the 1950s and 1960s and who was a regular at Wee Folks. When he offered to illustrate the cover and the book, I was flattered. Who better to illustrate my story than Mitch? Even though thirty years had passed since he was last in our store, he could still draw the Wee Folks logo from memory.

I also found hundreds of former Wee Folks customers and employees, children of former 79th Street merchants, and toy suppliers. Every one of them had something good to say about my parents. I was sometimes surprised by their recollections, particularly about how some individuals saved our store, once when it flooded and again when my dad hurt his back and couldn't work. I remembered the incidents, but not as vividly as they did. I learned more about my parents as people, as contributors to the community, and as friends from those who loved them.

Finding Mandy Patinkin, one of those former customers, was a thrill. My first letter to him went unanswered. I found another address and sent a second letter. When he contacted me, he admitted he rarely sees his mail as others open it for him. But my second letter had somehow made it through to him directly. *Bashert?* Mandy told me how years earlier, he had thought of writing a screenplay titled *Wee Folks*, whose main character, my dad, was modeled after George Bailey, the character played by Jimmy Stewart in *It's a Wonderful Life*. Mandy also told me how his passion for Lionel train collecting came from his time spent with Dad. Imagine my parents and their little toy store having such an influence on Mandy's life.

I researched other, now famous people who grew up in South Shore and who were our customers. I wrote to them and some responded, like Muhammad Ali. Then known as Cassius Clay, he was a devoted father. Through his assistant, Ali sent me best wishes on this project. Entertainer Corky Siegal also wrote and supplied a quote for the book.

The source of much of the information contained in this book was my mom. I interviewed her on tape in 1990, nine years before she died. My goal then was to preserve her memories, in her own words, for my children. She loved the experience, and even though there were gaps in her memory, she retold wonderful stories of meeting Dad, starting the store, and serving customers. Our sessions together revealed that Dad's parents were not originally from England as I had always thought, but from Russia. I encourage everyone reading this to preserve their priceless family memories for future generations.

I've written this book for residents of Joliet, Illinois, who can share Mom's fondest memories of the town of her youth as well as of the place where she met and married Dad. I've also written it for lovers of history, especially Chicago history, and for retailers who want to learn how retailing was done "in the old days." For followers of true-crime stories, the book is a chilling account of the real murder of a real neighborhood hero. Antique-toy buffs might learn something from the "Toy Stories" appendix, which details how famous toys of that era came to be. And I've written this book for members of Women's American ORT—the Organization for Rehabilitation through Training—for doing the good work that my mom, a former Women's American ORT president, believed in so much. I honor that organization and Mom with a donation for every copy of this book that I sell.

But I've written this book especially for you South Shore-ites who remember those days and that place with so much fondness. In fact, I had so many inquiries about the old neighborhood from former customers and neighbors that I wrote "Remembering 79th Street," an appendix that includes their recollections and mine about the neighborhood stores we all loved. It amazes me that even today, former South Shore residents hold annual reunions all over the country.

I have so many people to thank for making this book a reality. Thanks to my friend and speaking partner Carol Pietrus, who encouraged me and showed me that there really *are* two women who can think alike. Thanks to friends and fellow authors Sheila Glazov, for her unflagging enthusiasm, for sharing the Iowa Summer Writing Festival experience with me at the University of Iowa, and for so much more; Linda Brakeall, for leading me to the MegaBook Marketing Seminar weekend; and Carol Campbell and Sue Dobbe, who praised and cheered me when I was feeling down. Thanks also to Melanie Stone, who helped me research my father's murder case file and stayed with me while I read all three thousand pages of testimony.

Thanks to everyone at the Schaumburg (Illinois) Township District Library, who helped me with research at night and on weekends, both live and online.

Thanks to Lon Otto, my teacher at the Iowa Summer Writing Festival, who said, "This is an important work," after reading my outline and one poorly done chapter. His words kept me going through the times I needed them most.

Thanks to Michele Hodgson, my editor and book shepherd, who loved the book from the first moment. It was Lon who introduced me to Michele, and she was my rock and my guide through this intricate maze called publishing. She patiently put up with my incessant questions, and I owe some of the richness of the storytelling to her equally incessant questions.

Thanks to Shelley Sapyta at BookMasters, who continued where Michele left off and took the rest of my questions in stride to see me through the publishing and printing process.

Thanks to Mandy Patinkin, whose loving memories of my dad grace the beautiful foreword to this book.

Thanks to Mitch Markovitz, for lovingly designing the cover and interior illustrations, which re-created the store, the street, and the Avalon Theater so that it all looks just as it did when we lived in South Shore.

Thanks to Ozzie Roberts, columnist for the *San Diego Union Tribune,* who interviewed Mom in her eighties, saw the value of her story, and portrayed her in such a thoughtful and wonderful way in his newspaper.

Thanks to Dorothy Mavrich, my mother's good friend (and mine), who helped me research my parents' past in Joliet.

Thanks to my aunt, Carol Hyman, who located some of the old family photos you see in this book.

Thanks to Jack Lazar, Dad's youngest brother, whose inheritance made financing of my book possible.

Thanks to my children for their loving encouragement. One big perk of writing this book has been finding out how proud they are of me. They are also amazed to learn the facts of the lives of their grandparents and great-grandparents.

Thanks (and an extra big hug) to my husband, Bill, for editing, not laughing, and for doing the grunt work, keeping my butt in the seat, and telling me I could succeed at this author thing. It has been a new journey in our relationship that has made us even closer.

Thanks to the hundreds of people who shared with me their stories about my parents and Wee Folks, including members of the Overflow and Stony Island groups and the Classmates Web site. I am still amazed by how much everyone remembered, even after forty years. So many of you were then just children and now are doctors, scientists, writers, professors, housewives and husbands—all great people. Thank you for each and every one of your memories. It was difficult to choose which ones to feature in the book. If space had allowed, I would have included them all. Feel free to continue sharing those memories with me at comments@chicagospiedpiper.com.

Throughout this journey, I discovered how much my parents' little toy store on 79th Street touched the lives of so many people over so many years. Yet Wee Folks also benefited from our relationships with faithful customers and friends, from the boom times of the 1940s and 1950s through the decline—and ultimately the tragedy—of the 1960s and the sociological changes they brought to the world we knew as South Shore. My family experienced both humanity and history from inside our store, from behind the counter and through the front windows.

And so I save my last and deepest thanks for my parents, Belle and Manny Lazar, who not only taught me the value of hard work, but who also created that special and magical place where I first learned my marketing skills, the power of promotion and advertising, and, most important, the right way to treat people.

The Pied Piper of South Shore

Dad and Mom at the 1957 grand opening of Wee Folks on 79th Street in South Shore.

CHAPTER 1

The Day the Laughter Died

Friday, February 6, 1970—2:00 P.M.

MANNY LAZAR EDGED HIS WIDE frame through the back room of his Chicago toy store as he had done thousands of times, his arms laden with merchandise to stock Wee Folks' shelves. He had just finished pricing the toys, placing round white stickers on every box. The sleeves of his green-and-white houndstooth flannel shirt were rolled up to his elbows, revealing muscular, hairy arms. The shirttails hung out of his dark brown baggy pants. His black leather belt with the white metal buckle rode low beneath his middle-aged belly. The heels of his black laced shoes were terminally worn on the outside, with no hope of seeing a repair shop soon. Beads of sweat popped out of his wrinkled forehead as his short, stocky body heaved under the load. His sparse gray hair hung in his eyes. Large, thick, dark-rimmed

3

glasses, essential since his cataract surgery, slid low on his ample nose, giving him the air of a hardworking Santa Claus.

Today, it was the Barbie display's turn to be the center of Manny's attention. He stepped carefully, peeking around the stack of boxed dolls and outfits he carried that was almost as tall as his five-foot, eight-inch frame. He staggered slightly down the main aisle of the store toward the display island to set the boxes down.

"Don't move or I'll shoot," commanded a husky male voice. Guns weren't new to the store or to Manny, who had often demonstrated his fanning prowess with the latest Mattel Fanner 50s and Roy Rogers cap guns for awestruck young cowboys. Manny loved to mosey around like the sheriff of Wee Folks, wearing a holster and packing two pistols.

Manny saw the shooter and instinctively turned to look for cover. A bullet tore into his back, whirling him around to face four more rapid-fire bullets that ripped through his chest and arms. The force blasted him backward against the large display, splattering Barbies and boxes with blood. As he fell, he grabbed for the island, pulling dozens of dolls with him. A dark red pool spread from his chest across the cream-colored vinyl tiles, saturating the hair and clothes of the Barbies that lay next to him. He didn't move.

The transaction that day had started as many did at Wee Folks on 79th Street in Chicago's South Shore neighborhood: with the cheery "ding" of the doorbell announcing a customer. A slim, six-foot-tall black man had entered the toy store, telling Manny's wife, Belle, that he was looking for a doll for a niece's gift. As always, Belle, a petite woman in her late fifties, sat behind the cash-wrap counter, her hair permed and coifed, her pressed pantsuit covered with a teacher's smock with big pockets. The young man was new to the store, so she showed him around the place, making her usual experienced recommendations.

But something didn't feel right to her. The man was neatly dressed and clean-shaven, but he seemed like trouble. Belle wished Manny would hurry up and finish pricing the toys. She went back to the cash-wrap counter to wait as the man selected a Gingerbread doll and placed it next to the cash register. He continued to roam the store, up and down the aisles, past the games section, around the trucks, past the toy guns. He picked out a musical Roly-Poly toy and handed it to her.

Belle was leaning on the counter, waiting for him to choose the paper she would wrap the gifts in, when she saw him pull a pistol from his jacket pocket. By now, he figured she was alone and the store was an easy mark for a robbery. The gunman had no clue that anyone else was in the place until Manny emerged from the back room.

Barely nineteen, the gunman wasn't a regular. He wasn't even a resident of South Shore. He was a high-ranking member of the Blackstone Rangers, Chicago's infamous street gang.

The gunman didn't usually rob, but he needed money, now. Jeff Fort, the leader of the Blackstone Rangers, was in jail on local and federal charges and everyone in the organization was ordered to get bail money for Fort any way they could. The gunman had already robbed two other stores on 79th Street that day. Manny's sudden appearance had startled him so much that he never even asked for money. His first thought was to escape.

The young man panicked, fired five shots, and tried to rush out of the store. Unfamiliar with its layout, he first ran up an aisle that dead-ended at one of the large plate-glass display windows, covered, as usual, with the nose prints of wishful children. Realizing he was trapped and terrified to launch himself through the thick glass, he frantically sought another way out.

Two peach-colored display islands welded together stood between the gunman and the double glass entry doors. The islands stood five feet tall and, being made of steel, could withstand great weight. He attempted to vault over them but lacked the room for a running start. With the superhuman strength of intense fear, he began pulling the welded units apart, the metal slicing through his jacket into the flesh on his arms. The two pieces toppled forward, crashing onto the cash-wrap station. He scrambled over them, merchandise scattering every which way, and rushed out of the store, bleeding but free. In his haste, his watch banged against the display, ejecting a jagged piece of crystal. The tiny glass fragment rolled to a low spot on the floor, stopping to rest under the rubber ball display near the doors.

The happy little ding of the doorbell that usually meant more customers and more sales announced his departure.

A bus driver waiting at the 79th Street and East End Avenue stop about fifty feet from Wee Folks saw the shooter run into the parking lot adjacent to the store. So did other witnesses, who would later tell police he moved like a cat on fire as he jumped into the passenger side of an awaiting black Cadillac with Indiana license plates.

The car sped off. The gunman had escaped. He had also killed Manny Lazar. He had murdered my dad.

Belle, my mom, had hidden under the cash-wrap counter when the shooting started, jabbing at the security buzzer she and Dad had recently installed, "just in case." As she ran to Dad, she slipped on a trail of blood near his body and fell to his side. She cradled him in her arms, crying "Manny, Manny" over and over and telling herself that he would be all right. But he felt so cold. She got up, raced to the back room, and returned with her red plaid Pendleton blanket to warm him while waiting for the police to respond to the store alarm. She didn't know that he was already gone.

Passersby began to gather in front of the store. The bus driver came in to see what was going on and how he could help. Someone called an ambulance.

The security service pulled up within minutes, and realized soon enough that even seconds would have been too late. A young police officer burst into the store. He was new on the beat, but he knew Mom and Dad. Mike O'Rourke wore badge number 61, my dad's age.

When the ambulance arrived, two white-coated paramedics asked Mom to step aside while they tended to Dad's wounds. They hoisted him onto a stretcher and told her to meet them at Jackson Park Hospital, a few minutes' drive away at 76th and Stony Island Avenue.

Mom anxiously watched the ambulance disappear down the street, then looked at her pantsuit and white nurse's oxfords stained with her husband's blood, trying to make sense of something she could not. Within seconds her head snapped up, her heart pounding with a new terror. My son and daughter, her beloved grandchildren, would soon be dropped off at Wee Folks after school so she could watch them until I was off work. She couldn't let them see this grisly scene. She hurriedly dialed my number.

It had been a typical day for me in the research lab at the University of Chicago Hospital. I worked as the sole lab technician for a pediatrician who was looking for ways to save the newborns of diabetic mothers. In those days, many such babies died within twenty-four hours of birth. I had just finished dissecting a rat when the phone rang. My mother, who usually was so calm in emergencies, said in a trembling voice, "Don't have the children delivered to the store today. Come to Jackson Park Hospital, quick! I need you—your father has been shot!"

I started to panic. "Shot? What do you mean he was shot? Where is he? Are you all right?" Questions tumbled out of my mouth like Jack and Jill down the hill.

"There was a robber in the store. He got away. But he shot Daddy!"

I hung up, called my backup sitter to ask her to pick up Kim and Ian and keep them at her house, grabbed my coat, and fled down the hallway to the elevator. Once outside, I ran to the parking lot, my thin lab coat flapping in the cold breeze under the hem of my winter parka. I jumped into my old green Plymouth sedan, my fingers shaking as I put the key in the ignition. I sped down 59th Street to Lake Shore Drive toward the hospital, a long fifteen minutes away. But as I turned onto the drive, I realized I was heading toward home, not toward Jackson Park.

It was the middle of the afternoon, but traffic on the drive was heavy. *Hurry up, hurry up!* My heart pounded like thunder. What if Dad needed blood? I knew he was my type from a previous trip to the emergency room, when he had been burned in a furnace explosion at the store. What if he had been seriously hurt? What if he needed to be hospitalized for a long time? Who would help Mom in the store? Her life had been tied to his since the day they met more than thirty years ago. They had worked together every day since opening Wee Folks back in the summer of 1945.

As I turned and headed back west, I felt like a skydiver who had pulled the ripcord on a chute that wouldn't open. I was free-falling, my mind buffeted by a windstorm of unimaginable thoughts.

What about Kim and Ian? The man they called "Toy Toy" was the only father figure they knew. My husband had abandoned us when Kim was three and I was seven months pregnant with Ian. Dad was the only person who could show my three-year-old son how to grow up to be a good man. Who would light up Ian's face by giving him the daily Matchbox car when he came to the store every afternoon? How would Kim react? At six, she was the apple of Grandpa's eye.

I looked at my watch and realized in horror that in just one hour, my children would have been in the store after school to play until I finished work. I couldn't believe my mother's presence of mind. Her first concern in a moment of fear and confusion was the safety of her grandchildren.

Once I reached Stony Island I turned south toward Jackson Park Hospital. In that moment I knew that, even though I loved Mom, I had always been closer to Dad. This was strange, because I had often felt the sting of his discipline during my wild teenage years. But he was still the one I turned to in emergencies. He was the one who had picked me up from my bathroom floor and taken me to the hospital when I hemorrhaged after Ian's birth. With no husband around to help me, I counted on Dad as the one who fixed everything.

As I neared the hospital, an ambulance sped by, sirens blaring. How had Dad gotten to the hospital? A wave of nausea washed over me as the thought finally hit me: Dad could die. It was cold outside, but suddenly I felt sweaty. My moist hands clenched the steering wheel as I remembered childhood friends whose fathers, police officers and firefighters, had died in the line of duty. Never, during all the time I was growing up, did I imagine that one of my parents would be shot.

My younger sister, Marta, was already in the hospital's waiting room with Mom, crying, when I burst through the wide emergency room doors. Mom had been crying too. But as I rushed past other waiting families, in all stages of misery, I saw Mom's face become taut and her jaw set. She seemed determined to get through this unthinkable experience. I sat and put my arm around her shoulder. I didn't know what she had been told by the doctors and I was afraid to ask. Before long, Dr. Neil Strong, the emergency-room physician, came out of a room at the end of the hall.

"I'm so sorry," Dr. Strong said, his face grim. "We tried our best, but we couldn't save your husband. He was dead when he arrived. I'm so sorry. I know how much everyone loved Manny." I remember thinking at the time that he looked familiar. Had he been one of our customers?

We barely had time to comprehend what he said before two police officers appeared, asking for someone to officially identify the body. I volunteered, and left Mom and Marta in the waiting room. The officers led me down a corridor, past another room where even more people waited in dread, to the end of the hallway.

As a lab technician, I should have been used to this environment. I thought I was immune to the smell of death. But as I stepped into the room where my father lay, the stench of formaldehyde made my stomach lurch.

The aura of death filled that room like fog. A shelf filled with glass jars containing organs of previously autopsied occupants lined one of the sterile white walls. Trays of bloody surgical tools awaiting cleanup and sterilization sat along another wall. And there, on a stainless steel slab atop a rolling cart in the middle of the room, covered by a white sheet up to his chest, lay my father.

Feeling queasy, I moved slowly to the center of the room and forced my eyes down to look at Daddy. He looked tired. He always looked tired. But his face had the same determined expression he always had. I could see several holes in his chest and arms. Five bloody bullets lay nestled in a towel on a small metal tray on a rolling table next to the slab.

Two crime lab technicians stood to one side of the room, completing their report. They fingered the dry bloodstains splattered over Dad's green-and-white flannel shirt, examining the gunshot residue around each bullet hole. I later learned that the residue meant that he had been shot at close range. They had already identified the type of weapon the killer had used and the caliber of bullets. These items and more would later become exhibits at the trial.

I turned to the doctor in green scrubs standing next to me and said, in a small voice that seemed to flow out of a long, dark tunnel, "Yes, that's Manny Lazar—that's my dad." Somewhere down the hall I heard the cry of a newborn baby, probably an emergency-room delivery. Only much later did the old saying dawn on me that as one life ends another begins.

Two hours later, after Mom signed endless forms for the hospital, the police, and the funeral home, we left the emergency room. Someone guided us toward a police car, where two detectives waited to take Mom, Marta, and me back to Wee Folks, or what would thereafter be known as "the scene of the crime." I sat in the back seat, lost in my own thoughts. My mom and sister got in. Nobody said anything. All I could think about was Mom having to return to the store and close out the register tonight as she had done every night for the past twenty-five years. But this time she wouldn't make change at the bank to put in the till the next morning. This time she wouldn't prepare for another day of working side by side with her husband. Her life would never be the same. My life would never be the same.

I grieved in silence for my dad, who never knew what hit him. He would never return to the suburban house in Glenwood he and Mom had built and moved into a few months ago. Just a few weeks ago, he had signed a lease that would have moved Wee Folks from South Shore's increasingly dangerous neighborhood into a shopping center around the corner from the new house.

I grieved for my mom, who was forced to hear the gunshots that ended Dad's life while she hid helplessly beneath the counter. For the next thirty years, she would relive that day over and over in her mind and wonder how she could have changed things.

I grieved for myself and wondered how I could explain to my children that "Toy Toy" was gone and wasn't coming back.

I didn't want Mom to see me cry and so I held back my tears. It would be a year before I let them fall.

Friday, February 6—4:00 P.M.

It was two hours after the shooting and word was out on the street about Dad. A group of youngsters gathered in front of the store for any news of "Mr. Wee Folks." Their breath hung like icicles in the wintry air.

The sun was setting as Mom, my sister, and I arrived at the store in the detectives' squad car. The two men probably never knew my dad, but they seemed sympathetic. As we stepped out of the car, they patted Mom on the shoulder and said how sorry they were. She still clutched the Pendleton blanket she had used to cover Dad. His blood had already become part of the deep red plaid pattern. The wind whipped the fringe on the blanket, reminding me of the fringed prayer shawl, the *tallis,* which Jews use at temple, especially when saying prayers for the dead. I thought of Dad's tallis laying in a satiny case in his bureau drawer.

I didn't feel the cold. All I could think about was that my parents, who had such great plans for their later years, would never grow old together.

The kids outside the store became respectfully quiet as we walked past them. They wanted to comfort Mom, to tell her that everything would be all right, but they didn't have the words. No one did. They could only watch through the display windows as "Mrs. Wee Folks" walked down the aisle to where the shooting had taken place, blood-covered Barbies still strewn across the floor.

As I entered the store, I smelled a strange odor, like spent fireworks at the end of a Fourth of July celebration. Four crime lab investigators had arrived to fingerprint everything. Balls, trikes, trucks—nothing escaped their dusting powder as they scoured the store for the killer's fingerprints. They made their way up the book aisle, down past the games, around the Mother Goose puppets, behind the toy guns. Once in a while, one would comment to the other, "Hey, look at this." Most of the time it wasn't a clue he drew attention to but a toy his child might like for Christmas. The investigators covered every inch of the store, yet they found only one partially identifiable print.

As late afternoon darkened into evening, the neon Wee Folks sign blinked on and off. I stood at the front of the store, waiting for the lab people to finish packing up their gear. Mom busied herself by cleaning out the register while my sister wandered through the store. Looking down, I noticed the glint of a prism reflecting off the fluorescent lights overhead. The jagged piece of crystal that had broken free from the gunman's watch poked out of its hiding place under the ball rack. I called it to the attention of the detectives, who placed it in an evidence bag. The crystal would later prove to be valuable evidence and force me to testify at the killer's trial, even though I had not witnessed my father's murder.

Three hours after the shooting, a large crowd of children and adults still congregated outside the store, talking quietly about the death of Mr. Wee Folks, tears streaming down their cold cheeks. I guessed that most of the kids had never known anyone who died, let alone anyone who was murdered. Dad had been like a grandfather to them. Their sad voices resounded against the glass storefront like tender eulogies in the night.

"I'll bet Mrs. Wee Folks is going to close the store now for sure."

"We won't have no toy store 'round here no more."

"If a guy didn't have 'nough money to pay for the thing he wanted, sometimes Mr. Wee Folks would give it to him anyway. He was the kind of man that would let a boy do some chores around the store and give him a cup of cocoa as well as pay."

A thirteen-year-old black kid from the neighborhood stood watching it all. "I thought Mr. Wee Folks just fell down at first and knocked down all those Barbie dolls," he said to no one in particular. "But then I saw Mrs. Wee Folks and the funny look in her eyes. Her mouth was open like she was screamin' or somethin' but the door was closed so I couldn't hear nothin'. When I looked at Mr. Wee Folks again, his eyes were closed. But I knew he wasn't sleepin'. Right then I knew'd he was dead."

A burly, well-dressed black man tried to step inside the door of the store. "You know, ma'am," he called out to Mom, who was talking with the police, "he was one of the best sons of bitches on the street. Every time I'd bring my kids here he would give them a toy. I'd say to him that he shouldn't do that, but he'd say, 'Kids should have toys.' Why would anyone do such a thing to Mr. Lazar?"

Watching Mrs. Wee Folks tell the story over and over to newsmen arriving on the scene, a boy in the crowd turned to one of them and said, "You gotta promise me not to use my name in your paper. If you do, that man's gonna come and kill me for sure."

In the days that followed, we were deluged with comforting sentiments from all over Chicagoland. A young black customer later told me, "My life was never the same after that day. I had lost a good friend, and my whole view of innocence had been shattered. I remember I tried to say something to your mother and I'll never forget the look in her eyes. . . . Nothing was ever the same."

Another former customer touched my heart when she wrote, "In some small way I hope I can give back a little something for all your parents gave to the children of South Shore. The day 'Mr. Wee Folks' was shot was, for many of us, the day that South Shore died."

Tuesday, February 10—10:00 A.M.

It was twenty-eight degrees and starting to snow when our family led a procession of black limousines to Westlawn Cemetery on Montrose Avenue. Hundreds of mature trees lined the paths at Westlawn, one of the largest Jewish cemeteries in Chicago. Finding the gravesite my parents had long ago reserved for themselves wasn't easy. Thousands of other souls were buried here, and their graves were marked by an intricate system of numbers and letters. I knew the site was close to the graves of the rest of Dad's family, including several of his siblings.

Snowflakes hit my cold face as I looked at the wooden grave marker that simply read "Emanuel Lazar." I knew we would be back in a year, as Jewish tradition dictates, to dedicate the official headstone. But I also remember thinking that the hole in the ground was too small for this man who had been such a giant in the eyes of his community.

This was not the end foreseen by my parents in 1945 when they opened their first Wee Folks store, just a small toy shop on 79th Street and Constance Avenue in Chicago's South Shore neighborhood. This was not the future they had envisioned in 1957, when they moved into an abandoned music store farther west on 79th Street, across from the ornate Avalon Theater, transforming Wee Folks into Chicago's first self-service toy store.

Under my parents' expert supervision, Wee Folks had become a celebration of everything that was good about our South Shore neighborhood and postwar America: honesty, sincerity, a willingness to work hard, and a love of all people, regardless of race or religion. Through the years, they watched as the melting pot passing through the store's portals became doctors, lawyers, teachers, and just plain good citizens.

In the 1940s and 1950s, the neighborhood had been mostly Irish Catholic and Jewish. As years passed, other ethnic groups moved in. By the mid-1960s, the area had turned predominantly black. Who could have predicted how dramatically the racial mix would change or how fast terror fueled by bias and greed would escalate? Wee Folks stood like a beacon for twenty-five years, through decades of change: retailing highs and lows, a life-threatening fire, a flood that almost ruined the business, a historic blizzard, and the fury of the 1960s, when white and black residents clashed. My parents saw South Shore through a quarter-century of evolution, revolution, and, finally, dissolution.

In the year following the murder, blacks and whites alike left South Shore. Merchants closed their businesses and moved away. Wee Folks closed too. The playroom at the back of the store, a haven where so many children had worked on craft projects or read books while their mothers shopped, fell silent. The store stood empty, stripped bare of its fixtures, even the two display islands so violently torn apart by the assailant. The store was left as it had begun: abandoned.

On February 6, 1970, Clayton Moore, the Lone Ranger, opened his first fast-food franchise in Chicago. Abbie Hoffman and the Chicago Seven went on trial for inciting riots at the 1968

Democratic Convention. The first U.S. Cabinet meeting outside the White House took place at Chicago's Field Museum.

And on Friday, February 6, 1970, Thomas Gunn murdered my father, Manny Lazar, the Pied Piper of South Shore. The era of Wee Folks, one of the city's most beloved stores, ended with a series of gunshots. It was the day the laughter in South Shore died.

Ironically, it was gunfire in the distant past that had brought my father's family to this place in time. The shooting of Jews in czarist Russia had forced both my mother's and father's parents to leave their homeland for a more peaceful place in which to raise their children. My father's family first settled in England while my mother's came directly to America, a land where hard work would bring good fortune.

Mom and Dad courting in Joliet, July 1936.

CHAPTER 2

The Folks behind Wee Folks

Russia, 1800s

DURING THE NINETEENTH CENTURY, the world's Jewish population increased fourfold, from two-and-a-half million to more than ten million. In countries where they enjoyed full equality, Jews were quickly integrated into society, adopting the language and culture of their new home. Where only partial freedoms were granted, the process took longer. By the end of the 1800s, more than four million Jews lived in Russia.

In the 1860s and 1870s, Czar Alexander II began to change the way Russians lived. He instituted reforms providing greater freedoms, among which was the formation of labor organizations. But people became less and less willing to be limited by the czar's power.

In 1880, Alexander kept Jews from leaving the "Pale of Settlement" for the interior of Russia. In 1791, the Pale had been created after Russian empress Catherine the Great restricted Jewish residence to either the territories annexed from Poland along the western border or the territories taken from the Turks along the shores of the Black Sea. Later, when other annexed territories were added to the Pale, Jews were permitted to settle there. Jews were not allowed to settle outside urban districts encompassed by the Pale. They continued to be barred from the old Russia.

Certain labor organizations began to plot the czar's murder as a way to obtain even more rights for themselves. A bomb thrown at the czar in St. Petersburg killed him in 1881. As many labor organization members were Jews, they were blamed for his death. Alexander's son and successor, Czar Alexander III, gave the order to exterminate the Jews. In his eyes, Russian Jews were a problem that had to be solved, either by enforced assimilation or expulsion.

Russian Jews didn't fit into the new government's plan to merge all of its ethnic groups into a single nationality, speaking one language and practicing one religion. Enforced assimilation became difficult because the Jews resisted joining a society that would accept them only if they renounced their language and faith. They also preferred their traditional village existence to living in overcrowded cities. Village life ensured greater independence from the government, which now wanted to regain the economic power it had delegated to the Jews.

The Jewish economy had its flaws like any other, with many members living in poverty. Rubles were scarce and Jewish peasants didn't buy anything they could make themselves. What they did acquire, they acquired through trading. Unemployment was a particular problem, since new legislation in the 1880s prevented Jews from working in certain occupations.

Those who were employed were involved in commerce, crafts, day labor, domestic work, and agriculture. Others joined the military service. Jewish artisans—cabinetmakers, butchers, dressmakers, bookbinders, tailors—abounded in small Russian towns, but these small-time enterprises yielded little income. Many artisans worked long, hard hours, but felt demoralized when they still didn't earn enough to properly clothe, feed, and shelter their families.

Jews were seen as outsiders who prospered while native Russians went hungry. Deep resentment between the two groups forced the government to adopt harsh restrictions against Jews. They were strangled by taxes on the staples of Jewish life. There were double taxes on kosher meat, first on the animal and then on the meat itself. There were taxes on the candles Jews used in worship and on wearing the yarmulke (skullcap). Laws prohibited where Jews could live. A Jew couldn't hold office unless he renounced his religion. Few did. Only 10 percent of university students in Russia were allowed to be Jews. The government felt that enlightened Jews were a threat.

Emanuel Lazar—Kovno, 1880

In *Year of Crisis, Year of Hope,* Stephen Berk writes:

> In the 1860s, studies in the province of Kovno revealed that it was common for several Jewish families to occupy a single room. As time passed, their lives worsened. Ninety percent of Jews were found to be living from hand to mouth in the worst of hygienic situations. Russia was a backward country in the nineteenth century and it suffered one economic downturn after another. It was especially severe between 1873 and 1880. The emancipation of Russian serfs during this period caused the movement of peasants away from the countryside and into the villages where they were able to compete with Jewish artisans for business. Also at this time, the construction of railroads hurt Jewish haulers. New textile and shoe factories were built, some even owned by Jews, and were fierce competitors with Jewish artisans.

This was the atmosphere into which my father's parents settled. The families of Anna Berman and Morris Isaac Lazarus had moved to the small town of Kovno, 550 miles southwest of

Dad's mother, Anna Berman
Lazar, in Chicago, ca. 1950s.

St. Petersburg, in 1880. In 1863, Kovno's population was 24,000. By 1903 it had grown to 74,000, with nearly one-half being Jews.

Anna Berman and Morris Lazarus married in May 1895. Petite and feisty Anna was nineteen; big and muscular Morris was twenty-one. Morris, a carpenter, earned only seventy cents a day, and his ten-to-twelve-hour workday was backbreaking. It seemed to him that he was always working. He longed to use his skills as a cabinetmaker.

By 1900, Jews began leaving Russia, forced to flee economic hard times and ethnic cleansing by the Russian empire. While not much is known about how they left, Anna and Morris immigrated to England in July 1900. They settled in Manchester, about twenty-five miles east of Liverpool and 150 miles north of London. At that time Manchester was more progressive and open than Kovno. Discrimination by the government was not yet an issue and opportunities for employment were better, although not ideal. Morris found work as a carpenter.

Throughout the nineteenth century, German Jewish business-people made up the primary flow of Jews into England. In 1880, English Jews numbered 60,000. But by 1914, the influx of immigrants caused the country's Jewish population to swell to more than 100,000. As England was primarily a Christian country, the rapidly growing presence of Jews strained the community's goodwill. It led to the Restriction of Immigration Act in 1905. Morris and Anna Lazarus had arrived just in time.

A gulf of respectability separated the rich and poor, and the manual worker became stuck in an inflexible class system. Upper-class English families typically had two or three children; working-class families had four or five. The Orthodox Jewish Lazarus family had ten children, although two did not live past infancy. Given the 15 percent infant mortality rate among the families of manual workers, this was not surprising. Morris and Anna's first child, Barney, was born about 1900. Their last two children, Jack and Ethel—twins—were born in 1914. In between there was Max, Harry, Alice, Phil, and Emanuel—"Manny," my dad, who was born September 9, 1909.

As a journeyman cabinetmaker, Morris earned about forty-six shillings a week. Like most working-class families, the Lazaruses spent half on food—thirty pounds of bread and flour, fifteen pounds of potatoes, nine pounds of meat, two pounds of butter, five pounds of sugar, a dozen eggs, nine pints of milk, and a half-pound of tea. They rarely bought fruit, vegetables, or fish. Housing costs like rent, heat, and lighting consumed another eight shillings, leaving only fifteen shillings for clothing, repairs, beer, and tobacco. Little, if anything, was spent on outings and family amusements. The least unexpected expense would be enough to tip them over the poverty line.

By 1911, the labor force of craftsmen, factory hands, laborers, domestic servants, and transportation workers throughout England numbered fifteen million. The rich grew richer and the poor just stagnated. Hundreds of thousands of people were condemned to underemployment and poverty. It wasn't that they were lazy. They were victims caught within a poorly functioning social system that prevented workers from regular employment or a decent wage.

By 1915, a burst of emigration resulted in more than two-and-a-half million people leaving Great Britain, mostly for America. Seeking religious freedom and dreaming of a more prosperous life in an industrialized nation, Anna and Morris Lazarus decided to come to the United States early in 1917. It meant leaving friends and family and home for a place they knew only from word of mouth, but they had hopes that life in America would be worth the sacrifice. They spent most of their meager savings on tickets for their family from Southampton to New York. Second-class tickets, which cost $50 per adult and $25 per child—and which provided exemption from departure and landing scrutiny—were too expensive. Their only affordable choice was to travel third class, or steerage, at $25 per person.

Early on the day of departure, the Lazarus family stowed their packed trunks, boxes, and baskets on a train and rode from Manchester to the Port of Southampton. They were required to arrive early to allow time to have their baggage fumigated, take an antiseptic bath, and be examined by the steamship's doctor. Many an immigrant's hopes were dashed when he or she was deemed too unhealthy to travel for two weeks in cramped quarters below decks.

Anna, Morris, and their eight children walked the long distance from the station to the ship, carrying everything they owned onto a 10,000-ton steamer called the *City of New York*. Built in Scotland in 1888, the ship had an official capacity of 1,740 passengers—540 in first class, 200 in second class, and 1,000 in third class. Yet more than 2,000 packed into the ship. The steamer's manifest crudely stated the ethnicity of each Lazarus family member as "Hebrew" instead of their town of origin, which was the way non-Jewish passengers were listed.

As it crossed the Atlantic, the *City of New York* was not unlike a floating town, partitioned into haves and have-nots. Third-class quarters were called "steerage" because they were on the lower decks where the steering mechanism of sailing ships had once been housed. Here, in long, narrow, noisy compartments divided into separate dormitories for single men, single women, and families, the Lazaruses stayed. They slept on three-tiered, metal-framed bunks that, by the end of their journey, were rank with the smells of spoiled food, seasickness, and unwashed bodies. Lice were rampant. Privacy was non-existent and toilet facilities woefully inadequate. Meals consisted of potatoes, soup, eggs, fish, stringy meat, and whatever foods people had managed to carry with them from home. Unlike other ships that made the crossing, this one provided no kosher food.

After two long weeks, the *City of New York* approached the Port of New York. As he peered through the ship's rail, eight-year-old Manny Lazarus caught sight of Lady Liberty. Who, he wondered, was this? Was it a statue of some famous military leader? Not until much later did my father realize that a New York Jewish woman of privilege, one with the same name as his family, had written a poem about the Statue of Liberty in 1883. "The New Colossus" by Emma Lazarus had been engraved on a plaque at the base of the great lady as if to welcome this newest Lazarus family to their new world:

> Give me your tired, your poor,
> Your huddled masses yearning to breathe free,
> The wretched refuse of your teeming shore.
> Send these, the homeless, tempest-tossed to me,
> I lift my lamp beside the golden door!

It was an early spring day when Dad stepped from the ship onto the noisy, crowded Hudson River pier in his long-sleeved wool shirt, tweed knickers, and long wool socks. The rest of his belongings were crammed inside a little bag he carried in one hand. Thousands of other passengers from other ships disembarked in the same area, all to be hustled by ferryboat to Ellis Island.

Between 1880 and 1930, more than twenty-seven million immigrants entered the United States. Roughly twenty million came through Ellis Island. During its peak years from 1892 to 1924, Ellis Island processed thousands of immigrants daily.

After waiting for hours on the ferry, the Lazarus family joined thousands of others who slowly made their way into line on shore. Three abreast, they climbed the steep stairs of the brick and limestone building to a cavernous Registry Room that reverberated with voices speaking many languages. Trained watchers scanned the line, looking for signs of physical or mental impairment or disease. Someone asked Dad his name, just to make sure he was able to talk.

The name of each person on the ship's manifest had to be found and transferred to the inspector's record book. In a moment of confusion or power, the inspector changed our family name from Lazarus to Lazar. Dad always said of the experience, "When we came to America, they made us drop the 'US.'" Tags pinned to their clothes listed their ship, manifest page, and line number.

Once identified, they joined an endless stream of immigrants awaiting America's permission to live and work in this new land. The bureaucratic indignities they suffered began with immigration officials and public health doctors. The newly named Lazar family was forced to endure physical and psychological examinations. Literacy tests and interrogations as to their political views increased their rising apprehension. They waited in more lines to speak with the legal inspector, who asked a dizzying series of questions, the answers to which were already contained in the manifest. One determination he had to make was whether a family should be on welfare. He accomplished this by simply looking at them.

Despite all the humiliations, the Lazar family felt lucky to have made the trip. Immigration would slow dramatically after April of that year, when America joined the fight against Germany in World War I, and Ellis Island went from being an immigration gateway to a detention center.

Chicago, Illinois—1917

Morris Lazar traveled to Chicago with his family to live with relatives. He found work as a furniture-maker, handcrafting beautiful coffee tables, end tables, and cabinets, but money was tight. The Lazar children started working as soon as they were able, including my dad, who took any job a youngster his age could get and scrounged the streets and alleys for the saleable discards of others. The family needed all of the children's wages, so Dad and some of his older siblings quit high school so they could work even more hours.

Barney married. Max and his wife, Raye, had four children: Morrie, Allan, Betty, and Sara Lee. Alice and her husband, Jack, had two children, Lawrence and Rhoda. Harry married Milly, an English girl, and they had two children, Barbara and Seymour. Harry worked for the same Chicago women's foundations manufacturing company for more than forty years. Brothers Phil and Jack never married. After suffering injuries in World War II Phil spent his retired life reading and adding to his extensive stamp collection. After serving in the Navy Seabees during the war, Jack became an engineering consultant for Lindbergh Aircraft, where he spent his entire career. He traveled all over the world. His twin sister, Ethel, married Sidney Sharpe and had Marcia, a child who died in infancy, and Karen and Mark.

In 1924, when he was fifteen, Dad began working in the stockroom at the Davis Company Department Store on State and Van Buren Streets in downtown Chicago. On a visit to the store, a buyer for Chicago's Pullman Couch Company witnessed Dad's hardworking style and told his boss, Lawrence Schnadig, "If you want a guy who will last you a lifetime, go to the Davis Company store and get this Lazar kid." Schnadig himself went to the store and talked with Dad. He liked what he saw, and Dad hired on at Pullman in the early 1930s, making living room furniture. As the story goes, the company's two founders, Jacob Schnadig and Julius Kramer, were German Jews who, when they came to America, kept hearing the name of Pullman Coach, the railroad car manufacturer. So in 1909, when they went into the furniture business, they named their company Pullman Couch.

Kiev, Russia—April 1881

Near the close of the nineteenth century, Kiev was a good place to live if you had money and a trade—and weren't Jewish.

Thirty hours by train from Moscow on the banks of the Dnepr River, this Ukrainian/Russian city was a major water and rail transportation center. Its rolling green hills were rapidly being replaced by a haphazard system of urban growth, with houses set close to the street.

But for Jews, who lived as best they could under the tyranny of the czars, Kiev offered a tenuous existence. The city was infamous for its lack of sanitation. During those germ-ridden times, Jews typically lived in low-lying areas where cholera epidemics often got their start. At the outskirts of town people dumped excrement, garbage, and junk, creating an unbearable stench. There, stray dogs foraged for food and children played, hoping to find a lost kopeck. Soapy water from public bathhouses ended up in the street; in springtime the baths used foul-smelling river water. Newspapers urged residents to boil their water, bathe often, and disinfect their clothing, but it was easier said than done.

Water contaminated by human waste was the primary source of cholera, smallpox, scarlet fever, and diphtheria. Some months, the number of deaths in Kiev exceeded the number of births, and children under five were usually the victims. There was only one physician for every 700 residents.

Rent was often 30 percent of a person's wages. One small, dank room often housed four or five people. Beggars roamed the streets, joined by gypsies and charlatans who pickpocketed at the crowded Jewish bazaars on Sunday afternoons. In the bazaars, unclaimed railroad freight was sold in a flea-market-like setting. Since many Russian Jews could not read or write, merchants in the bazaars used pictures on signs to advertise their offerings.

More than 4,000 permanent stalls operated in Kiev's nine major bazaars. Rows of handmade carts run by hundreds of barefoot peddlers sold anything they could without fear of paying taxes. Some goods were contraband, some were handmade, and some were inexpensive homegrown food. Wandering minstrels and puppeteers entertained for a kopeck or two. Professional matchmakers, looking to make a *shidach,* combed the bazaar for likely prospects. Ruffians raced down the narrow aisles, sometimes knocking over strolling shoppers. Horse-drawn cabs and electric trains clattered along crowded cobble-stone streets. Residents dreaded these noisy wonders and lived in fear of the occasional runaway on the steep hills. New electric streetlights twinkled unreliably on and off.

Gentiles in Kiev were uneasy with the Jews, who often spoke Yiddish, not Russian. Many Jews were merchants and land-owners. Fed up with the inaccuracy of Kiev's postal system, Jews had started their own mail service, which quickly became known for its efficiency. But the authorities found it threatening and closed it.

As throughout Russia in general, much hostility was building toward the Jews in Kiev. Any Jew who failed to comply with Czar Alexander III's edict—assimilate or be expelled—would be punished. His 1881 pogrom—his organized effort to perse-cute and massacre Jews—included nightly roundups of "illegal" Jews, who then were banished or killed. A Jew living in Kiev did so at the whim of city officials. Jews were forced to hang crosses and other Catholic icons on their doors and windows to protect their true identities. In *Year of Crisis, Year of Hope,* Stephen Berk vividly describes the pogrom of April 1881 in Kiev:

At twelve o'clock noon, the air echoed with wild shouts, whis-tles, jeering, hooting, and laughing. An enormous crowd of young barefoot boys, artisans and laborers was marching. The entire street was jammed with the barefoot brigade. The de-struction of Jewish houses began. Windowpanes and doors began to fly about and shortly thereafter the mob, having gained access to the houses and stores, began to throw upon the streets absolutely everything that came into their hands. The sounds of broken windowpanes, the crying, shouting, and despair on one hand, and the terrible yelling and jeering on the other, completed the picture. The mob threw itself upon the Jewish synagogue, which, despite its strong bars, locks and shutters, was wrecked in a moment. One should have seen the fury with which the riff-raff fell upon the many Torah scrolls. The scrolls were torn to shreds, trampled in the dirt, and destroyed with incredible passion. The streets were soon crammed with the trophies of destruction. Everywhere fragments of dishes, furniture, household utensils, and other articles were scattered about.

Acts of violence against Jews were common during this time. Jewish children were beaten or made the butt of cruel jokes and verbal abuse by anti-Semitic teachers. Every week the Russian Jewish press reported cases of murdered families and raped women.

On January 9, 1905—Bloody Sunday—participants in a peaceful demonstration of St. Petersburg workers were brutally gunned down by order of the czar. Mass political strikes and demonstrations swept over Russia under the slogan of "Down with Autocracy," marking the start of the revolution of 1905–1907. From that day through 1917, controlling the size of the Jewish community was the main preoccupation of Kiev city officials.

During the insurrection of 1905, hatred of the Jews ran deep. The Kiev city council raised taxes on stalls in the Jewish bazaar. Inflated food prices resulted in even more starving Jews. Butchers in blood-stained aprons, cleavers in hand, ran down the street chasing Jewish women who held children in their arms. Nobody defended the Jews, not even the police, whose salaries benefited from the heavy tax imposed on kosher products. Police even pointed out Jewish-owned shops to prospective plunderers and often stole more from them than civilians did.

Belle Rosen

During this time, my great-grandparents William and Fanny Decikovici were trying to survive in Kiev. William managed a match factory while Fanny stayed home with their fifteen children, including the three daughters of Fanny's dear friend who had died. William and Fanny adopted the girls, whom they raised and married off as if their own.

Like other Jews, William and Fanny tried not to call attention to themselves and their family, especially during social activities. They ate together in their home, talking over steaming bowls of borscht and homemade cheese dumplings. After dinner they sang while the girls embroidered shirts for their favorite young men. A red light in their window indicated it was a safe time for friends to visit.

Non-Jewish young people, on the other hand, could freely stroll the streets, eyeing members of the opposite sex, listening to street minstrels, or ice-skating while trying to avoid the peddlers, gypsies, and thugs.

In 1905, the czar refused Jewish children an education. Some Jews who ran tearooms and reading rooms held free evening classes in back rooms. Half of the students were young women. Rabbis put their school-aged sons and daughters under sacks of potatoes in horse-drawn wagons and drove them to the closest yeshiva, where students read the Talmud along with their other studies. A Russian Orthodox priest and friend of William's managed to get some of the Decikovici children into a Russian Orthodox school, where each wore a Christian cross to protect their Jewish identity. Among these fortunate children was Celia, my grandmother.

Even as a child, Celia had Russian features: a chiseled nose, delicate lips, and clear, white skin. She grew into a high-spirited youngster whose idea of fun was diving under the logs floating on the Dnepr River with her friends. One day, one of her friends drowned under the sea of timber and Celia never played the game again. When Celia had typhoid fever and lost all her hair, the other village children teased her mercilessly. So Fanny and William sent her to live with Fanny's parents in a nearby town until her hair grew back.

Celia's impulsiveness ultimately led to her escape to America after being sentenced to expulsion to Siberia. Her journey was precipitated by the pogrom on October 18, 1905, which resulted in a bloody confrontation in front of Kiev's city hall. More than 100 bodies lay on the ground. The attacks against Jews and their property lasted three days. Jews were accused of toppling the monument to the czar, sacking the local monastery, and tying portraits of the czar to the tails of dogs and cats, which were then let loose to run through the town. The czar's troops fired on a crowd listening to speeches. Eighteen hundred homes and shops were plundered, leaving 300 injured and 3,000 without a place to live or work. Frightened Jews, whose homes were but a few blocks away from the rampage, huddled together in hotels to plan a defense attack. But it was too late. Police and right-wing elements had armed the city's hooligans, young boys often egged on by elders whose contempt of Jews ran deep. The arrest of suspected Jewish militants was imminent.

More than 8,000 Jews were arrested for petty crimes in 1905. Roundups and expulsion of Jews suspected of subversive operations against the czar were conducted nightly. The "killers of Christ," as they were called, were targeted as exploiters of peasants. Acts of violence were committed against Jewish bread peddlers, chicken sellers, and shopkeepers. Vodka-filled hoodlums preyed on the weak, the old, and the poor.

The revolution in Kiev, led by the Society for the Dissemination of Enlightenment, published 3,000 leaflets urging a general strike at the Southern Russian Machine Works. The Jewish organization stood for democratization of Russian and Jewish life and for the use of Yiddish rather than Russian or Hebrew as their main language.

In February 1907, Celia's younger brother, Morris, was caught carrying subversive literature that criticized the czar. Russian soldiers told William and Fanny that they had one day to prepare to send their sixteen-year-old son to Siberia. The soldiers promised to return the next day to start young Morris on his long journey. Celia stepped forward, claiming that the literature belonged to her. Morris was absolved, and Celia was banished. Because she was a girl, however, she was given thirty days to prepare for the same Siberian trip. With the help of William's friend, the Russian Orthodox priest, she was smuggled out of Russia on a false passport. Later that week, seventeen-year-old Celia Decikovici was on a ship bound for America.

Celia's true love, twenty-year-old Max Rosen, had preceded her to America from Kiev to set up his contracting business. Max was a cultured young man, a musician and a writer of poetry. Word came to him to meet Celia at the dock in New York, but plans went awry and she wound up in Philadelphia. Not knowing a word of English, she was confused and terrified. She entered the lobby of a hotel for sanctuary. A large, black porter came her way to inquire how he might assist her. Celia, who had never seen a black person, dropped her luggage and cried out in Russian, "Please, sir, don't hurt me!"

Max at last tracked Celia down through a network of Russian immigrants, and weeks later they were reunited. They returned to New York, where they joined the thousands of other European and Russian immigrants searching for jobs and a decent place to live. Max and Celia were married in the spring of 1907 and moved into one of the better tenements on the lower East Side. Recent fair-housing regulations made these buildings more livable than most, often with such luxuries as heat and hot running water. Because the Rosens had many Russian friends in the same circumstances, they could live a full life without ever having to learn English.

The Rosens' first child, a sixteen-pound boy, died in childbirth because he was too large for the tiny, four-foot-ten Celia to deliver. The experience also left her paralyzed. While Max struggled to make a living in his newly adopted country, Celia sat at home in a wheelchair, condemned to loneliness, befriending a rat that lived in their apartment as her only companion. Every day before he left for work, Max would knock on the neighbors' doors, saying, "Don't forget to look in on Celia today." He searched all of New York to find a doctor to help her. Finally, one specialist said that the only cure for her was to have another child. She did, and that child was Belle Rosen, my mother, who weighed fourteen pounds—almost as much as her stillborn sibling—at her birth on July 26, 1911. A few months later, Celia, inexplicably, was able to walk again.

Everyone in the neighborhood told Celia and Max that Mom was an adorable baby. The proud parents decided to enter her in a baby contest held by their medical clinic. Every patient was to line up that day for a smallpox vaccination, but the clinic, not wanting to photograph a child with a vaccination mark, neglected to give her the shot. Mom won the baby contest but promptly got smallpox. For six weeks Max had to stay away from his quarantined apartment. The doctor who came to the house daily wore what looked like a diving suit to call on his afflicted patients. Mom recovered, and two years later, in 1913, her sister, Fanny, was born.

Mom's parents, Max and Celia Rosen, in New York, 1912.

Just one year later, when he was twenty-eight, Max Rosen died suddenly of complications from asthma. Mom was three and Fanny eleven months. Celia spoke no English and knew no one in New York who could take her in. So she took the girls to Newark, New Jersey, to live with her Tanta (Aunt) Rifke Burstein, her mother's sister, in five rooms over the Burstein hardware store. The close quarters became stifling, so, in 1917, Celia and her young daughters took the train from Newark to

Joliet, Illinois. There they moved in with Celia's cousin Rose Atkin, who was married to a rabbi and had five children.

Joliet, Illinois—1917

In 1917, Joliet was the hub of a railroad transportation system with more than seventy passenger trains arriving daily. The year also heralded the opening of the stately 102-room Inn at Scott and Jefferson. Its brass beds, oak dressers, and Wilton velvet carpeting made it one of the finest hotels in Illinois. Then under construction, Joliet Community College was America's first public junior college at a time when the concept was unknown. With its thirty-two-foot-high, fourteen-inch-thick walls, Stateville Penitentiary, also under construction that year, would earn Joliet the name of "Prison Town." Joliet's grand motion-picture house, the Princess Theater, had just opened its doors, while the "Mecca of Gladness"—the 650-seat Crystal Stairs Theater, known for its flight of glass steps with colored lights dancing on cascading water—was destroyed by fire.

Joliet became home to Grandma Celia and her little family in the spring of 1917. Not long after their arrival, Grandma took the children downtown to watch the parade of 12,000 marchers wind their way through the streets as World War I draft inductees were escorted to the railroad depot. A gigantic electric American flag beamed "America First, Then Joliet" from the top of the courthouse.

The following month, on May 26, a tornado cut a five-mile-wide swath through Joliet, killing three people and injuring sixty. Homes were flattened, cars were demolished, and almost every barn and silo was destroyed in the 100-mile-per-hour winds.

Grandma Celia and her two girls lived down the street from David Hyman, a tall, slightly built Lithuanian with dark, curly hair, a large nose, and long, delicate fingers. David had married at seventeen, but had lost his wife in childbirth. He was a graduate rabbi, but early in his studies he decided he didn't have the political skills necessary to lead a congregation, so he started what became a successful scrap-metal business.

David was twenty years her senior in June 1917 when he spotted Grandma Celia in the neighborhood, but he loved her on sight. She and the girls still spoke no English, but David spoke Russian, not to mention several other languages. He and Celia were married one year later, in 1918. Mom was seven and Fanny was five.

Nobody would rent to the couple because of the two children. So when David learned that a two-story cottage surrounded by a white picket fence was for sale at 511 South Joliet Street, he bought it for his new wife and family. Mom said that for the rest of her life her heart would always leap when the clock hands showed 5:11.

David loved Mom and Fanny like his own children. Soon after they were married, Grandma Celia and David became concerned that Mom was drumming her fingers in her sleep. Their doctor said there must be something she wanted to do with her fingers, so David bought her a piano. He knew nothing about music, but he knew he wanted the best for Mom. He insisted that all of her sheet music come from the Shermer Music Library, considered the top sheet-music publisher of the time. Mom studied piano with Florence Scholl, who came from Chicago once a week to their home.

Right after David married Grandma, Mom was also diagnosed with tuberculosis. David insisted on taking her to Chicago to see the top specialist, Dr. Robert Black. Dr. Black leaned back in his chair and just laughed and laughed. "There is nothing wrong with her except bad tonsils, which poisoned all her teeth. We'll take the teeth out first, and when she is well from that, we will take the tonsils out." Mom was home from school for a year. When she went back during the winter of 1919, David took her to Eliza Kelly Grammar School on Joliet Street every day on a sled.

Mom's teacher told Grandma Celia that she and mom needed to learn English. While David was happy to read to Grandma from the Talmud, translating the ancient rabbinical writings into Russian, he encouraged her to go to night school to learn to speak English. So while Mom went to grammar school, Grandma went to night school at Joliet Community College.

Mom often walked the mile to the Joliet Public Library, where she buried herself in books. Her love for reading started early and was nurtured by her family. "My mother was funny about reading," Mom later recalled. "You weren't allowed to read junk. I knew the classics before I knew Jack and Jill, and I had read Dostoyevsky and all the classics in Russian by the time I was ten." Eventually Grandma learned to read. Her accent never left her, but she became a U.S. citizen in 1921.

Grandma Celia had a bad heart, so David was constantly warning Mom and Fanny not to slam the door as it would startle their mother and she could drop dead on the spot. To help out Grandma around the house, Mom and David did the shopping, visiting the Lincoln Bakery and Grocery Company on Bluff Street. It was here that Mom learned a lifelong respect for high-quality fruits and vegetables from the Greek owner whose shop boasted the slogan "Good Things to Eat for Less Money."

Even with her heart condition, Grandma desperately wanted to have a child with David. They had a stillborn child during the flu epidemic of 1918, when they were first married. When she became pregnant again soon after, she sought help from her family doctor. He referred the couple to famed obstetrician Joseph DeLee, founder of the Chicago Maternity Center and the Chicago Lying-In Hospital.

Dr. DeLee ordered Grandma to stay in Chicago for eight weeks before delivery and two weeks after to recover. At the appropriate time, in December 1918, she and David left for their Chicago pilgrimage, a fifty-mile trip taken in an open, horse-drawn carriage—their surrey with the fringe on top. During Celia and David's absence, Mom and Fanny stayed at Guardian Angels Orphan Home. A friend of Grandma's picked them up in an electric automobile and took the solemn waifs to their temporary home to await the return of their parents with the new baby.

Working with top specialists in Chicago, including Dr. DeLee, Grandma finally delivered a child in her eighth month. Too large for normal delivery, thirteen-pound Maurice (my Uncle Mac) was born on February 18, 1919—reportedly Illinois's first caesarian section operation. Mom was eight and Fanny was six.

Later that spring, after the family was reunited, they rented the upstairs apartment in their house to the first black people in town: Dr. Williams, a physician, and his wife, Clarice, a teacher. Day after day, Grandma and Clarice would sit on the back stairs for long hours, sewing and talking. Every two years, the Williams family would bring a girl up from Clarice's hometown in Tennessee. They would provide her room and board and send her to Joliet Community College to earn her teaching degree, then send her back home to educate others.

It was not an easy time for blacks in Joliet. By 1925, membership in the city's Ku Klux Klan chapter had mushroomed. The KKK was not just anti-black; it also sought to punish aliens, liberated women, Roman Catholics, and Jews. Its slogan was "Kill the Kikes, Koons, and Katholics." The Klan had Jews in Joliet shaking in their boots. By the late 1920s, the violence inflicted by the KKK offended the sensibilities of the entire nation, resulting in indictments of Klan leaders. It was then that the white-sheeted barbarians found their world dissolving.

When the stock market crashed in October 1929, America fell on hard times and Joliet was no exception. During the Great Depression, children with buckets in hand walked up and down the city's railroad switchyard and along the tracks, collecting pieces of coal that would help heat their homes. Members of the Good Fellow Club drove trucks through the streets, collecting food and clothing and preparing "bundles of good cheer" for needy workers year-round. The Morningstar Mission dispensed food to hungry families. But it was never enough to satisfy the needs of the town's unemployed workers. Steelworkers were hit especially hard when their hours were cut and jobs were eliminated. The WPA—President Roosevelt's Works Progress Administration—provided much needed jobs, and, as a result, Joliet's west side sewer system was constructed.

As a survivor of the Jewish pogroms in czarist Russia, Grandma Celia had learned to look at the world as one large family. Even during the depression, when food was scarce, she opened her tiny home and kind heart to anyone in need of a meal. Jobless and often homeless strangers showed up regularly at her back door. Grandma would invite them in, give them breakfast, pack them a lunch, and send them on their way.

But feeding all these people cost money, so Grandma Celia started cutting corners to pinch pennies. Her method was unorthodox, to say the least. Grandma had always kept a Jewish home, strictly kosher. It was thought to be a sin to eat *traif*—non-kosher meat. One day she discovered that her butcher down the street traveled to Chicago to buy non-kosher meat for less and then sold it at a bigger markup as kosher. For an entire year, Grandma bought and served non-kosher meat to her family without telling them. One night at dinner she announced that they hadn't eaten kosher meat for a year and it didn't kill them. "If I am going to commit a sin, let the butcher have the sin too," she said.

In 1929, Mom was attending Joliet Community College and studying to be a teacher. After she graduated, she looked for a teaching job but was rejected because she was Jewish: "I remember the many rejection letters saying boldly, 'Under the circumstances, a Christian would be hired.'" Luckily, Fanny went to night school with a girl whose father was clerk of the Rockdale school district. The girl encouraged Mom to apply for a teaching job there. During the interview, the school board asked her to stand up and talk about herself. "The first thing I will tell you is that I am Jewish," she said. "If that doesn't please you, there is no sense my telling you how wonderful I am." The interview continued, and she got the job.

Thanks to her piano lessons as a young girl, Mom had also become a proficient piano teacher. After the American Can Company, a large Joliet area employer, closed in nearby Rockdale, she knew money would be especially tight for families. Even so, they believed it was good for their children to learn music and to play the piano. So did Mom, so she started a piano group for twenty-five cents a lesson. This was a pittance, but Mom knew how hard it was for families to scrape together even a few quarters. One particular student, a ten-year-old named Dorothy Mavrich, stood out among Mom's pupils. Dorothy had crossed eyes and wore braces on both legs due to polio, but she was a gifted pianist. One day, when Mom found out that Dorothy's parents could no longer afford lessons, she met with them to convince them of Dorothy's promise and to offer to continue the lessons in their home for free.

Dorothy shone under Mom's tutelage, memorizing more than sixty pages of concertos at a time. She would listen to piano rolls at the library and from memory play anything she heard. A physician heard about her and dedicated himself to fixing her physical problems. He uncrossed her eyes and paid for numerous operations on her legs so she could wear regular shoes. When Dorothy's recovery was complete, the doctor committed suicide. Mom always wondered whether he killed himself because her recovery meant that his life's work was over.

"I was in fourth grade when Belle came to Rockdale. My dad was on the local school board and at that time they hired a young Jewish teacher. She also gave class piano lessons for $.25. It wasn't long before there was no money at my home for more lessons. My dad thought I could learn on my own, as he was able to pick out simple tunes on the piano. But the teacher, Belle Hyman, decided to give me free private lessons to set a good example for the class. Our families became friends. Many times she would have the evening meal with us. Dad would take her home to Joliet Street. Her mother, Celia, a short, lovable woman, came to our rescue many times. [For some unknown reason,] my sister was unable to walk. Celia came [to our home] and said [to her], 'Walk to me,' and she started walking. In 1933, after my first ankle surgery, I picked up head lice. Celia was there pronto with some awful-smelling stuff. She covered my head with it and it killed them.

"Belle saw, in my inability to tackle life, that using my hands could be my avenue of pursuit in obtaining happiness. My dad's purchase of a Cable piano was the key to a full life. I credit Belle with my love of music. Today, my happiness continually reminds me of Belle. Belle shared her knowledge with me, and this one person made all the difference in my life. Teaching piano provided me with a good living. I know I have passed the love of music on to countless others."—Dorothy Mavrich

Mom taught first through eighth grades, boys band, and other academic classes in Rockdale for four years. Then President Roosevelt put out the call for teachers for his WPA nurseries in 1934. So, as her gift to the children of America, Mom took a job in a Rockdale WPA nursery for half the pay she could get in Joliet at Eliza Kelly Grammar School.

The tough times continued. Grandma collected safety pins and socks from neighbors so Mom could take them to school. The safety pins replaced lost buttons that families didn't have money to buy. And when the kids got their feet wet at recess, Mom had dry socks to give them. It seemed nobody noticed these good deeds at the time, and yet every Christmas Mom found a lot of anonymous hand-crocheted doilies on her desk.

In 1935, Grandma had a heart attack and died. She was forty-five years old. This was the darkest day of Mom's young life. Her black hair literally turned white overnight and she began to have migraine headaches. Her younger sister, Fanny, had moved to New York some time ago after studying accounting at Joliet Community College and had married and begun raising a family. At twenty-four, Mom was a spinster Jewish schoolteacher, living at home with a widowed stepfather and younger brother to look after.

Manny and Belle—June 1936

Mom's luck changed on June 20, 1936. She was teaching Sunday school at the Joliet Jewish Congregation, where the youngest boy from the Lewis family attended her class. His father and three brothers were responsible for building the temple. Their father's sister and her family would often come up from Chicago to visit. They didn't own a car, but a friend did, and he occasionally drove them in for daylong visits. On that June morning, Mrs. Lewis called Mom to say she had guests from Chicago arriving that day. Would Mom mind keeping their friend, the driver, company? "I want you to come so he will have someone to talk to," she told Mom.

Mom was reluctant to go, but David and Uncle Mac ganged up on her and insisted. She arrived by cab at the Lewis residence and rang the bell. The door opened and there stood Manny Lazar, filling the doorway. She first saw the face of this handsome, dark-haired man of twenty-six. Then she saw his hands, calloused and leathery from being cut by too many screwdrivers and box cutters.

"Hello, I'm Manny," he managed to blurt out.

"After the party he brought me home and said he wanted to see me again," Mom later recalled. "I told him it was OK if he happened to come to Joliet." He happened to come to Joliet a lot in the next few weeks, often with a bunch of posies behind his back, freshly purchased from Sterling Florist. They picnicked. They took long walks on the winding footpaths in Bush Park. They stopped at the Sweet Shop on Jefferson for a soda. On especially hot days, they would grab a bunch of friends and go for a swim down at the beach. They went canoeing at the Joliet Beach Club. Dad taught timid Mom to enjoy horseback riding, and together they rode through Higginbotham Woods.

Mom also saw Dad in Chicago. It was unusual back then for an unmarried woman to take a trip to visit an unmarried man, but Dad's youngest sister, Ethel, would put Mom up at her house, so everything was kosher. "Manny thought coming to Chicago would be a nice break from my job and all my household chores," Mom recalled. "He and I would take long rowboat rides in Douglas Park."

Sometime in July, Dad broke the news to Mom that he was going to be transferred in early 1937 from the Pullman Couch factory in Chicago to a plant in Warren, Ohio. Lawrence Schnadig Sr., Pullman's owner, wanted Dad to be the plant's supervisor, so he was distressed when Dad said he would prefer to stay in Chicago near Mom. Mr. Schnadig called Mom and asked her to prevail on Dad to take the job. By then, Mom and Dad were very much in love. Encouraged by Mom, Dad went to Ohio to check out the job and wrote her every day for two weeks. Then, suddenly, the letters stopped. On July 26, Dad showed up at Mom's door with a ruby ring for her birthday and he asked her to marry him. After a whirlwind courtship, this nice Jewish couple married on Christmas Day, 1936. It was the only day Dad could get off from work. It was also the start of many memorable Christmas Days together. Every year their anniversary would be a holiday that practically the whole world celebrated.

Since Dad hadn't finished high school, the superintendent's job was a terrific opportunity. The newlyweds moved to Warren,

Dad surprised Mom with a ruby ring and a marriage proposal for her birthday, July 1936.

Ohio, the day after they were married, and in January 1937, Dad started his new job at the Newton Falls factory. He always had a funny way of describing things. He would later say of the town, "It must have been where Newton fell because that was the size of the town." The town looked cheery, still decorated for Christmas with trees and lights. But their apartment wasn't clean and Dad refused to bring his bride into it. So they lived in a hotel opposite the town square for two weeks until their new home was ready.

Dad left early every morning for the factory. It was a place he loved to be. When he first walked into the plant, he had noticed piles of junk and scraps. He decided he could raise money by selling it. He used the money to start a fund for employees, most of them young men fresh out of high school. If they ran into debt buying a new car or an engagement ring for their girl, Dad would lend them money from the fund. In Ohio at that time, if someone reneged on a bill, the sheriff could arrest him. Dad's fund paid the bill before the sheriff could collar a valuable worker. As this happened with some frequency, the men appreciated it and always repaid the fund.

When a man would ask Dad for a ten-cent-an-hour raise, he would say, "Let me watch you work. I'm not going to snoop. Just work at your own pace and when I walk through the factory, I'll pay special attention to what you're doing. If I feel you deserve it, I'll give you a raise." Under his management, the company never had a union and never had trouble. Morale improved considerably and workers started pitching in.

After Dad had been at the factory for two years, his father, Morris, died at the age of sixty-four. (Dad's mother, Anna, would live to be over 100.) The elder Mr. Schnadig passed away the same year.

When Lawrence Jr. took over the business, Dad felt that morale suffered, and the resulting conflict caused the firing of many of his best and most experienced upholsterers. The new people that were hired had little experience making expensive furniture. They also expected Dad to gather the upholstery, padding, frame, and other materials for each piece of furniture and bring it to them at their workstation. Only then would they assemble the item. They were the production workers and he was the supervisor, yet he was doing the gathering and lifting. Dad no longer went to work happy.

When a man at the factory decided he wanted Dad's job, he did everything he could to make it tough for Dad. He would make sure a piece of furniture wasn't on the loading dock when the truck arrived to pick it up. If the truck reached its destination without the shipment, the company (and Dad) would look bad. But Dad was on to this guy. He would tie the piece of furniture to the roof of his car, catch up to the truck (Dad knew all the routes), and load the piece himself.

For a brief time Dad was Mom's boss at Pullman. She was his secretary. "His former secretary taught me to keep the books, file, and run an office," Mom recalled later. She didn't know that what she was learning would translate directly to running her own business someday. She worked for Dad until she became pregnant with me in 1940 and had to go on bed rest. When Dad got home from Pullman, he would do all of Mom's chores, scrubbing floors and washing dishes. I was born March 2, 1941, in Warren, Ohio.

At home with my parents in Warren, Ohio, 1941.

Sofa beds were the backbone of the Newton Falls factory. Because they required a lot of steel and steel was needed in the war effort, the factory closed shortly after the United States entered World War II. Dad was transferred back to Pullman's Chicago plant in November 1942. His new position was department manager.

I was eighteen months old when we moved into our third-floor walkup in Hyde Park, at Fifty-seventh and Drexel. And on a warm day in May 1944, Manny and Belle Lazar began their greatest adventure together. My two culturally mismatched parents had been products of the Great Depression. Dad, the rough-around-the-edges English immigrant with little high-school education, and Mom, the first-generation American of Russian descent who taught school and piano, began to live the American dream. They opened their own business.

*Mom and Dad in their first store on
79th and Constance, 1947.*

CHAPTER 3

Baby Steps:
The First Store

Chicago, Illinois—May 12, 1944

ONE MAY MORNING IN 1944, after he had been working at Pullman Couch's Chicago plant for eighteen months, Dad looked across the breakfast table at Mom and said, "Kid"—he always called her Kid or Kitten—"how would you like to go into business for ourselves? This is the perfect time."

"The perfect time? You have to be out of your mind. How would we do it?"

"We'll work it out somehow."

"But the war—how will we get merchandise? What would we sell?"

"We'll work that out. Let's just try it."

All the while Dad was working at Pullman Couch, he knew he was making the company prosperous with his dedication and hard work. An out-of-the-box thinker, he dreamed of making his own fortune, of making his own dreams come true in his adopted country. He had vision and the heart of an entrepreneur. And, as it turns out, he had pretty good powers of prediction: Pullman Couch would be sold in 1951.

My parents had no money saved. Dad had never earned enough at Pullman to put away and Mom had quit work to stay at home with me. But Grandma Celia had always told Mom, "If your husband is a thief, then you get up on the horse behind him and rob with him." If Dad was sure their own business would work, that was enough for Mom.

"Marrying Manny was like putting a sandwich together," she once said. "He was not a professional man, but when the two of us put our strengths together, we succeeded."

Both of my parents loved children and, after talking about their combined skills, they decided the children's toy and furniture business was a perfect fit. Mom liked the idea of offering families the benefit of her teaching experience. Dad enjoyed being a craftsman. Both had been brought up with the Jewish philosophy that everyone was worthy of respect and kindness. They believed this new venture would give them the opportunity to make a good, honest, meaningful living.

When it came time to christen their business, Dad said to Mom, "You're the poetic one, Kid. You give the store a name."

"I remembered the story of my little Irish Granny Dolan when we lived in Joliet," Mom later told me. "She was the grandmother I never had. She lived at the end of my street and had lots of children. Granny loved me because I would let her show me the pictures in her many photo albums. She was so proud of her children, many of whom were priests and nuns. As Granny Dolan lay dying, she looked around at her family and said, 'Go get Hyman.' When Grandma Celia came, Granny looked at her and said, 'God bless you,' and passed peacefully to sleep. Grandma Celia believed that blessing was for a purpose. She always said that she never expected any return on anything she did. She just wanted God to chalk up blessings for her children.

"I can still remember Granny Dolan saying to me, 'I will tell ya the story o' the little people, the wee folk, the leprechauns who made Ireland a magic place,' " Mom continued. " 'They are merry little fellows gaily dressed in old-fashioned green clothes, with a red cap, a leather apron, and buckled shoes. These small sprites do small labors for humans. Sometimes they ask small favors in return. Then they give humans those things that bring luck and good fortune. The story goes that leprechauns possess a treasure—usually a pot o' gold— which a human can obtain if he succeeds in capturing one of these wee folks.' "

So Mom said to Dad, "Let's call the store Wee Folks, after Granny Dolan and the little people." And from that day on, she said, it was like magic, "like unseen hands were watching over us, helping us, because we had nothing . . . really nothing."

The uncertainty of World War II hovered over their plans. U.S. troops were fighting in Germany and Japan. Ration books limited how much sugar, coffee, and meat Americans could buy, as well as tires and gasoline. Gas had risen to twenty-five cents a gallon, making it too expensive to use a car anyway. Mom and Dad decided to sell their old Buick for $500, and with the money—and Granny Dolan's blessings—they started searching for the perfect place in which to open their toy store.

Mom examined the ads in the city's major newspapers—the *Chicago Tribune,* the *Herald American,* the *Daily News,* the *Sun-Times*—and carefully considered each area in which she thought a toy store would be welcome. She studied books on retailing at nearby Blackstone Public Library. She had a strong vision of the right location. They made a list of the most promising sites, and in the evenings after Dad came home from work and on the weekends, he and Mom would climb aboard the red wooden streetcar in Hyde Park and ride from one neighborhood to another. The fare was eight cents, but thankfully transfers were free. For countless miles they rode, perched on seats whose caning had unraveled like an old sweater and now poked them with sharp fingers. If the streetcar was crowded, they stood and clung to the leather straps for dear life as it rattled along.

Some sites were too far from our apartment; others showed no sign of retail diversity. One already had an established toy store; another seemed to have little foot traffic for a Saturday in Chicago. At last months of searching brought them to South Shore. Mom would always remember the day they stepped off the Stony Island Avenue "Rocket" streetcar and discovered 79th Street. South Shore was five miles south of Hyde Park and ten miles south of downtown Chicago. "It was just a couple of miles west of Lake Michigan, had a good mix of goods and services merchants, but no toy store," she said. "We were standing at the front of the streetcar, looking around, when the driver asked,

Mom and Dad enrolled me at the Lab
School of the University of Chicago in 1944.

'Did you want this stop, lady? There are a lot of good stores right along here.'

"Maybe this was a good place to look," she continued. "We got off the streetcar in front of Lawrence Interiors and watched customers going in and out. I remember saying to Dad, 'These are my people.' Almost every face going by was Irish. I knew the Irish and I knew they made wonderful friends. And the many churches nearby made me believe these were religious people. We walked the neighborhood and visited Our Lady of Peace Church, St. Phillip Neri, and Mount Carmel High School."

"Unlike the melting pot of New York, Chicago in those days seemed to section off its ethnic groups. From 79th and Muskegon to Exchange and on to 95th Street and beyond was a Polish area. From 71st to 76th and Stony Island to the lake was Irish Catholic. The area north of 71st Street from South Shore Drive to Stony Island was more cosmopolitan, consisting of Irish, Jewish, and other nationalities, as well as groups with religious differences, including many with a large Protestant following. Jackson Park Highlands was a restricted (no Jews allowed) area until the late '40s. The largest Jewish community stretched from 76th to 79th and Jeffery to Muskegon. As more professional people moved from Hyde Park, a new demographic was created. So many doctors had built beautiful homes south of 95th between Jeffery and Stony Island that they called it Pill Hill."—Harriet Grady, owner of Circus Nursery School

Real estate was scarce, and Mom and Dad weren't sure what size store they needed. They asked a realtor on 79th Street to show them available locations. Eventually he brought them to a corner store at 79th and Constance. Housed on the first floor of a brick building, the store was small, about 3,000 square feet. Three floors of apartments rose above it. Mom's heart sank as she stepped inside 1832 East 79th Street. The store had most recently been a butcher shop, and it still smelled of rotten beef. The front door was heavy and its glass window was broken. Both of its display windows, one of which was cracked, had been painted over. Two bulbs dangling from the ceiling dimly lighted the filthy space. A gaping hole consumed the back wall where the electrical panel should have been. The tiny bathroom had no sink and its window had bars on it. The back door was weak and in need of repair. There were no display fixtures and no storage space. The realtor said there was an unfinished basement, but it was inaccessible.

Mom didn't like the store at all. How could they ever turn this dismal spot into a place where children and parents would choose to spend their time and money? She waited as Dad paced up and down the floor. After a thorough tour, he came back with a gleam in his eye. "This place has promise, Kitten."

"It does? Where?"

"We can put balconies along those two walls and we can stack things to the ceiling."

Dad could already see their dream store laid out and in full swing as he looked at its empty shell. He was an adventurer, and could always see the possibilities. Mom was less of a risk-taker and more of a realist. She knew Dad was more than capable, but she wondered whether even he could change this horrid place into the inviting engine of commerce he imagined. But she did have faith in his judgment, and she did like the idea of having their store in a neighborhood with so many of her beloved Irish people, so she reluctantly agreed. The realtor offered them a three-year lease at $85 a month. Mom's face fell. They weren't sure what they might sell in this store, let alone where they would get that kind of money. Seeing her reaction, the realtor said, "You know, it's been vacant for a long time. How about $75 a month?" After a brief discussion, my parents agreed.

Mom recalled, "The University National Bank in Hyde Park had enough faith in us to give us a loan."

"Dad's brothers and sisters helped raise more money," Mom added. "Uncle Jack, the bachelor in the Seabees, had his twin sister, Ethel, sell some of his short-wave radios and war memorabilia. Uncle Phil, the unmarried philatelist, sold some of his stamp collection. Some borrowed on their life insurance. My brother, Mac, was in Germany, a captain in the army medical corps. He sent us the $75 rent every month, and never kept

Dad's brother Jack, who served in the Seabees during WWII, helped Mom and Dad pay the rent on the first store.

track of anything he ever gave us. But I did." They paid him back every penny after a few years.

David Hyman, Mom's stepfather, wanted to mortgage his property to get them started. She refused. "Just give us $300 to put into the bank for luck, Daddy," she told him. Anyone to whom David lent money had become wealthy, and she hoped a little of that luck would rub off on her and Dad.

Dad was a genius when it came to craftsmanship. He studied the site to make the best use of its tiny space. Because of the war, all building materials were at a premium. Since the government had frozen the supply of lumber, he bought used shelving and scrap wood from nearly defunct lumberyards. He never measured anything. He'd just stare at a wall for a while, decide on a design, get the materials, and start to build.

Almost a year to the day after Dad and Mom first talked about starting a business, World War II came to a close. Germany surrendered in May, and Japan would follow suit that August. My parents spent that long, hot summer of 1945 building the store. Dad propped open the front and back doors to keep air moving through the place while they worked. Air-conditioning was a rarity in those days and they couldn't afford a fan.

Dad often worked late into the night after putting in a full day at the factory. Hands bandaged to cover cuts and splinters, he sawed, nailed, and screwed two-by-fours together to make a wooden balcony that hung about six feet above the floor and circled the store. Climbing a rickety wooden ladder, he hoisted and fastened a railing to the balcony to keep wagons, strollers, and bikes from rolling off. Along the length of the store he fashioned a narrow stockroom, with shelves from floor to ceiling.

"What toys and furniture should we sell?" Mom wondered early on. "We had to buy merchandise, but we had no retail experience. We had no connections and little credit. We had to prove to the bank and the people who had staked us that we could do it. We went to jobbers and wholesalers and bought closeout merchandise to resell. When the children's furniture manufacturers would give us only limited credit, we decided to add soft goods and then we added toys."

Inventory was determined by what they could buy on extended credit. Metal goods were still at a premium because of the war, so Mom and Dad emphasized babies' and children's clothing. At the front of the store Dad crafted a large built-in wooden frame with tongue-in-groove drawers to house tiny socks, T-shirts, underwear, and pants in sizes 0 to 6x. Some time later, after Mom almost lost me while visiting Marshall Field's, they decided to stock kiddie harnesses.

Mom's teaching experience was invaluable in choosing merchandise. She knew what kids liked and needed. She knew she wanted to sell educational toys, and Fisher-Price and Playskool were first on her inventory list. She bought books and games; Dad gave his input on model kits and boys' toys. Wheeled goods like doll buggies, baby strollers, scooters, and bikes all required assembly, but with his handyman skills, Dad was a whiz.

"Mattel, which started in business the same year we did, wouldn't sell to us," Mom recalled. "We bought off-brand children's clothes, toys, furniture—anything we thought we could sell. Once we had a credit rating, we were able to purchase brand-name goods, like Carter's and Hanes. Even though money was tight, as we gained brand clothing, we donated some of the non-brand clothing to area churches to support the community."

Dad built a big workbench in the back room. Over the years, I would watch hundreds of metal and plastic parts tumble out of cardboard boxes onto this table to be transformed into toys kids loved. Eventually, customers congregated around that table, drinking coffee and eating delightful whipped-cream pastries from Dressel's Bakery across the street. In an emergency, the table served as a place to diaper babies or an escape for Mom to drink strong coffee and recover from one of her vicious migraines.

From used lumber now freed of bent and rusty nails, Dad built the area's first self-service display islands. As fast as he built them, Mom painted them a walnut color to make them look like the rich wood shelving they couldn't afford. Because the wood soaked up so much paint, and because Mom wanted them to look brand new, she applied two coats to each of the eight islands. She was a sight, standing on her tiptoes to reach the top shelves, head wrapped in a terrycloth towel to absorb her perspiration so she would look presentable should anyone stop by.

One day an old man popped his head in the door. He was short, thin, and a little disheveled. "So what are you going to make of this place?" he asked Dad, waving his finger in the direction of the shelves.

"It's going to be a toy store."

The old man looked around and immediately took a liking to Dad.

"You don't have a big store here, but if you hang a series of motors from the ceiling, attach a wire to them, and put merchandise on the wire, it will look like a bigger place. If people see more of the merchandise in action, they'll be more interested. People like things that move. You'll sell more, you'll see."

Dad took the advice. On the ceiling above every display island he suspended small motors from which he sent gas-powered airplanes, toy trucks, and cars spinning on fishing test wire. All types of merchandise would whirl above customer's heads here for the next twelve years.

The old man told Mom, "Your husband will make a go of this thing. He is good at it."

Day after day, the old man came to the store's front door, and soon Mom and Dad would have coffee waiting for him at the back room workbench. Sometimes he would go to the greasy spoon across the street for a big bowl of potato soup. He loved potato soup. He would disappear for a couple of days every now and then. "You know," he once told Mom, "I am ninety-two and my doctor is thirty-two. And *he* is telling *me* what to eat."

On every visit, the old man imparted pearls of retailing wisdom to my parents on how to purchase and display merchandise in ways that would be irresistible to buyers. He kept track of them and their progress that summer and for a while after the store opened. I'm sure he told them his name, but they never really knew who he was until they read his obituary a few years later. It told the story of a man who was the main buyer for Marshall Field's. The department store had sent him around the world to find one-of-a-kind merchandise, unusual goods for the high-profile retailer. Until he died, nobody in our neighborhood had known where the old man came from or where he lived. But Mom always believed it was her parents' wisdom and the luck of little Granny Dolan that sent him to them.

Uncle Mac had returned from the service about that time, and was doing his medical internship at the University of Illinois in Chicago. His girlfriend, Genevieve, was from Joliet, and would often spend weekends at our Hyde Park apartment. That way, she could see Uncle Mac when he was off rotation. Aunt

Gen, as I called her, also babysat for me in the evenings while my parents were working, and brought me home from school. I attended the University of Chicago Lab School nursery, where I had been given a scholarship when I was three.

Before Wee Folks opened, Mom wrote up a formal document she called the "Basic Principles of Operation." The list seems as sound now as it did then: You must work three years before you know you have a success. You need to meet and know your competition, view the business from the customer's point of view, and use good timing for buying and advertising. You should strive to become a leader in the industry. You need to understand that a customer's taste is not a matter of money. Most important, you must always back up your word. It was also imperative to be a good housekeeper, teacher, friend, and citizen. This document underwent many revisions in twenty-five years, but the basics were always upheld. This was the real secret of my parents' retail success.

Their Irish luck continued when, just before opening, an older man offered to wash the walls and windows for $10 as a welcome to the neighborhood. Dad's hand-lettered multicolored paper signs for the windows had been up for two weeks. GRAND OPENING! WEE FOLKS! CHILDREN'S CLOTHING AND TOYS!

October 26, 1945—9:00 A.M.

Mom and Dad stood in the back room of the dark store next to the newly installed electrical panel. Together, they stood ready to flip the light switches. It might not sound all that romantic, but to them the moment was the culmination of all their hopes and dreams. One by one, they flipped them all. Flip! All the fluorescent lights down the single, middle aisle flickered on, illuminating cases of merchandise on the left and five-foot-tall shelving units on the right. Flip! The lights over the baby clothes in the display cases at the front of the store blinked on. Flip! The lights in the display cases holding the most fragile dolls on the west wall glowed. Flip! The ceiling motors sent planes and trucks circling slowly through the air. As Dad gave the store one last walk-through, Mom double-checked the contents of the

National push-key register. They had been to the bank that morning and had $25 in the till. That was all the cash they had.

Curiosity had been building, and as Dad propped open the heavy front glass door, a few area residents stepped into the store. As they strolled around, they looked from floor to ceiling, seemingly amazed at the selection, presentation, and neatness. Everything was in order, thanks to Mom. Toddlers and young children could easily find what they liked in their own sections while older brothers and sisters checked out model kits, paint, and glue. That day, the first pebble was cast into a pond that created ripples all over South Shore. Wee Folks was here!

During the store's first few weeks, our family settled into a routine. Mom awakened at five o'clock to get me ready for school. After she dropped me off a few blocks from our apartment, she took two streetcars so she could open the store promptly at nine. The trip took almost an hour one way. She had to be on time—couldn't disappoint a waiting customer. If I was sick, she brought me to the store with her and made a bed in the back room where I could quietly play or nap. Summer and winter, in all kinds of weather, she waited for the often-tardy streetcars. The first one to stop was usually so over-crowded that she was often forced to wait for the next. For the first eighteen months, she took this trip alone as Dad continued to work at Pullman Couch.

Dad was already on his way out the door to Pullman by the time Mom's five o'clock alarm went off. He showed up at the store about three o'clock every afternoon to assemble shiny new bikes and buggies and to repair whatever needed fixing. They had no car that first year, so Dad delivered toys in the evenings and on weekends on the streetcar, even in the snow on Christmas Eve. Later, a young couple needing money sold my parents a car for $300. Mom and Dad put far more money into that rattletrap than they ever got out of it.

After closing the store, Mom and Dad came home, often past midnight, and prepared for the following day. Mom sat at the dining room table and read books about retailing, poring over catalogs and trade magazines, trying to find educational toys she could recommend to a customer. Dad sat across the

*I had the snazziest trike on my Hyde
Park block in 1945.*

table or lay sprawled on the brown tufted couch and studied toy
and wheeled-goods assembly instructions. Mom was the brains
behind the operation. She ordered all the merchandise and han-
dled all the paperwork. Sometimes the stacks of bills for merchandise as yet unsold overwhelmed her. Early the next
morning, it was time to start again. During Wee Folks' first five
years, my parents had little life outside the store.

Aunt Gen was always there after school and in the evenings
to watch me. I remember one August afternoon in 1946 when
she brought me home from school. We climbed the three flights
of tattered carpeted stairs to the apartment. She put the key in
the lock, but when she tried to open the door it was chained,
and we heard banging from inside the apartment. We were
being robbed! Our arrival surprised the robber and he quickly

escaped through the window. But he did manage to steal Uncle Mac's surgical tools that were left with us for safekeeping.

We didn't know it at the time, but the robber was a seventeen-year-old University of Chicago student named William Heirens. He was also a serial killer. After his arrest, Heirens confessed to murdering two women and a six-year-old girl whose body he dismembered and disposed of in Chicago's sewers. When police raided his room at the university, they found several incriminating items, including Uncle Mac's surgical kit. Lab tests showed that the instruments had never been used on a human being, but Chicago newspapers had a field day with the information anyway. Headlines screamed "DISSECTING KIT FOUND." Heirens's confession and, later, his triple life sentence came as a relief to Chicagoans, who felt they could now safely walk the streets at night again. And Uncle Mac got his tools back.

With Dad still working his day job, Mom did just about everything. It was a sight to see this four-foot-ten woman lugging the wobbly six-foot wooden ladder to the balcony to retrieve a stroller or into the stockroom to reach something on the fourth tier of shelves.

One day Mom was in the store alone when a sales rep from the *Southtown Economist* came in to sell advertising. "I've come to sell you something" was his cheery opener.

"Well, you sure came to the right place," Mom said jokingly. "We don't have enough money to buy merchandise, let alone advertising."

"OK," said the fellow, "if I can't sell you something, I will give you something—an idea. Register every parent who walks into your store. Keep their name and address, and their kids' names and birthdays. Then, print a nice-looking card promising a free gift and send it to the child on his or her birthday. When the child brings in the card, give him or her a small gift."

The Birthday Book became a cornerstone of Wee Folks sales for the next twenty-five years. Mom dressed up a cardboard box with brightly colored wrapping paper and cut a big slit in the top so tots and their parents could drop in their names and addresses and be added to the Birthday Book. She placed it prominently on the counter. At first the birthday cards were small, printed in one color on flimsy paper. Over time they became a half sheet of glossy stock in full color. The free gifts the cards promised never cost us much—less than a dime—but in the eyes of children, those gifts were gold. The treasured prizes were usually closeout items and discontinued merchandise from jobbers: bamboo finger tricks, a monkey that climbed when you pushed the sides of his ladder together, little puzzles, miniature trucks and cars, plastic dolls with stringy hair. When kids proudly brought in their cards, Dad would often joke around with them, asking them if they were married yet and how they were doing in school. Mom would find out how old they were and what they liked to do, then rummage through the gift box under the counter for something that fit their particular interest. Hardly anyone left without buying something, especially after Dad showed off the latest toy in their age range.

> *"My father owned the Cash Erler Photo Finishing and Camera Store on 83rd Street, and our dads knew each other well. Birthdays were never complete without Dad saying, 'Do you want to go to Wee Folks?' Of course, at Christmas we were not asked what we wanted, but Mom and Dad found our treasures there. My wife Kathy's uncle, John Dunn, owned Dunn Brothers Movers, and Kathy's cousins were allowed to spend $100 each on their visits to 'Heaven on Earth.'"—Name withheld by request*

The Birthday Book was so effective that, at the close of business in 1970, Wee Folks was sending out more than 10,000 birthday cards every year.

Mom and Dad promised that they could find their customers any item the store didn't carry. If an item had to be special-ordered, customers would always say, "We'll wait!" rather than go elsewhere. Customers like Marg Flanigan wouldn't buy anywhere but Wee Folks. She recommended the store to many of her friends, who appreciated the personalized service as well. That kind of loyalty kept Wee Folks going during the struggles of those early years.

At that time, only a handful of Jewish families lived in South Shore. Right after Wee Folks opened, a Jewish woman came in and told Mom, "You're going to have a lot of trouble doing business here and I don't think you'll make it. These people are very anti-Semitic." Mom told her, "If you treat people right, it shouldn't matter what religion you are." Mom was just like Grandma Celia. She didn't judge people based on religion or race, and neither did Dad. Things like that didn't matter for this nice Jewish couple, known as Mr. and Mrs. Wee Folks, who sold toys in a predominantly Irish Catholic neighborhood. "The neighborhood people were wonderful," Mom recalled many years later. "They took to us like a duck to water. I guess God sent them to us."

The store took on the characteristics of my parents. People felt warm and comfortable there. "We never lowered our prices—never," Mom recalled. "We never had to. But when a box got knocked around and looked too shabby to sell, we put it aside. If we knew of a customer who wanted that toy, we would call them and offer it for a discount. Or we would donate it to the local church. In the late fifties, when the discount houses started up, people still bought from us at full price. Discount houses didn't offer free advice, gift-wrapping, delivery, and humanity!" For me, Wee Folks was where I learned to read, sitting in a kid-sized wooden musical rocker in the book section, paging through *The Bobbsey Twins* and studying Richard Scarry books.

> *"I remember the store, because if I got a good report card my parents would take us there to pick out a small toy."—Linda Mayeroff Spitz*

After eighteen months in business, Dad walked into Wee Folks one day and told Mom, "I just quit Pullman Couch."

"That's great!" she said as she gave him a big hug. "Now you can run the business like you want to."

As business picked up, they hired kids from the neighborhood to help out, often from Our Lady of Peace Church, St. Phillip Neri, and Mount Carmel High School. Many of them grew up with the store as customers. Several came back as seasonal employees after going away to college.

By the third year, Wee Folks had access to the Merchandise Mart, an enormous building constructed in 1931 by Marshall

Field's in downtown Chicago to consolidate its thirteen whole-sale warehouses into one. At that time, its 6.2 million square feet made it the largest commercial building in the world. In 1945, ownership passed to Joseph P. Kennedy, former ambassador to Great Britain and father of the future thirty-fifth president. At the mart, hundreds of wholesale showrooms brought wholesalers and retailers together from around the country. In one fell swoop, retailers could see the latest merchandise and talk with representatives from hundreds of new and established manufacturers. Mom and Dad bought stuffed plush toys from Jay-Bee Creations and Steiff and Gund, microscopes and mechanical drawing sets from Skill Craft, wagons and scooters from Radio Steel, beach toys and pools from Eyerly, toy luggage and doll trunks from Luce, swing sets and slides from Gym Dandy, steel toys from Structo, puppets and dolls from Atlanta Playthings, educational toys from Playskool and Fisher-Price, trains and accessories from Lionel, games from Milton Bradley and Parker Brothers. Major toy companies began to extend credit to my parents.

Mom and Dad also made semiannual pilgrimages to A. C. McClurg, a gigantic wholesale storehouse at 333 East Ontario that carried everything from patio sets to televisions to toys. They set up a network of distributors, with folks like Steve Marienthal and Julie Kagan. In those days it seemed that most everyone in toys was Jewish.

When Miss Margery's and Miss Evans' Dance Studio moved into the second floor of a building across the street, Mom added pink and white tutus, black leotards, and black and white ballet shoes to the inventory. She custom-fit the tutus in the back room while would-be ballerinas stood in front of a tall mirror to see the full effect. The large selection of sizes soon appealed to other area dancing schools, which started sending their aspiring dancers to Wee Folks.

"It was just a little toy store, but there was love and warmth there. Nobody was just a customer. Your customers were your friends and we were their friends. We shared our life stories. My daughter was taking dance downtown and we lived at 85th and Wabash. We were a long way from the store. But the word got around that Wee Folks

carried dance shoes and outfits and there was no place near us that came close to your selection. Word was, you can get anything at the Lazars'. Belle was the woman behind the man, as were many women in those days. But if there was a decision to make, she would look to Manny. She was fun and charming and shared little stories with you. But Manny was Mr. Wee Folks. He would run from the back of the store to the front very quickly when he heard me come in and pat me on the back. He always had a joke or two. Then he would drag me all over the store asking, 'Did you see this new item?' He was flamboyant. My husband was obsessed with airplanes. Manny would take him out to lunch and, on the way back, they would fly radio-controlled planes."—Dr. Jane Brown

"Wee Folks was on the way to a friend's house and the show. I took dancing lessons across the street at Miss Margery's and Miss Evans' Dance Studio, and I recall buying a balsa wood plane and birthday presents."—Judi O'Brien

Within five years, Mom and Dad's hard work paid off. "For the first five years, we couldn't buy anything for ourselves," Mom recalled. "We were always borrowing. The day we paid our last debt was a glorious day. And, after that, we were never in debt again. We closed our door every night not owing a penny."

A Sister—March 7, 1950

I was nine when my sister, Marta, was born. As this was Mom's second caesarian, it took her longer to recover. But since the store was established by then, she also didn't need to hurry back to work. By then, our family had moved into one of the third-floor walkup apartments over the store. Between the baby stuff and Mom's baby grand piano she had brought from Joliet, it was a tight squeeze. And though our new quarters above the store eliminated their long commute, my parents simply put that time back into their work.

My parents hired a lovely German woman to take care of my sister, allowing Mom to eventually resume her store duties. We called her Oma, or "Grandmother," in German, and she was a godsend. Oma had lived in Nazi Germany during the war and escaped on a train just before her house went up in flames. She often made us dinner and we loved her old world cooking, especially her "Oma" salad dressing made with fresh lemon, oil, and a pinch of sugar. She sang as she worked and taught me many German songs, several of which I can sing to this day. Oma was invaluable to our family. She stayed with us for about four years until she left to care for her daughter's baby.

I like to think I helped Dad a lot in the store after my sister was born. My parents always intended for me to be part of the business. When I was five, Dad made a wooden step stool so I could reach the cash register. I learned early that my parents would reward me with love and attention for being good with customers. Mimicking my parents, I demonstrated toys with exuberant descriptions of what great play value they had. Customers appreciated a child's point of view and often asked for my recommendations. Like Mom, I loved to match a customer with just the right toy. I was one of the few store employees who could shimmy up the stockroom wall to retrieve toys, a task I quickly volunteered to do.

As I grew older, I helped out even more at Wee Folks. One evening shortly before Christmas, a man sat on a stool at the front counter, waiting for his wife to finish shopping. As I waited on her, he turned to Mom and said, "Don't turn that kid loose on me! She can sell anyone anything." I loved helping customers.

Dad's passion for the toy business and his excitement about toys showed on his face. To this day, I can see him bounding up to an unsuspecting customer with his childlike enthusiasm. With a crooked little smile and a wink, he would blurt out excitedly, "Want to see what just came in?"

"It was in 1950 when one of our most treasured friendships started. We were in the planning phase of Circus Nursery School on 79th Street. We came to Wee Folks to see what they had in materials and toys. Everyone in the neighborhood knew that Mr. Lazar was the only person with expertise in the toy field. We spent many evenings at the store. Manny let us look through his toy catalogs and pick out items that he would order for us. He came to the school many times in the months before we opened and gave us resources to help

us construct the school. My husband, Bill, was the main developer and created big equipment that had never been seen in a nursery school before: the giant fire engine, a four-room house, a bowling alley, a gas station, and a beauty shop. They were all larger than life and ready for action. Manny would just order toys with us in mind and then call us over to see them. His decisions were never wrong."—Harriet Grady

Dad always did extra things for customers without giving it a second thought. If mothers or daughters came in with squeaky buggies, Dad would squirt a little oil on the wheels. It never mattered if the item had been purchased at Wee Folks. For a woman without a husband or whose husband wasn't handy, Dad assembled toys and set them up on Christmas Eve. People often told us that their children would never have had a Christmas if it weren't for Dad. Customers would kiss and hug him. Dad was like a father to all of them.

Mom always said that the store was the best thing that ever happened to Dad, and made him feel that his life was worthwhile. "His parents didn't have much time to give him individual attention while he was growing up," she said. "But his instincts were to do things for people without ever worrying whether or not it would be good for business. The store was his humanity."

The customer list became longer, as did the hours. We were open until nine almost every weeknight and all day Saturday. We were closed Sundays, which was supposed to be our day of rest. But every Sunday turned into a catch-up day for Mom, who would address that week's Birthday Book mailings and do the bookkeeping and ordering. Dad checked in orders and searched toy catalogs for the newest and latest childhood wonder. And yet, even though the store was their life, the Tooth Fairy always remembered me and left a dime. Somehow my homework was always checked. Somehow I learned the stories of the Quick Running Squash and other favorites from Mom's nightly readings from the Book House Books.

In short order, Wee Folks had become one of the best-known stores in Chicago. It was a local leader in the toy industry, just like Mom's "Basic Principles of Operation" said it should be. She always said she felt Grandma Celia's hand on her shoulder and credited that feeling with the store's success.

"I can really feel my mother touch me," Mom would say. "When I am troubled, she provides a solution. She told me that if anything should happen to me, my father, Max Rosen, would keep me safe.

"We were really at home in the store. It was like being in church."

Wee Folks was famous for holding birthday party contests and other promotions.

CHAPTER 4

The Fabulous Fifties

Chicago, 1952

WEE FOLKS THRIVED DURING THE prosperous postwar years, and, from a business standpoint, was in the right place at the right time. After four years of rationing, scrap drives, and Victory Gardens, America was ready to get back to the business of living and playing again. The baby boom took off and toys were in demand like never before.

It took more than five years after rationing ended before toy manufacturing truly changed, and the early 1950s were a time of great creativity in toy design. When supplies of steel, rubber, and nylon were limited, toys were made of other materials, most commonly cardboard and wood. Manufacturers also experimented with plastics. That surge in creativity and diversity contributed to Wee Folks' early success.

Bigger was better when it came to the latest in toy design, and Dad's hand-hewn balconies now groaned with larger strollers, bigger buggies, heavier bikes. Many other toys grew in size, including those still swirling from the ceiling motors. The variety of toys and the demand for them grew as well. By the early 1950s there were more toys we wanted to sell than we had space to house. Toys were tucked into every cubbyhole and piled to the ceiling. Overnight it seemed that the self-serve aspect of the store disappeared as toys became harder for small visitors to reach. We weren't a retailing giant like Chicago's Goldblatt's or Spiegel, but business was booming. I always said that toys were *us* long before Toys 'R' Us, Babies 'R' Us, and Kids 'R' Us.

South Shore was undergoing changes too. The old electric streetcars that had lurched, bumped, and grumbled along 79th Street were replaced by buses. The trolley rails were now buried under layers of asphalt along with the copper pennies we once put on the tracks to be crushed. As the bus schedule was beefed up, more connections were added, making it easier for customers from outside the area to find Wee Folks. Route 79 was a popular one and it connected all over Chicago.

Seventy-ninth Street changed dramatically. Once-empty storefronts bloomed with merchandise. It seemed there was a merchant for every need. Brandt's store for ladies and children near Jeffery Boulevard carried nicer clothes for every occasion. Horney's Dime Store on Bennett was a treasure-trove of notions and potions, this and that, a little something for everyone. There were bakeries, cleaners, shoe stores, beauty shops, barbershops, food stores, and florists. There was even a funeral home, assuring people that they could live their whole lives, die, and be buried, all on 79th Street.

One of Dad's favorite stores, and mine, was Slutsky's Hardware, just a half-block east of our store. Dad was always at Slutsky's, hunting for a specific-size washer or screw that was missing from the box for some stroller or bike he needed to assemble. The only person who could find everything in that dimly lit store was Morrie Slutsky himself. Built into the wall on one side of the store were hundreds of small wooden boxes that held screws, brads, tacks, nuts, bolts, and washers of all sizes. If Morrie didn't have it, it probably didn't exist. He was a fix-it genius, and he and Dad were real pals.

When Wee Folks first opened, South Shore was primarily an Irish Catholic neighborhood. But a lot of other ethnicities were thrown in. You could hear accents from all over the world ringing through open store doors. The Greek food store owner, the Italian pizza man, the Jewish deli owner—all had immigrated here to make a better life for themselves in America.

Looking back, I guess people outside South Shore considered us an upper-middle-class Jewish community. By the early 1950s, while Jews made up just 2 percent of the nation's population, our neighborhood was about 40 percent Jews. More than 20,000 Jews of mostly Eastern European descent lived here. Initially, the Jewish population of South Shore was largely Reform or Conservative. In the early 1950s, an influx of Orthodox Jews from Eastern Europe started moving in from Chicago's Lawndale area.

Several area synagogues practiced various facets of the faith. South Shore Temple on Jeffery Boulevard represented the Reform movement. South Side Hebrew Congregation on 74th and Chappel Avenue was the Conservative *shul* (synagogue). After 1950, more Orthodox synagogues like Anshe Kinesses Israel and Torah moved in from Lawndale. Soon there was even a *mikvah* (a ritual bathhouse for women), a kosher bakery, and the Akiba Day School, where children learned Hebrew starting in the primary grades. Agugath Achim, an ultra-Conservative (almost Orthodox) congregation at 79th and Yates, held four-hour-long Hebrew school classes every Saturday morning. In the sanctuary, Orthodox male scholars stood on the *bema* (altar) with their *tallises* (prayer shawls) over their heads. As is customary in Orthodox Judaism, men and women sat in separate sections. The only English spoken was the occasional calling of page numbers.

In my early years, our family belonged to South Side Hebrew Congregation. I'm not sure why. By the time weekly services started on Friday night, Mom and Dad were too exhausted to attend. As Reformed Jews, my parents sent me to South Side to attend Hebrew school, but I was a less than ideal student. I know I gave Mrs. Garbo, my Hebrew teacher, a lot of trouble. Needless to say, I didn't reach the level of learning to be a *bat mitzvah* (coming-of-age ceremony at age thirteen).

When I was twelve, my folks enrolled me in Sunday school at Chicago Sinai Congregation in Hyde Park on Lake Michigan. This ultra-Reform congregation, founded by German Jews, was so nontraditional that we called it St. Sinai on the Lake. It was here I received most of my Jewish education and was confirmed. My parents went to Sinai's Sunday services. They loved to hear the inspiring sermons of Dr. Louis Mann, a brilliant rabbi of national prominence. Sinai also had frequent enrichment programs. I'll never forget hearing Louis Armstrong play in our sanctuary. After I became a semiprofessional singer, I sang with Sinai's choir for several years.

(I also sang with Max Janowski, a nationally known Jewish composer. A true taskmaster, Max taught me a lot. I sang with his choirs at KAM Temple in Hyde Park, for an Israel Bond ceremony in Chicago, and at churches throughout Chicago. For a while in my teens, I had an agent, Mr. Zamzow, who got me gigs at a few nightclubs, weddings, and other local events. I sang arias and classical music when most people wanted to hear rock 'n' roll. I was the soprano soloist for the Girls Chorus at South Shore High School all four years. I won a Chicago television amateur hour contest and met with someone at Capitol Records in Los Angeles, but my fame as a singer was not to be.)

Rodfei Shalom near Pill Hill, with a membership of more than 800 families, made it the largest center of Jewish community life in Chicago at that time. Many people also belonged to the Henry Hart Jewish Community Center at 91st and Jeffery and spent their summers at the swimming pool. B'nai Bezalel and Habonim were Conservative synagogues that supported the B'nai Brith, an international organization that helps Jews connect with their heritage and expand their cultural richness.

Two Jewish teen groups—AZA for boys and BBG for girls—were based at the large Jewish Community Center. Located at 76th and Phillips and sponsored by the Young Men's Jewish Council, the JCC sponsored activities and social functions for its members. Among the featured performers was Mandy Patinkin, who later achieved international prominence for his singing and acting abilities.

In addition, high school fraternities and sororities at Hyde Park, South Shore, and Bowen High Schools were almost entirely Jewish, totaling some 600 teenagers who met at the JCC. These non-school-sanctioned groups structured themselves to be similar to the college organizations, Greek names and all.

Several Jewish-owned retail establishments opened in the area between 71st and 79th Streets, like Hy's Delicatessen, Lazar's Drug Store (Dad's cousins), and Shapiro's Drug Store, at whose soda fountain I spent many an hour sipping Green Rivers and chocolate phosphates. Store signs appeared in Hebrew on shops like Jessleson's Fish Market. Along the main drags you could hear the cheerful sound of Yiddish words being exchanged between the merchants and the grandmothers. *"Arein, arein,"* ("Come in, come in") shopkeepers would call from the comfort of their chairs behind the store counters.

Yiddish is a spoken language, handed down from parent to child. Every geographic region in Europe had its own version. I knew Yiddish firsthand, as Dad and Mom spoke it often when they didn't want us kids to know what they were talking about. I caught on to the important phrases pretty quickly. In the store, it was often Mom warning Dad about a kid who might want to take a toy without the formality of a purchase. *"Gib a kuk"* meant that Dad should watch the kid, that he might get into trouble or steal something. From her perch on a stool behind the counter, Mom relied on her teacher's instincts to give her control of most situations. She trusted children to behave properly but watched the few she felt couldn't be trusted.

The 1950s were the dawn of the convenience era. Local stores *had* to be convenience-oriented, as most families had only one car and the father drove it to work. Delivery, which Wee Folks had offered from the get-go, was now the norm. We knew all the deliverymen as if they were friends. Phil, the Bowman Dairy milkman, delivered glass-bottled milk with cardboard stoppers from his horse-drawn wagon. Jerry, the iceman, still did cometh, and kids followed his creaking wagon to catch pieces of ice as they fell to the street. We sucked on the icy fragments until our hands were freezing and our clothes were sopping. Dave, the knife-sharpening man with his singsong pitch—"Scissors, knives, razors, blades"—showed up weekly at the back door. The junkman, Mr. Siegel, drove his horse-drawn wagon up and down the alleys, looking for good junk. Every summer evening neighborhood kids would wait for Harry, the Good Humor Man, who rode a bike with a cooler box in front. Abe, the fruit and vegetable man, was a regular at the store's back door. The postman delivered twice a day. And you could always get a kid to carry home your groceries for five cents.

It was a simple time, and folks never worried about the dangers we know all too well today. Kids rode their bikes all over the neighborhood and entered friends' unlocked houses without knocking or ringing the bell. We stayed outside until dark and our parents didn't worry. Somehow, we were safe even though we rode in cars without seat belts. Babies slept peacefully outside Wee Folks while their mothers shopped. We sat on front porches, front stoops, or street curbs, eating Twinkies and candy from Pete's Karmelkorn and Sweet Shop next to the Avalon Theater or from Crane's Rexall Drug Store on 79th and Bennett. We gorged ourselves on ice cream and sodas. Somehow, we never got fat.

As money was scarce in some homes, children often had to improvise playthings. We made up games with sticks and tennis balls. Boys built go-carts out of wood scraps and raced downhill, dragging their feet on the sidewalk to stop. We used hubcaps, paint can lids, and paper plates as early versions of Frisbees or as *laggers* (game pieces) for hopscotch. We pulled catalpa pods off the trees and set them a-sail down water-engorged gutters on rainy days with notes tucked inside, like Moses in the bulrushes.

Creativity in games and amusements ran especially rampant during the warmer weather. We played Stinkfish, a tag-you're-it game, plus hopscotch, jump rope, jacks, marbles, "baseball" with a Pensington Pinky hi-flyer rubber ball, Mother May I, Red Rover, hide-and-seek, blind man's bluff, and kick the can. We ran pell-mell through the sprinkler or through gushing water on those rare and glorious days when they opened the fire hydrant. We played cops and robbers and cowboys and Indians. We climbed trees, made backyard forts, ran lemonade stands, caught fireflies, had pillow fights, and laughed so hard we could bust. In the winter, we went ice-skating on a frozen pond at any of several area parks. When someone bought a new appliance or television set, the empty cardboard boxes became forts or play-houses, or vehicles for rolling down the grassy hill at South Shore High School.

By 1948, more than 200,000 people owned TVs. We didn't have one until 1952, when I was eleven. So after school, I went to a friend's house to watch my hero, the Lone Ranger (Clayton Moore), and his Potawatomie Indian friend, Tonto (Jay Silverheels), on an eleven-inch black-and-white. "The Lone Ranger" radio show had started in Detroit in 1933, sponsored by Wheaties, and aired three times a week. I was glued to the radio whenever the program was on. After twenty-one years, 3,500 half-hour radio shows, and 220 television shows, the run ended in 1954. During their reign, the Lone Ranger and Tonto had brought more than 22,000 bad guys to justice using 13,000 silver bullets. Lone Ranger merchandise was a main-stay in Wee Folks. We carried everything, from the Lone Ranger board game to the costume set, complete with guns and cloth mask.

Growing Up at Wee Folks

In those days, most moms stayed home while dads went off to work. I often envied the kids whose moms welcomed them home from school with a plate of freshly baked cookies.

In the early days of Wee Folks, I spent my afternoons after school in the back room doing my homework. I did my science projects there, many of them involving bugs. Mom hated bugs. After homework, I could play with friends or work in the store. If I worked, I got twenty-five cents an hour. Since working was how I earned spending money, I often chose to stay at the store. Once I turned ten, I worked every day for fifty cents an hour. By then, it was not an option. We were so busy I had to help out.

We were open every weekday evening at first, and later just two nights a week. There usually wasn't time to go home for dinner. Besides, Mom didn't have the time, inclination, or talent for cooking, so eating out was better for everyone. The many 79th Street restaurants were our constant haunts. We were the best customers at Miner Dunn's, a hamburger joint, as well as the St. Moritz, a little fancier restaurant; Lorentzen's, a nice sit-down place; the Chatterbox, close to Stony Island; and, if we had time to sit a while, Frank Sylvano's on 91st and Stony Island.

On nights when the store was open late, we sometimes ate at a strange place called the Kickapoo Inn. It was housed in an odd-looking triangular building at 79th and Stony Island. The Kickapoo always seemed rundown, and it looked like it could collapse at any minute. A sign outside boasted the sale of Kickapoo Joy Juice, whatever that was. There was a big bar and lots of eating space in the back. I remember it seeming seedy, with tables of unkempt men sitting together, smoking big cigars, talking in low voices, and exchanging money. Story is that the Kickapoo was a front for a bookie joint.

After Dad paid for the evening's meal, he often gave me a penny to put into the gumball machine next to the counter. The ball rolled down the chute and into my hand. Getting a gumball with stripes meant I had won a candy bar, given to me by the old man behind the counter. Sometimes we'd stop at the newsstand on the corner owned by the Streeter family. "Crippled Johnny" (no one seemed to know him by any other name) worked there during the week, while Mark and Phil Streeter worked on weekends.

On Sundays, we forayed farther from 79th Street for special dinners. We liked Phil Schmidt's on Calumet Avenue in Whiting, Indiana. They were famous for their frog's legs, and Dad loved them. I could never bring myself to eat them, even though Dad said they tasted like chicken. I especially began to dislike them when I started dissecting fermented frogs in high school biology class.

Sometimes we would stop at the Tropical Hut in Hyde Park after a family outing to the Museum of Science and Industry at 57th and the lake. (The museum is the only building remaining from the Columbian Exposition of the 1890s.) I could always get a Polynesian kiddie cocktail with a little umbrella in it.

I attended Horace Mann Elementary School at 80th and Chappel Avenue, about half a mile from the store. I couldn't make it home for lunch and back in an hour, so I often ate alone at the noisy Pla-Mor Bowling Alley counter, watching the pin boys do the set-ups and unemployed and retired men bowl. Sometimes I went to Walgreens or, on special days, to White Castle for a slider.

Since I knew all the merchants on the street and they knew me, I was never far from my parents' sight. I couldn't get away with anything. I practically lived next door at Mr. Schaider's Delicatessen. To this day, I believe heaven smells of fermented garlic, sour new pickles, and corned beef, pastrami, and beef tongue. It was at Schaider's that I learned to love *halivah,* a flaky Jewish delicacy made with sesame. I visited the deli daily, perusing the penny and nickel candy, my store wages burning a hole in my pocket.

I paced in front of the long case that held three rows of glass jars covered with tight lids. Should I choose wax lips, candy cigarettes, Red Hots, Coke-shaped wax bottles filled with colored sugar water, or Bulls Eyes, those caramel circles with soft, white candy inside (still my favorite)? Or should I buy candy dots on a long strip of white paper, Green Leafs, red or black licorice sticks, lollypops, Mary Janes, malted milk tablets, or a candy necklace? It was a tough choice and took time. And whatever I chose, I had to make it last the entire day. Mr. Schaider was a patient man, but after following me back and forth, white paper bags in hand, he grew tired of me and said, *"Gib zich a shukl!"* ("Shake it up—hurry!").

Life's passages took place in our store's back room. Parents talked over plans for their kids' Christmas, worried about staying within a budget. From the safety of the back room, I could hear parents in the store admonish their kids, "Keep that up and I'll give you something to cry about" and "Because I said so, that's why."

The Movies—1952

Dad had hundreds of ideas for promotions, but the best were cooperative ventures with movie theaters. He felt that theaters could be used for more than showing cartoons and films. He devised promotions to showcase toys, then visited area theaters to pitch them. As with most new ideas, it was rejected at first. But soon it was the beginning of a win-win situation for both the movie houses and us.

Dad's biggest break came when he met Pete Paisano, manager of the Avalon Theater. Pete and Dad became instant buddies and established a long-standing relationship as well as wildly successful promotions.

In the 1920s and 1930s, almost every Chicago neighborhood had one or more movie houses. As profits grew, so did the size of the theaters. By the end of the 1920s they were called movie palaces, and for good reason. The city's theater owners, most notably Balaban and Katz, expected their palaces to draw audiences from across the city, not just the immediate neighborhood. They hoped that the theaters' classical architectural details would allay fears that movies were corrupting the minds and morals of the city's youth. It worked. By the end of the 1920s, movie attendance was one of the city's most popular leisure activities.

The Avalon, at Cornell and 79th Street, was one of the largest, most ornate, and impressive theaters in America—and *the* cinema mecca in South Shore. It was close to bustling Stony Island Avenue, across the street and a few blocks west of Wee Folks. John Eberson, a designer of 500 theaters nationally, including the Paradise in Chicago's Garfield Park, created the huge structure in 1926. It looked like a Moorish temple with its towering minarets. A Persian incense burner that Eberson had found in an antiques market inspired his design.

The Avalon's interior displayed an immense oriental rug, said to be the world's largest, hanging from the lobby's twenty-foot ceiling. We kids were convinced it was a flying carpet. The lobby also boasted a gigantic Wurlitzer organ. Five murals made of tiny inlaid mosaic tiles adorned the walls along with a series of floor-to-ceiling mirrors. The entire place was encrusted with imitations of semiprecious jewels. A working fountain and a grand piano graced the balcony. A winding marble staircase enhanced the splendor of the theater's rich yellows and blues. The ceiling's small electric lights twinkled like stars. It created an atmosphere of an imaginary courtyard surrounded by exotic buildings under a starry sky. In the 2,400-seat auditorium four fierce gargoyles guarded the stage. It all looked like pages from the stories of the *Arabian Nights.*

Wee Folks held seven or eight promotions a year at the Avalon in the fifties. Dad would set up an elaborate display of toys in the lobby so kids could see what they might win in next week's drawing. In addition, the theater would play a brief "trailer" about our store. On the big day, a kid could see twenty-five cartoons for twenty-five cents and perhaps win the toy of his dreams right from the stage. Dad and I coordinated many of the events. I had my first onstage moment at the age of eleven, when I awarded prizes to the kids with winning tickets. Later, promotions expanded to include the Rhodes Theater, farther west on 79th Street.

I particularly remember the annual Christmas promotions that started in the 1950s and continued for years. Dad put a glass and wood display case in the Avalon lobby and filled it with the hottest, most tempting toys of the season. Enormous signs told moviegoers four weeks in advance that a big toy giveaway would take place on stage the Saturday before Thanksgiving. The theater showed one regular kids' feature and twenty-five cartoons, and then Dad and I took the stage. We drew winning ticket stubs for bikes, cap guns and holsters, and all things Mickey Mouse. Only a handful of kids won each time, but those who did remember the thrill to this day. The drawings pulled in so many kids that theaters started approaching Wee Folks with dates and ideas for cross-promotions.

"I have many fond memories of Wee Folks even though I never set foot inside the store! My older sister and I would save our allowance money and once a month we would walk to the Avalon Theater from 81st and Phillips. Twice a year the Avalon Theater would have a big toy giveway, with all of the toys from Wee Folks. Each person would receive one raffle ticket and between the cartoon and the movie they would call out number after number. There were so many toys and bicycles, and with tickets in hand we would dream of winning something really big. The first numbers called could pick any toy or bicycle they wanted. One by one, the numbers would be called and the big prizes would leave the stage. How we longed for a big prize, but alas, it was not to be. My older sister never won a toy, but I was usually lucky and would win something every year. Often it was a coloring set or a game and I really cherished the toy. Often, it was the only toy I would receive the entire year. When I think back now, I realize that I thought only parents went into toy stores and bought toys. Having never been in a toy store until I was a parent, it seems quite logical for an eight-year-old's thinking. Unfortunately, my parents also didn't go into toy stores, so toys were not among my memories."—Sandee Cohen Kosner

"I distinctly remember the fly-back paddleball contests in front of Wee Folks. I stood outside in front of Wee Folks with fifty other contestants. We would hit the ball over and over until we missed. I was one of the last survivors and I went on to the contest on the stage at the Avalon with ten other kids. The contest was between the Saturday movies. Yes, we got to see two movies for the price of one. I came in second, missed the bike, and got a model airplane."
—Larry Schimmel

When Dad sponsored Yo-Yo competitions, kids from all over the area were eager to show their skill. The Duncan Company awarded embroidered badges prized by Yo-Yoists. The Super Tournament model, made of American hard rock maple, was the inspiration for all of the classic Yo-Yo tricks. Other popular models in the 1950s included the Butterfly, whose wide string gap made it easier to do tricks like "the Trapeze," "Double or Nothing," and "Shoot the Moon."

*"We would go in a group of boys to the twenty-five-cent double fea-
ture at the Avalon Theater almost every Saturday morning. I remember that there often were special theme matinees, and your store
sponsored the Yo-Yo exhibitions between features. I do remember buying my first Duncan Yo-Yo at your store and just wandering through,
looking at all of the toys, almost every Saturday."—Doug Schwartz*

*"I lived on the East Side, and for many years we rode the bus to
the Avalon for a double feature. Can you imagine sitting through
two movies? We never checked the times—just walked in, and at a
certain point, we just got up and said, 'Well, this is where we came
in,' and then left in the middle of the movie. Sometimes before the
show, I would beg my Aunt Dorothy to take me across the street to
your store. Thanks for the memory!"—Sharon Kookich Nasella*

"Theater events are a natural for a toy store," Dad told a
reporter for *Toys and Novelties* magazine. "What better spot for
a display of Disney character toys than in the lobby of a theater
featuring eight Mickey Mouse cartoons?"

My perk from Pete and Dad's relationship was that on many
Saturdays, I could walk up to the Avalon's ticket booth, ask for
Pete, and be escorted into the theater for free. In those days,
parents didn't think twice about sending their kids to the show
alone without an older chaperone or parent. Most movies were
clean-cut and so were the kids.

I always got candy at the Avalon counter too. They had all
my usual favorites—Milk Duds, Chunky Chocolate Bars, Al-
mond Joy, and Clark Bars. I still recall the advertising with the
camel saying, "I want a Clark Bar." I knew Pete would give me
all the popcorn I wanted, but knowing I would be at the
movies for several hours, I also bought a box of Indian Head
sunflower seeds and candy from Pete's Karmelkorn and Sweet
Shop next door.

Adding On

By 1952, Wee Folks was bursting at the seams. Dad needed
more storage space for Christmas merchandise. One day, while
prowling around the rear of the building, he followed a rusty
metal staircase to a basement area he knew nothing about. It

was home to thousands of ugly black water bugs, which terrified me. Dad told the landlord he would finish the space as long as there would be no increase in rent. The landlord agreed.

At first the space seemed like one room, but when Dad took a pickaxe to the concrete walls, he heard a hollow sound. He hacked his way through two more walls, creating three rooms under the building. I remember crawling through the round holes to go from room to room. There was never enough headroom in the connecting areas for anyone over four-feet-five to stand upright. But we somehow managed to squeeze ourselves and a stack of merchandise all at once through each of the holes.

During our first year with the new basement, Dad poured a concrete floor, added a sump pump, and built floor-to-ceiling wooden shelves at three-foot and six-foot levels that held even the heaviest toys. He added an electrical panel and lights. I was always amazed at the things Dad could do. He wasn't a highly educated man or trained in electrical work and plumbing, but somehow he just knew how to do everything.

He built wooden stairs that led out of the depths of the basement to a trap door he cut into the floor of the east stockroom. When we needed merchandise, we had to lift the heavy wooden trap door by its metal ring, prop it open with a two-by-four, and carefully pick our way down the narrow wooden stairs. Even Mom could do it after a while. I never had any trouble, but because of the dreaded water bugs I tried not to be the first one down for the day, the one who turned on the lights.

This storage area saved Christmas almost every year thereafter. It was the place that hundreds of layaways resided, waiting for their new owners. Large cardboard boxes were filled to the brim with gift-wrapped toys, each with a sticker bearing a child's name. They stayed there until Christmas Eve when Dad and I would deliver them.

Manny's Inferno—December 5, 1953

It was the first week of December, and most of our Christmas shipments had arrived. Dad had unpacked them and hundreds of brown cardboard boxes now sat empty and stacked all over the floor of the back room. We used many to hold layaways, but dozens more were left over. Garbage day was three days away, and the landlord wouldn't allow Dad to store boxes in the basement because of the fire hazard. And he wasn't allowed to put them into the dumpster outside before garbage day.

Dad knew the rules, but he was an impatient, impetuous man. He knew it was dangerous to add other fuels to the sub-basement's coal furnace, which heated the store and the apartments above it, including ours. But the extra boxes were in his way and we needed the precious back room space to receive even more merchandise the following week. Near closing on Saturday night, December 5, Dad had had enough.

"Let's get this stuff outta here!" he roared at me.

We shoved several piles of boxes out the back door and into the alley. My job was to flatten and sail them down the snowy concrete stairs to the basement. Dad opened the door to the furnace room and dragged them inside. After I was finished at the top, I joined him. I had never been in the furnace room before. It was large, dark, and filthy, with junk scattered all around the walls. A single light bulb swayed from a long cord, and when it was turned on the ever-present water bugs went scurrying. In the middle of the room stood the cavernous old furnace.

I jumped on the boxes, crushing them even flatter so Dad could fold them in half. He opened the door of the furnace and started stuffing boxes into its gaping, fiery mouth. It seemed like he was going to put all of the boxes in at once.

BOOM! WHUSH! The explosion sounded like a car crash and then like air being sucked from the room. Flames leaped out of the furnace and enveloped Dad. He screamed as his flannel shirt caught fire. I was near the rear of the room, far enough away to be unharmed. Looking around, I saw several filthy moving-company pads lying in the corner. I grabbed one and threw it on top of him. Remembering what firefighters had taught us during our visits to the firehouse, I rolled Dad in the first pad and ran for more. After three pads, the fire was snuffed out, but his face and chest were severely burned. His glasses were askew, but they saved his eyes. Somehow I needed to get Dad up to the first floor and into the store where Mom could fix him up. I started dragging all 200 pounds of him across the sooty basement floor, now filled with burning pieces of cardboard. When we got to the bottom of the staircase, I didn't have the strength to continue.

"Wait here, Dad, I'll get help."

"Hurry . . . hurry."

I ran up the stairs into the alley, entering the back room to get Mom. She called the fire department and within minutes they had Dad loaded onto a stretcher and on his way to Jackson Park Hospital. They told us he would be there for several weeks.

What would our store do without Santa for the month of December?

Compassionate customers stepped forward, posting a list in the back room and signing up to work two- and three-hour shifts. Many volunteers were wealthy people who had cooks and maids, but when Mr. Wee Folks needed them, they wanted to help.

When Joseph Schoeneman, a long-time customer, heard about the furnace accident, he knew Dad's absence would be hard on Mom. Even though he already had a full-time job, Joseph often stayed to help until the wee hours, preparing the store for the next day:

"With the holiday season approaching, there were deliveries every day of huge boxes of merchandise. Each carton had to be taken to the basement for storage and handling, opening and pricing, and then carried back upstairs and stocked appropriately in the store. It was a daunting task for a woman alone because she also had to tend to customers, keep records, and still make a home for her daughters.

"At that time I was in the installment business. Since it was a very busy time for retail sales, I was out working till very late in the evening, delivering purchases and making collections. I could imagine how overwhelmed Belle must have been, and I had great empathy for her and understood her dilemma. I offered my help and she wisely accepted. After work I came to Wee Folks and stocked shelves, carried cartons downstairs, did whatever needed doing and kept occupied until one or two in the morning. When Belle locked up the store, it was ready for the next day's business. It was hard and tiring work but very satisfying. I guess it was a real mitzvah *[good deed].*

"After Manny was healed and was back to a normal working schedule, he and Belle wrote a very beautiful letter of thanks. They invited my wife, Marian, and me to be their guests at a beautiful evening at the Chez Paree, the finest nightclub in Chicago at the time. We enjoyed a special dinner and dancing and each other's company and made a wonderful memory."—Joseph Schoeneman

This was the first time I saw my dad as fallible, more like a man and less like a hero. After that, I think I was always afraid that something terrible would happen to him.

The Big Flood—October 2–4, 1954

It was nearing Christmas and, once again, new merchandise was arriving every day. For weeks, Wee Folks employees had been opening items, tagging them, and storing them downstairs. The battery-operated toys were especially amazing: drinking bears, clapping monkeys, drink-mixing bartenders. But all the toys seemed bigger this year, and it was a struggle going up and down the stairs with an extra-long Tonka Hydraulic Aerial Ladder fire engine, Rallye Race Car set, Casey Jr. Disneyland Express, or Fort Apache. Even the stuffed animals had grown to gigantic proportion, and some of the Steiff toys were a full five feet tall. The storage area was stuffed with Christmas merchandise.

"I think often of the privilege of working in a toy store and under such wonderful people as your parents. I still have the Steiff bear they gave me for my high-school graduation. He has moved with me many times and, now eyeless, rests on a shelf in my office."
—Susan Richardson McKelvey

Because South Shore was prone to flooding, Dad had installed a second new sump pump in the basement storage area. But on Saturday, October 2, Chicago was hit with one of the biggest rainfalls on record. By midnight almost four inches had fallen. Union Station in Chicago flooded, as did the main post office. Pumping equipment shorted out, sending water cascading through the drains and into the basement of the *Chicago*

Daily News. Paper stock valued at a quarter of a million dollars was ruined and the machinery was put out of service. CTA transportation buses ran hours late. The Red Cross evacuated thousands of families, many of whom searched for each other by motorboat. Marooned motorists tried to escape in their cars, but got trapped in roof-high water under flooded viaducts. One person died.

To save downtown, the locks between the Chicago River and Lake Michigan were opened, the first time since 1900, when the flow of the river and its sewage was diverted south from Lake Michigan and into the Mississippi River through the newly built Sanitary and Ship Canal. A gigantic swell of water roared into the lake, but the river kept rising. South Shore received more than six inches of rain and the sewers couldn't hold it.

By early Sunday morning the worst of it seemed over, but a second wave hit. Another two inches of rain fell during the afternoon. Hardest hit was the area between 69th and 87th Street. That day and the next, a heat record of seventy-three degrees was set.

Dad was working in the store that Sunday. If he had had the radio on, he would have heard the latest warnings about basements flooding all over the city. He heard a loud GRUMPH from the basement as the new sump pump groaned, growled, and erupted out of its pit, spraying sand for yards around it.

Dad ran downstairs, took one look at the rising water, and ran back up to call Mom. Mom called me at Southfield Methodist Church, where I was attending a Youth Fellowship meeting, a philanthropic group that always seemed to be helping the community. At their regular Sunday night meetings, Reverend Bill Yandell would talk about issues of importance to teenagers between seventh and twelfth grades. The church planned activities, retreats, and discussion groups and worked on charitable projects such as serving at soup kitchens. While I wasn't Christian, I was welcomed with open arms.

When the call came in, Reverend Yandell called me over. "It's your mom, Caryn," he said. "There's trouble!" I don't remember asking them to help, but Reverend Yandell and the entire group of thirty-some teenagers ran the three blocks with me to the store through the hard rain. The heat and humidity were oppressive.

Three feet of rainwater had already risen in the basement. One by one, the group jumped in, even Jack, the boy with a game leg and crutches. They formed a line that started at the last room addition, snaked to the stairs, then climbed to the first floor. Hands held high, they passed dolls, trucks, games, and magic kits overhead, piece after piece, from one kid to the next. The upstairs group loaded the store's back room with all the goods.

Three feet, four feet—the water kept rising. Dad's brother Jack, the engineer, called from California to see if we were all right. When he heard about our flooded basement, he told Mom to get all of us out of there before the water reached the electric meters or we would be electrocuted. Everyone tore out of the basement but not before we had saved over half of our Christmas merchandise. Clothes clung to us like a second skin, and even though it was over seventy degrees outside, we shivered after standing in the chilly floodwater. Mom made hot chocolate for everyone and tried to look cheerful, but she knew our Christmas was in trouble. Even if we had had the funds, it was too late to reorder merchandise.

An even more serious rainstorm the following weekend dumped as many as twelve inches on Chicago, especially in the south and west areas, making October 1954 the wettest October ever. Flooding during that second weekend alone caused an estimated $25 million in damages.

Wee Folks made it through that Christmas, thanks to local toy jobbers who extended us credit before the holidays and got us a few of the harder-to-find and more in-demand toys. In January, Mom and Dad gratefully made a donation to the Southfield Methodist Church's building fund and to the MYF group.

The floods of 1954 were followed by the seventeen-year locusts (cicadas) of 1956. These giant grasshoppers crunched their way through the crops of Illinois and the entire Midwest. I remember when they swarmed over Chicago, covering the sky like a dark cloud of doom. Their calling and mating sounds could be heard from blocks away. Their two-inch-long black bodies and blood red eyes were never more frightening than when they became tangled in women's beehive hairdos. The abundance of hairspray we used in those days made it practically impossible to extricate the cicadas, whose legs were often left behind when their bodies were pulled free. Maybe they thought our hair was a good nesting place to lay their eggs before dying. Layers of locusts covered the sidewalks as I walked to school, crunching thousands of their bodies under my feet.

Family Time

After the flood, our family began to experience a period of good times. Business at Wee Folks was gangbusters. Toy manufacturers started seeking us out to make sales presentations on new products. We could always spot a toy salesman. He wore a suit, even in summer, and carried a big, wide briefcase that opened from the top in two parts. I'm not sure if Mom and Dad made appointments with them or if they just strolled in, but in any case, the salesmen seemed to come when we were at our busiest. The other employees and I would mind the store as my parents and a salesman would go into the back room to see what was new. I was dying to see too, so I often sneaked back to listen.

I feel that growing up in the Wee Folks family made me an honor student at Toys and Games University. I learned how toys worked, how to demonstrate them, and how to explain their play value to a customer.

We had been around long enough to see families grow up and have families of their own. Many of the young people who grew up with the store would stop at Wee Folks to show us their new babies. "Mazel tov, mazel tov," we said to our Jewish and Irish customers, who received blessings from Mom and a quick hug from Dad. By now, we had more than 5,000 names in the Birthday Book and Mom spent more and more time on the cards, hand-addressing each one of these customer generators.

For the first time, my parents could take time to enjoy themselves. Dad, who had not had a vacation since the store opened in 1945, started taking the four of us on short summer trips to nearby dude ranches and resorts, like the Nippersink Resort in Wisconsin. It looked like the set of *Dirty Dancing.* In later years, we stayed at the Wagon Wheel Dude Ranch, where we all rode horseback. I loved to ride. I had started riding English saddle at a Jackson Park stable when I was five and was pretty good at it.

As a child, I had gone to Rainbow Day Camp run by Horace Mann Elementary School's gym teacher, Dan Trahey. In my early teens, I went to a Wisconsin riding camp for six weeks. Campers had their own horses to train and saddle break. This was a joyous time of my life, and it kept me off the streets and out of trouble. During the school year, I took the bus to a western-style stable at 95th and Kean. We often went on hayrides with hordes of kids and few chaperones. Looking back, I realize my parents probably couldn't afford this extravagance, but they wanted me to have good experiences.

Our family especially loved summer because it wasn't Christmas. We weren't a real family at Christmas, just merchants working side by side to make a living. Even though Chanukah fell in December, we never had a chance to celebrate it. On Christmas Eve, long after midnight and the last delivery was made, Dad would put up our Christmas tree and set up a Lionel electric train around it, complete with houses, switches, and buildings, just as he had done for so many customers during the holiday. I was never sure why he thought my sister and I would like trains, but he did and that was what counted. He played with them all Christmas Day. That evening my parents would try to celebrate their wedding anniversary. No restaurants were open, but Mom—never the accomplished cook—made brisket as a special dinner for Dad.

Even though they didn't have sons, Dad and his fellow merchant and good buddy, Morrie Slutsky, didn't let that stop them from enjoying typical father-son outings with their daughters. For several summers in the 1950s, Dad and I went with Morrie and his daughter, Edabel, on annual fishing pilgrimages to a quiet lake somewhere in Wisconsin. I was about eleven when we started and Edabel was a couple of years older. We'd all pile into the boat early in the morning and wouldn't return until sunset. Dad made lures and put me on a first-name basis with worms and minnows. Sitting in the aluminum fishing boat on the silvery lake with the sun glittering on the water was my idea of heaven. It was the only time I really saw Dad relax. There were no phones, no orders to fill, no schlepping of merchandise— only the ker-plunk of lures and the clear water rippling against the side of the boat.

I learned to bait the hook, cast the line, and take the fish off the hook. I also learned more about my dad as a human being and a friend. He could be a tough taskmaster in the store, but never harder on anyone than he was on himself. Dad seemed closer to Morrie than almost any other person, other than Mom. Dad could relate to Morrie. He was Jewish like Dad, but I don't know if that was the reason. They both were merchants whose young lives had been hard. I always thought Morrie looked like Yul Brynner with his shaved head. He and Dad laughed a lot. Edabel and I shared a cabin and giggles over girl stories.

One day during the summer of 1956, my fishing pole doubled over and a big muskie led me on a merry chase. Dad showed me how to work the mighty fish close to the boat. After what seemed like an hour, the muskie was close enough for Dad to scoop it into the net, tail flailing and jerking. Everyone caught something big that day. We took pictures, Morrie did the cleaning, and we all did the eating. It was a great day for fishing and an unforgettable summer.

Dad loved cars, all kinds, but especially souped-up ones. At that time he owned a "woodie," a station wagon with wooden side panels. When I was fifteen, I wanted to learn how to drive. Many kids' parents had sent them to driving schools, but my dad wanted to teach me himself. He let me drive alone for the first time in the Sears parking lot on 79th Street. He was unbelievably patient while I let out the clutch too fast and killed the engine over and over and over. I suppose it was because Dad taught me to drive that I drive just like him: with a lead foot. He taught me to change the oil, fix a carburetor, and love cars. So while other girls my age primped for dances, I followed the car crowd to the Friday night drag races on 95th Street. Afterward we'd go to Melody Lane for a Rocket Sundae or the largest banana splits in Chicago.

When I was sixteen, the '57 Chevy was my dream car. It may have had something to do with my first boyfriend, who owned one. We cruised 79th Street to the Overflow, the South Shore necking spot at 79th and Lake Michigan, to watch the "submarine races." That was code for sitting in our boyfriend's car on a double date, listening to the Top 10 Hit Parade, and looking out over the water. Or we would drag race on side streets, laying rubber with stations WLS or WJJD blaring on the radio. We had "Moments to Remember," and it was not only on "Blueberry Hill." We hung onto every word from Jim Lounsbury on "Chicago Bandstand" as he played the latest hits and interviewed DJs from all over the country. We joined the Bill Haley fan club.

For a brief time after I turned sixteen, I decided that my parents were much too hard on me. They bawled me out for not working hard enough or forgetting to do something. And they did it in front of the other employees. So I decided to quit and get a job where people treated me better. I went to work at Burny Brothers Bakery on 71st near Jeffery. After a couple of months of standing during my shifts, for hours on end behind the counter in my perky pink uniform, and suffering bleeding cuts on my hands from tying cake boxes, I begged my parents to let me come back to Wee Folks. They did. Same salary.

As my sister grew older, Mom had more time to become involved in community affairs. She became a Brownie leader for Troop 719, which met at the Southfield Methodist Church. In addition to my sister and Reverend Yandell's daughter, a cross-section of our South Shore neighborhood belonged: Roberta Goodman and Mary Lou Flynn, Susan and Beth Kupper, and Patricia Murphy. When the Brownies became Girl Scouts, Mom took over as a troop leader for several years. She used her teaching skills to make this troop the star of the area. Hugh Celander, 79th Street's "official photo studio," photographed Brownie Troop 719. His son, Charles, is the author of *Chicago's South Shore,* which features many of his dad's South Shore memories.

"It was special just to be in your mom's Girl Scout troop. Wee Folks and Circus Nursery School had a big impact on South Shore and had a positive role in the development of its children."
—*Harriet Grady*

Customers and Service

At this point, many merchants started carrying store credit. To keep track of credit purchases, Mom created a system of little brown envelopes that she kept in a file cabinet under the register. We wrote up orders in triplicate on the old Uarco machine. One copy went to the customer, the second onto the layaway item, and the third into the envelope.

We often started Christmas layaways in January, but many customers weren't able to pay them off by Christmas. We carried them anyway.

Wee Folks offered to get any toy that customers wanted. A call to Regent 4-4510 got you a "personal shopper"—my mom—who would listen patiently while you described the birthday boy you forgot or the sick child who needed entertaining. She would select the most appropriate item and wrap it as a gift. Either Dad delivered it later in the day or a mom could send one of her kids to pick it up. Of course, we put it on the charge.

"Why did people shop on 79th Street? In those days, people's shopping focus was narrower. In the 1950s and 1960s, South Shore's Jewish and Irish customer mix gave the neighborhood merchants the first shot to get everything. It was the birth of relationship marketing. People didn't have the mobility they have today. There was only one car in the family and Dad took it to work. So moms called stores and had things delivered or sent kids for it. Stores extended their own credit, gift-wrapped purchases, assembled items for free, and even delivered. They served a definite niche in South Shore. In 1957, there were few credit cards and to get them you had to have money and a bank account or a credit history. Taking in-store credit was a significant way to develop and keep customers. Much of Wee Folks' success came from the relationship that your parents created with their customers. They had good buying sense and had unique and novel things you could not find anywhere else. If they did not have it, they got if for you."
        —*John C. Melaniphy II, Chicago retail consultant*

"I remember getting a color-by-number set of Colonial Williamsburg when I was eight. From that toy, I fell in love with that place. I recently fulfilled a lifelong dream of visiting there."
        —*Cheri Brown Stute*

"I remember my younger brother David getting his Davy Crockett outfit there . . . down to the coon skin cap."—Jeanne Sager

"My father and grandfather owned Mel Turner & Son Auto Repair on 79th Street from 1929 to 1972. As a young boy, my mom used to take me to Wee Folks. Dad had been a pilot during the war and I loved airplanes, but the shiny silver airliners really caught my eye. Around 1952, your folks had just what I was looking for— a big, all-metal, four-engine DC4, with a friction-motor undercarriage. It was hanging from the ceiling and was pretty expensive, but I had my heart set on it. Dad was making only sixty bucks a week, but my mom saved up what she needed from her shopping allowance. When my birthday came in August, there it was. I have no recollection of what became of the plane, but it's funny how you always remember 'the want' and then 'the gift.' Seventy-ninth had plenty of little store gems . . . and your folks had the best one of them."—Don Turner

"My mom and dad used to take my older brothers and me there a lot. Two weeks before my father died in November 1955, we came to your store to purchase Christmas presents. I remember a small gray robot that walked along the floor. My dad bought that robot for us and we opened the present containing it that Christmas. I have few memories of my father. This story is one of my favorite ones about him."—Donald W. Larson

Early in my life my world had been filled with outstanding personalities: TV and radio stars like Laurel and Hardy, Howdy Doody, the Lone Ranger, the Shadow, and Roy Rogers and Dale Evans. But Wee Folks had many famous customers too. Cassius Clay and his wife came in often as they lived near the store. Clay, who later became known as Muhammad Ali, was definitely the buying kind of father. He has been quoted as saying, "I want to buy them horses! I want to buy them every toy in the world!" He did some of that at Wee Folks.

Several entertainers grew up in South Shore, including Mahalia Jackson, Steve Allen, and jazz musician Ramsey Lewis. Several entertainers were Wee Folks customers, including Bo Diddley, Corky Siegal, and Mandy Patinkin. Patinkin credits my dad with his long-time interest in Lionel trains. He still has one of the largest collections in the country. Patinkin also admits that his Yo-Yo proficiency came from the many contests we sponsored. He claims never to have won anything big, but says he still plays with a Yo-Yo while he rehearses for his concerts. And blues musician Corky Siegel recalls the toy he received when he was sick:

> *"When I had the mumps I received a pegboard with little wooden pegged houses. There was a light coming out of this little wooden toy, and I know the people at Wee Folks had a lot to do with that. They were that kind of people. I still feel this light and it still uplifts me."—Corky Siegal*

Sports figures like Pete Ward, Billy Pierce, and Sammy Esposito of the White Sox were our neighbors. Mary Levy, former coach of the Buffalo Bills, lived on South Shore Drive. George Connor, one of the first of the Chicago Bears greats, was from South Shore. Gayle Sayers of the Bears lived at 68th and Constance. Ernie Banks of the Chicago Cubs ran the car dealership on Stony Island.

People from many walks of life who later became famous began their lives in South Shore. Boxer Gene Tunney, Paramount Studios CEO Sheri Lansing, playwright David Mamet, singer Mel Torme, financial guru Suze Orman, Oracle president Larry Ellison, actors Amy Madigan and Robert Conrad— all were residents of our neighborhood.

But the real celebrity was the larger-than-life one who lived at our house. I never realized in those days what a legend my dad was in our neighborhood. To me, he was just Dad. The force of his personality drove the business. His brilliant promotional ideas created loyalties so strong that, even after the neighborhood changed and many customers moved away, they would call from all over the country to place their holiday orders.

> *"I remember Mr. Lazar as one of the most friendly and helpful merchants from my childhood. He always had the neatest toys and always seemed to be truly interested in us. I wanted the cream-and-blue Mercury equipped with a fully furnished house trailer in tow. It kind of reminded me of the movie with Lucy and Desi. To my amazement, the car and trailer showed up at my house and I was*

*the happiest kid in the neighborhood. I don't know what ever be-
came of that toy, but I will always remember it with fondness. I also
recall starting my Corgi car collection, which I recently took out of
storage to display in my septuagenarian father's collection. I'm sure
Mr. Lazar influenced my decision to collect Corgis and, for that, I
will always remember him."—Garry LaVine*

It was my parents' drive and my dad's moxie and policy of
aggressive promotion that was responsible for Wee Folks out-
growing its small quarters on 79th and Constance. The enthusi-
astic reception families in the neighborhood gave to Mom and
Dad made them long for enough space to make their customers
more comfortable. In 1956 my parents began looking for a new
79th Street location for the store. I was fifteen, my sister was six.

After a long search, Mom and Dad visited the empty shell
of Mr. Matay's Music Store. The rent was high and the space
was dirty, but it was a double store with a vacant second floor.
And it was just three blocks west of Wee Folks, kitty-corner
from the Avalon Theater.

They made their decision and started preparing to move in
June and July of 1957. They worked with the Avalon to pro-
mote a huge sale to reduce inventory. Every adult customer
who brought in the Wee Folks ad from the *Southtown Economist*
received a free ticket to the Avalon's latest features: *Tammy and
the Bachelor* with Debbie Reynolds, or *Midnight Story* with
Tony Curtis.

What started as a children's toy, clothing, and wheeled-
goods store would soon be expanded into the only self-service
toy store in Chicago. By the time we opened the new store in
September 1957, a second wave of exciting new toys like Barbie was being developed. Our sales skyrocketed, propelling us
to record success for the next ten years.

Mom and Dad on opening day in the new store, 1957.

CHAPTER 5

Grand Opening:
The Second Store

September 5, 1957

THEY STARTED LINING UP BY seven o'clock on that bright Thursday morning in September outside of 1708–1710 East 79th Street. Some walked to the corner of 79th and East End while others took the bus. Sure, they knew the doors to the new Wee Folks store wouldn't open until 9:00, but they just had to be there. By 8:30, a sea of excited kids and parents flowed down the street and around the block from the storefront, which had been spruced up with multicolored streamers that flapped in the cool breeze.

Those lucky enough to be toward the front of the line peered through the two large display windows on either side of

95

the entrance. For weeks, white paper signs promising a vast selection of dolls, carriages, bicycles, books, games, hobbies, and juvenile furniture had covered the windows. On Monday the signs came down. The east window was now chock-full of burp guns, Bonanza and Gunsmoke rifles, and Mattel's latest toys for boys. Prizes for the grand-opening contest were on display as well: a first-prize Rempel horse, Disney squeeze toys, Mattel's Mickey Mouse Club Newsreels, Mickey Mousegetar Jr., and Popeye Getars.

The west window—the "girls' window"—featured dolls and an eye-popping assortment of doll accessories, from buggies to bottles to layettes, all designed to hold little mothers spellbound. Some kids waited with dimes in hand for a chance to ride "the Champion," the mechanical horse outside the east window. But during the grand opening celebration, all rides were free.

Everyone knew it was going to be exciting. For weeks, the *Southtown Economist,* the *Chicago Tribune,* the *Chicago Daily News,* and the *Chicago Sun-Times* had run articles and ads about the three-day grand opening of Chicago's only 100-percent self-service "Supermarket for Tots." All 8,000 children in the store's Birthday Book had received postcard mailers offering a free gift with any purchase. A lobby display in the Avalon Theater had promised the birth of a great toy extravaganza at Wee Folks.

More than 5,000 toys awaited behind the double glass doors. Here at the new, larger Wee Folks, my parents finally had the space to make good on their slogan, "Everything for Little Folks." The 6,000-square-foot store, double the size of the old one, was awash in corals, greens, and yellows, offering a delicious mint-colored backdrop for a full menu of toys and baby-related merchandise.

The new store, which cost my folks a year in the planning and $20,000 to remodel, featured the latest in retailing design. Because they believed that more sales were made when customers knew the merchandise, they patterned the store after successful food marts. Wee Folks now boasted wide aisles, open displays, and a large inventory at all levels of affordability. Display islands of metal pegboard stretched throughout the store.

Shelves were divided into sections for models, books, dolls, action toys, and baby items. The layout allowed customers large and small to inspect the stock without supervision. As a boon to aunts, uncles, and grandparents, many toys were marked to show the appropriate age group.

At last it was nine o'clock! The double doors burst open as Mom and Dad greeted the crowd. Children and their parents swarmed through the entrance, each signaled by that cheery "ding!" again and again as they crossed from reality into a world of childhood fantasy. There were abundant hugs, as many of the children hadn't seen my parents during the remodeling.

> *"You felt when you went into Wee Folks that you were going into someone's living room. They knew all the adults' and kids' names. You were welcomed. You heard stories being shared about new toys coming out."—Dr. Jane Brown*

A three-foot-high replica of the red and blue Playskool Mailbox stood at the front of the store. During the holidays, children placed their letters to Santa in the box, but this weekend it was the place to register for $250 in grand opening prizes. Hundreds of eager contestants dropped in their entries, carefully cut from the Wee Folks newspaper ads. For weeks before the grand opening, young readers had studied the ads, looking for deliberately misspelled words to circle and correct, and now submitted them as their entry forms.

Boxes of free gifts awaited the eager fingers of children with birthdays in August and September. They redeemed their Birthday Book mailers for magic tricks, dolls, any item we could get for under a dollar. With the Christmas rush just around the corner, other kids came in to mentally prepare a wish list for Santa. But every child had the same agenda: to look and touch and dream.

> *"Wee Folks was like going to Disneyland. There was a toy horse in the front of the store that would move forward as your weight pushed it down. I didn't weigh enough to push it far, but your mom*

always put me on it to let me try. I remember the Birthday Club and how I came in to pick out my gift after getting my postcard."
                                                —*Michael Block*

"Wee Folks—those two words bring on an attack of nostalgia, a flood of beautiful visions of my own life as a wee folk with Mom and Dad and sister Joy in South Shore. I heard 'Wee Folks' when I was being naughty as a carrot to help get me on the right track. . . . Being there was heaven, and the two people who owned it were angels."—Corky Siegal

Girls peered inside two locked glass cases right at the front that held Madame Alexander dolls, created by the daughter of the owner of New York's first doll hospital. Beatrice Alexander started making doll costumes with her sister Rosie in 1912. At the height of World War I, Beatrice designed and sold Red Cross Nurse dolls. In 1923, she created a doll modeled after her daughter, Mildred. Backed by a $5,000 loan, Beatrice formed the Alexander Doll Company when she was just twenty-seven years old. Her creations are still prized for their lifelike eyes, rooted hair, molded limbs, and elaborate costumes.

Other locked cases held Nancy Ann Storybook dolls. The plastic dolls stood between three-and-a-half and seven inches tall and were produced in a variety of series: Days of the Week, Months of the Year, Countries, Nursery Rhymes, Sports, Powder and Crinoline, All-Time Hit Parade, Operetta, and, of course, the Storybook series.

"Wee Folks was my favorite place in the whole world. I had a collection of Storybook dolls as a child. My parents would take me to Wee Folks and I would stand in front of the glass case and stare with wonder at the beautiful dolls dressed in costumes of far-off lands. Each one was more beautiful than the next. I would stand there and try to decide which one I would secretly wish for next. It was such a difficult decision. I would magically receive that choice for my next birthday. I had quite a collection. As a young adult I moved out of my father's home and left my dolls there for safekeeping. Sadly, there was a fire that destroyed everything. My prized collection had been ruined by the smoke damage. To this day, when

I talk about the fire, I always mention the dolls that I lost and my memories of that wondrous store."—Michele Schwartz Gulli

"For every birthday party, we always went to Wee Folks to buy the present. Going to Wee Folks was the best part of growing up. We had all the Storybook dolls your folks sold. That was one of our most favorite items. Mr. and Mrs. Lazar always had time for us to help us purchase the best gift. If we had money to spend it was at Wee Folks that we spent it. My sister had great memories of the Yo-Yos and the contests to show off all the tricks we could learn. Too bad that there are not more shops like that!"—Barbara Flanigan Graf, daughter of longtime customer Marg Flanigan

A five-foot-tall Steiff lion and giraffe lounged on top of the doll cases, watching over all the excitement.

The west wall—the doll wall—held open displays of dolls like Ginny, Baby Ginette, and Muffie. Facing it was a large display island with rows and rows of doll clothes, where discerning girls spent hours selecting just the right outfit. A Noah's Ark of stuffed animals stood at the end of the aisle.

The island Mom called the "ladies' section," located opposite the doll shelves, displayed miniature household appliances like vacuum cleaners and sweepers and other things that little homemakers needed to play house. There were dollhouses, doll furniture, and figurines with bendable bodies that would sit at a child's command.

"My memories of Wee Folks are from my 'innocent' era, the time of my life when everything was good, things were easy to comprehend, and Mom and Dad took care of the big stuff. I remember going into the store and looking at the Muffie dolls and their clothes in a wooden case near the front store windows. I still remember that the 'feeling' of the store seemed magical to me. A toy could be anything you wanted it to be—even what it was supposed to be! Imagination was never limited with a toy. And so it was with Wee Folks. Your dad's store was where the magic was. To this day, I get excited about toys. My husband and I browse through 'antique' shops, hoping to find a Muffie or two. But I enjoy looking at the old-fashioned toys, the ones that ran solely on imagination."—Jan Weiland

"Every time I ponder whether to put my two Muffie dolls up for auction on eBay, I have a brief remembrance of being in the store where we bought them: Wee Folks! I spent many happy hours there with my mother and grandmother (both gone now), enjoying the wonderful assortment of dolls and doll clothes. For me, Wee Folks was heaven, and I'm sure that must be at least partly because of your parents' graciousness. We had very little money, so we probably spent a lot more time than cash there—but it was a real treat to take home an outfit for Muffie. Wee Folks will always have a special place in my heart."—Fran Langner

Boys made a beeline toward the rubberized rocking horse that overlooked a display on the east wall filled with hobbies and crafts. There were microscopes and chemistry sets for aspiring scientists, kits for making crystal radio sets, and car, boat, and airplane models conveniently parked next to all the necessary glues and paints. There were telescopes and walkie-talkies. For budding artists, finger paints, paint-by-number sets, and full-sized easels were housed on the balcony, where Crayola crayon sets boasted the hottest new colors of Prussian Blue and Carnation Pink. The hobby and craft section became one of the fastest-growing areas in the store, probably because Dad would leap at the chance to talk with any kid trying to decide which model kit to buy or which paint and glue to use for his project. He even taught his teenage disciples how to whittle with an Exacto knife. (I watched these demonstrations carefully, but still wound up in the emergency room when I tried to sharpen a stick with one and nearly sliced off the end of my finger.) Today, a group of teenagers stood looking at the models and begged advice from Dad.

"My first model car contest was at Wee Folks. I didn't win, but your dad encouraged me to continue building models and entering contests. I did, and subsequently won an honorable mention. It was a big deal for me. It helped me to understand perseverance and focus at an early age."—Bill Hill

"As I recall, there was a collection of plastic model kits at the back of the store. I used to walk there from my home at 78th and Jeffery

whenever I had enough money to buy one. The love of building plas-
tic models has been passed on to my sons and grandkids."
—Dennis Haffron

"Your father always seemed to know about the new toys. I thought
it was so cool to have a dad who knew and cared about toys. I
thought you were the luckiest kid. I was sure your dad brought
home every new toy for you. My younger sister was artistic and my
mom and I went to Wee Folks to buy her an easel when she was just
a few years old. She was happy with it, calling it her 'weasel from
Wee Folks.'"—Name withheld by request

"I lived at 7815 Constance and your father's store played a major
role in my childhood. . . . I used to see him when I went past the
store on the way to Horace Mann Grammar School because I often
stopped to look at the exciting things in the windows. Back then, I
liked to build plastic models of military aircraft and ships, and I
purchased practically all of them in Wee Folks. It was a natural
hobby to build plastic models of destroyers, cruisers, and aircraft,
perhaps due to the influence of TV. I used to watch 'Victory at Sea.'
Those models may also have had an impact on my early ambitions
of attending the Air Force Academy. Later in life I became more in-
terested in peace than in war. Perhaps all of the good fun I had
playing with other types of games and puzzles from Wee Folks also
contributed in some way."—Donald Smith

Hard-to-find metal toy soldiers from Great Britain, a special
favorite of the English immigrant storeowner, stood at attention
in locked glass cases. The handpainted figures were just three
to four inches tall, but the scale was perfect. The Matchbox,
Corgi, Tootsietoy, and Dinky vehicles shared the same cases.
That department also featured mechanical toys like drinking
bears and robots, all loaded with batteries and ready for a kid
to try them.

"I was a Tootsietoy freak. I recall cutting a lawn or shoveling some-
one's sidewalk for $2, maybe $3. I loved to head down to 79th Street
and Wee Folks to check out the latest batch of little gems. I have a
picture of myself at about three years old on my new Christmas tri-
cycle surrounded by Tootsie sets in their graphic boxes. This must

have been the beginning of my 'addiction.' I must tell you that I never saw your father frown. He was meant to do what he did. An amazing guy. Thank you, Mr. Lazar!"—Judi O'Brien

"I am sixty years young and I worked for my dad a block west of Wee Folks at Peterson's Cities Service Station. My mom would take us to your dad's store around our birthday to let us choose our own gifts. I loved Dinky toys from England. As a teenager, I bought Revell model airplanes. I would be back for a new one so soon that your dad could not believe I had built the kit. Your dad made me a deal. He was paying Revell $25 for a built display kit. We made a deal that he would give me two models every time, one for me and the other one to build for him to display."—Kenneth J. Peterson

The east wall near the front windows housed seven tiers of games for all ages. Candy Land, invented in the 1940s by a woman recuperating from polio, was still recognized as a child's first game. Scrabble, created in 1948 by an unemployed architect, was always a favorite. And there was Clue, with Professor Plum, Colonel Mustard, and all the other colorful assassins, plus Tudor's Tru-Action football with the vibrating surface that moved players across the metal field.

Wee Folks had the largest game selection in Chicago, and thanks to television, the section kept growing. Television broadcasts had grown from two stations in 1941 to more than 400 in 1955. More than 20 million people owned TV sets by the mid-1950s. When a new TV show became popular, a game by the same name was quickly created and in demand at Wee Folks. Milton Bradley, Parker Brothers, and other manufacturers marketed games based on "Our Miss Brooks," Art Linkletter's "People Are Funny," and "I Love Lucy." Cowboys and cowgals had their games too, featuring TV's "Bat Masterson," "The Rifleman," "Have Gun Will Travel," "Gunsmoke," "Maverick," and "Roy Rogers and Dale Evans." We carried TV-generated toys like the "Howdy Doody" hand puppets and theater and "Romper Room" Romper Stompers. We had "Mickey Mouse Club" everything.

"I remember your family's store. We bought board games and always enjoyed going shopping for toys. My dad had a trailer rental busi-

ness on Stony Island. . . . Wee Folks could be symbolic of my life growing up in South Shore. There was something great when you could stop for lunch at numerous homes in a three-mile area. The feeling of community, of a safe place throughout my days on the South Side, is a memory that still lives in my heart."—Bo Blinski

"My next-door neighbor and I purchased a set of toy telephones from Wee Folks, which we connected between our two apartments. Our mothers were friends also and we found ourselves on the phone a lot, so we thought we'd bring down the phone bill with the toy telephones!"—Carol (Hicks) McShan

From the fleet of toy trucks on the east back wall, boys picked up vehicles like Tonka trucks and scooted them across the floor. From anywhere in the store, you could hear the sirens from friction-wheeled police cars and fire trucks as they were being "consumer tested."

"Wee Folks was definitely an ideal location for me. I passed it four times a day when I went to grammar school in the fifties. The display window required careful examination with each passing. I am sure I was guilty of most of the nose smudge marks three-and-a-half feet from the ground. I bought caps for my cap gun and airplane, ship, and car models, glue, and paint. We had hobby day on Friday afternoon at school. Although I didn't have any, claiming model building was acceptable. My most poignant memory was of a green construction toy. It was a magnificent piece of equipment with a conveyor belt. A boy could shove dirt into one end, run the conveyor belt, and fill a dump truck. My real hobby at the time was digging in the dirt near our swing set in our backyard. I would make roads, miniature golf courses, dig to China—it was a wonderful yard. I was sure if I had that green machine in the Wee Folks window, I would be the happiest boy in the world and my life would be perfect. Alas, it was not to be. The pronouncement from my mother was, 'It's too expensive.' I don't know how long it was in the window; it seems like an eternity. It seems like birthdays, Christmases, any occasion where I would be likely to get a present, would come and go and always, 'It's too expensive.' On occasion I would be so fascinated by it in the Wee Folks window on my way home from school for lunch, my sister or even my mother would find me there, turn me around, and send me back to school; having wasted

my time, it was too late for lunch. When the store moved down the street, it was my first experience of change in the retail trade. Although I understood it was better for them to be in large quarters, it wasn't good for me. It was out of the way. It wasn't as cozy and I didn't like it as much."—Gerald Hochberger

The large display of Breyer horses became a favorite stop. Made of hard, durable plastic, they featured lifelike details added by hand, most notably the eye whites around the iris. Nostrils were painted pink and hooves were tinted with highlights.

"My brother went in to buy a red cowboy hat, and your dad let him buy it on time. It was probably all of $2 but in those days that was an astronomical sum. My dad was shocked that my brother bought it in installments, so he emptied out the penny jar and bought the hat. I just smile when I see the store in my memories."
—Sherry McGarry and her brother, John Hartigan

Bats, balls, mitts, metal roller skates, Hula Hoops, paddleballs, Yo-Yos, and outdoor action toys filled a back display island. If there were times when we couldn't find Dad, we knew where to look. He would often slip outside with a young customer to test the swing on a new bat, throw a few balls, or try a new glove. At the request of local Scoutmasters, we carried Cub Scout and Girl Scout knives, books, and other paraphernalia. Scouting offices and sporting goods stores usually offered this merchandise, but with Mom being a Scout leader, it was a natural to sell them at Wee Folks.

"I think I bought my first football from the store. I later played football in high school (South Shore), college (Purdue), and I was fortunate enough to play professionally: Dallas Cowboys and Minnesota Vikings (NFL), Chicago Blitz, New Jersey Generals, and Orlando Renegades (USFL), and Chicago Bruisers (Arena). So that was a very special football."—Marc E. May

Along the wall on the far north side of the back room—and extending across the shelves Dad built in the store's bathroom—was "Train Central." Orange and black Lionel train boxes sat next to those of rival companies, and housed "O," "O27," and "HO" cars and accessories like switches, cattle loaders, signals, and houses. Dad, the biggest kid in the store, loved this place most of all. Over the years he would assemble hundreds of complete train sets on the back table. No doubt this is the place where young Mandy Patinkin developed his fascination for trains.

"As a kid, my route to grade school passed Wee Folks, and I liked to stop and gaze at the model trains stored high up in, of all places, the bathroom."—Burton Pickard-Richardson

Mom's favorite spot was the book island near the rear of the store, just in front of the back room. A reader all her life, she was always ready to recommend books for any age. She started a book club for avid readers of the series books, like Nancy Drew, the Bobbsey Twins, the Hardy Boys, and Tom Swift. The club members came in weekly, many using their allowance to buy the latest volume. When readers were registered, Mom would hold a copy of the newest book from their favorite series and call to let them know it had arrived.

"Wee Folks was a big part of my childhood. I would save my allowance to buy Nancy Drew books. I bought so many books that your father gave me a bookcase to hold them all. I still have the books. The book collection outgrew the bookcase. I passed the store every day on my way to school. Thinking back on it I remember buying Ginny doll clothes too. I still tell the story about the bookcase. People just don't do nice things like that anymore."
—Brenda Porter Salinas

"I remember Wee Folks. At the front of the store were little wooden rocking chairs so kids could sit and read books."
—Barbara Blond

In the new Tiny Tots Playroom, toddlers could amuse themselves with educational games, toys, and books while their harried mothers shopped in peace or wandered into the back room for a cup of coffee. Snuggled into a corner at the back of the store, that playroom had been the subject of animated debate between Mom and the store's architect. The architect felt that a playroom would consume too much valuable selling space. Mom didn't care.

"You were never a mother," she told him. "When a mother walks into the store with kids, they will drive her crazy unless they have something to do. If the children are happy and their mother knows they are safe, she will be a contented shopper.

"I feel we are doing a service to humanity by giving Mother a breather, a few minutes' peaceful shopping time without crying tots pulling at her skirt."

Even after they learned their insurance wouldn't cover an unsupervised playroom, my parents persisted until they found appropriate coverage. They surrounded this sixty-square-foot slice of heaven with a wrought iron fence to keep grownups out. Kids dove into buckets of crayons and colored at a pint-sized table, plopped themselves into rockers to look at books, or expressed their artistic sides at a chalkboard along one wall.

To make space for other, larger sections, the new Wee Folks carried fewer children's clothes than the one on Constance. But along the west wall, decorated with plaques of Little Bo-Peep, Dumbo, and Mary Had a Little Lamb, you still could find layettes and clothing for the first year of life, along with gifts, rattles, and teething rings. And we still fit Capezio ballet shoes and tutus in the office in the back room.

"When I was three or four, I refused to leave until my mom bought me this small workbench with color pegs. You used a small wooden hammer to hit the pegs through one side and then turned the whole thing over and banged them through to the other side. I remember my grandparents going to the Avalon, but I wanted to stay in the store instead of going to the movies."—Ken Love

The Fisher-Price and Playskool sections were well stocked with everything for a little tyke's education: the Looky Fire Truck with its moving eyes and two firemen on the back, the Musical Sweeper that really picked up dirt—and probably made mothers crazy as it constantly played "Whistle While You Work." My favorites were the Snoopy Sniffer, Nosey Pup, and Happy Helicopter. They looked real to kids and weren't too noisy.

Every inch of space served a purpose. Even the three structural posts running down the center of the store were put to use. Covered with pastel-tinted metal pegboard, the posts held small, inexpensive cellophane-wrapped items geared to catch the eye of young shoppers. Kids on a tight budget swarmed here, trying to choose between cowboy and Indian figures, crayons, toy cars, balsa wood model airplanes, paper dolls, and more. At Christmas time, more than a thousand stocking stuffers hung there, each costing no more than a dime.

Dad's newest handcrafted wooden balcony, eight feet from the floor, surrounded the store and displayed doll buggies, strollers, bikes, wagons, rocking horses, and toy pianos. The twelve-inch Bicycle Pal bike cost just $12.25 on opening day, and the Murray Ohio pedal car was also on sale. Just as in the old store, merchandise slowly spun high above display islands, suspended by fishing line.

The back room housed the office and the table where things in mysterious cardboard boxes with dozens of parts became buggies, strollers, and gym sets. Wee Folks never charged for assembly.

If an item wasn't in the store, it was likely in the stockroom, which stood twelve feet high and ran seventy-five feet long on the store's west wall. No one was ever sure how Dad expected anyone to retrieve merchandise from the highest of his floor-to-ceiling shelves. The stockroom was only four feet wide, and the top shelves were accessible only by climbing two ladders we brought over from the old store. Since the ladders couldn't be fully opened in the narrow aisle, nimble employees had to climb to the top by bracing one foot on a rung and the other against a shelf. The exercise became a two-person event as the climber shimmied up and tossed items to the designated catcher below. I became an expert "shimmier." I wonder if customers ever knew why it took us so long to get their stockroom items.

The wrapping table/checkout area was a U-shaped counter. A pegboard pillar in the center held the wall phone, orders in process, and other elements of the day's communication. Wrapping and checkout were conspicuously placed together in the middle of the store and strategically set back from the front door. This way, customers wouldn't feel they were blocking the entrance if they lingered to talk while having their gifts wrapped. And linger they did, huddling with Mom over just the right toy for a child or grandchild or just catching up with her on their lives. The setup also prevented customers from feeling checked out before they left the store, as was the case in most department stores.

After a customer picked out paper and ribbon from the attractive selection, Mom's imagination went to work. She wrapped beautifully, and had a real knack with bows. She would slice several strips of ribbon into twelve-inch lengths and attach them to the package. I watched thousands of times as Mom curled each strip with the edge of a scissors until a bow appeared like magic, looking like a large flower. No purchase was too small for this level of attention, and even the youngest customer was assured a lovely gift-wrapped package. By the end of the Christmas season, Mom's fingers bled from cuts made while creating her intricate adornments.

Our grand opening was featured in *Toys and Novelties Magazine* with a headline that boasted, "Wee Folks Snares the Pee Wee Trade." The article gave glowing testimonial to my parents' "shrewd merchandising presentations," including our cooperative promotions at the Avalon and Rhodes theaters.

As a recognized retailing phenomenon, Wee Folks also was written up in a September 1957 feature in *Playthings Magazine*. The interview with Mom and Dad highlighted our window displays, saying, "The Lazars change their windows frequently, rotating various toys so passersby can see the large selection. One of the most successful windows Wee Folks ever had was one featuring a Bilnor six-foot plastic pool filled with water. Bath toys, sailboats, and even mechanical boats with batteries floated in the water. Five hundred pounds of sand made the window look like a beach. Many Doepke model toys such as road graders, dump trucks, and caterpillar trailers were spread over the sand."

Wee Folks became the first toy store in Chicago to put everything except the highest-priced items on a self-serve basis.

Emanuel Lazar, proprietor of Wee Folks, has a friendly visit with a lad who buys all his guns—self-service—at this store.

Teenage hobbyists can look over the stock to see what models their collections still lack. Almost everything's out in open.

ALL PHOTOS TAKEN AT . . .

Wee Folks, Chicago

Joe Cohn of M & D Store Fixtures points to supporting post with metal sheathing.

One "don't touch" display is glass case for dolls positioned at end of counter.

Adjustable shelving for preschool toys can be moved on pegboard.

The wrapping center and cash register are centrally located.

National toy magazines often praised Wee Folks' innovative merchandising.

A buyer for a large area department store once told them, "We wish we could put dolls, trains, wheeled goods, and toys on a self-selection basis, but we believe going through a turnstile has a psychological effect on pilfering." Wee Folks had few problems. With our policy of hiring and training employees who liked kids, few toys were stolen. If we did catch a child stealing, however, Mom's background as a schoolteacher came into play. She called the parents and invited them to pick up their child. While the child waited, he or she sat on a high step stool behind the counter to think about what to tell the parents. Mom then met with both the child and the parents privately to discuss how to keep the child out of trouble in the future.

Wee Folks was a fun place, but to Mom and Dad it was also a serious business. In addition to being merchants, they were a part of the community and felt a great responsibility to their customers. They believed they had a moral obligation to show by example how people should be treated.

"I remember one very important lesson my grandfather taught me, which involved Wee Folks. I was a Greek American kid in an almost all-Jewish community. It was hard to make friends and I was depressed. My grandfather would take the two-hour bus ride to our house. I told him I hated my parents for moving and the new school was a nightmare. He suggested we take a walk. We walked around the corner and I stopped in front of Wee Folks. A toy caught my eye, and I asked Grandpa if he would buy it for me. He said that he was sure I had enough toys, but asked me why I wanted it. I told him it was different and I liked toys that were different. He smiled and said that the toy was like me. I was in a bunch of toys that were not the same, but did it make the toy less of a toy because it was different? He told me that I was in a different school, but kids were kids; they would get to know me, and then things would be better. We went inside. Your mother was listening to us and said that time would heal all wounds. My grandpa didn't have enough money, but she insisted that he take the toy and enjoy it.

"Of course, at the time I didn't know my grandpa was very poor and couldn't afford that toy. I didn't know that I would never see him alive again. . . . I didn't know that a stranger would give us a toy when we didn't have enough money to buy it. . . . Funny how a little trip to the toy store would teach me so much about life. Thanks for making me remember."—Tim Thimios

The Wizards of Aahs

From the beginning the new store was a hit. The years 1957 through 1963 were the heyday of Wee Folks. Mom and Dad were toy wizards who recognized what kids wanted before the kids knew it themselves.

The grand-opening *Playthings* article had boasted, "The Lazars have a fondness for children and they feel if you sell a child, you can sell the parent. They have long been advocates of the right toy for the right child, and they use this formula in selling. Mrs. Lazar's training as a nursery school teacher has been a vital factor in her attitude towards children. Manny and Belle treat children like adults and have confidence in their opinions."

Her teaching background definitely gave Mom more formal expertise. "As each new stage in a child's life is reached, he needs new toys to aid in his full development," Mom told *Playthings Magazine* in 1958. "It is the parent's responsibility to recognize the arrival of each new period in his mental and physical growth. These needs are just as important as food, clothing and health. Properly selected toys are a powerful educational force that will enrich his character and development. Many people make the mistake of giving toys only at Christmas or on birthdays. Too many toys at one time only confuse a child. Toys should be bought with thoughtfulness, not generosity. They are not gifts. They are tools. As the child plays today, so will he live tomorrow."

Dad, on the other hand, instinctively knew what kids liked. Of course, sometimes he found out the old-fashioned way: he asked them.

After Wham-O's Hula Hoop arrived by storm in 1958, selling twenty million in six months, hundreds of our customers gyrated their way to prizes in contests held in front of the store. Some could keep the brightly colored hoops twirling around their waists, hips, or knees even while jumping rope.

"Our family business, Alpert's Food and Liquors, was at 79th and Essex. Going to Wee Folks was a special treat 'cause it meant taking the 79th Street trolley or bus. We couldn't afford much, but whatever goodies we got were cherished. I remember a 100-piece cowboy and Indian set I got for a birthday—wow. I recall they sponsored a Yo-Yo contest at the Avalon between movies and the

prize was a bike. Yo-Yos were not my forte, but they were fun. Seems they found a real Yo-Yo expert who demonstrated the tricks."

—Bobby Alpert

Wee Folks also sponsored the local junior league baseball team. Players in our uniforms often came into the store after a game to celebrate a win with parents.

Throngs of kids would follow Dad wherever he went. In 1958, a number of our customers and later the *Southtown Economist* and *Chicago Tribune* newspapers dubbed him "the Pied Piper of South Shore," after Robert Browning's charismatic Pied Piper of Hamlin. The title stuck.

"Your father was a great man, very well respected and liked. I used to see your mother in the store at times your dad wasn't there. She was just as sweet as your dad, but he was like having Santa Claus on the street all the time. Your father was always decent to everyone, even the kids who tried to steal from him."—Andre Nickerson

"I worked at Wee Folks for seven years. I was hired to do the guy stuff—assembling bikes, unloading shipment, and stocking shelves. I helped Manny with the physical stuff, with promotion, sales, fixing and painting, and putting together bikes and buggies. He allowed me to grow a lot. I didn't have a dad, so working closely with Manny meant a lot to me. He made me feel important and confident in myself. My mechanical skills grew. He involved me in the hobby section and we went to toy and hobby shows to select products. He was a steady and patient teacher and even though we often worked eighty hours a week at Christmas time, he was a rock. He ran his business smart, with lots of service and lots of caring. He was the institution of the neighborhood."

—Burt Pickard-Richardson

Of course, kids weren't our only customers. There were adults, from the working poor to the South Shore Country Club elite to celebrities. They had names like Goodman and Schwartz, O'Brien and O'Toole, Smith and Washington, Clay and Banks. There were teachers like Sister Mary Elizabeth, who stocked up on school supplies for the disadvantaged youngsters

ked them physically and with the donation of prizes and gift
ificates. He was beyond generous to every local nonprofit orga-
ation that asked him."—Harriet Grady

ur dad was the kindest man in the neighborhood. My dad
ned Al's Food Mart, and they were both members of the 79th
eet Business Men's Association."—Al Randel

Iy father [Abe Marienthal] closed his retail store in 1955, and
ncentrated on wholesale, helping Manny Lazar, Abe Grossman,
e Nadler, and others redevelop their businesses into dedicated toy
res. He helped turn a small souvenir counter into the Mart at the
useum of Science and Industry. He was such a large supplier
at, on the recommendation of the museum buyer, he created a sec-
d wholesale business, Active Import Sales, which was operated
t of Wee Folks' storeroom."—Jeff Marienthal

he Gradys often went to Merchandise Mart toy shows
my parents. Bill always said Dad was the finest, most in-
tive merchandiser he met.

ad made friends easily, often because he was always ready
lunteer and donate toys for special-drawing events. No job
ed too menial for him, whether it was building something
neighborhood event or cleaning up afterward. From him
ned the importance of giving and the treasured memories
make when volunteering.

Barbie Mania

parents were passionate about their dream and determined
ucceed. Their vision to offer exceptional service—making
customers knew that Wee Folks had or could quickly get
item needed—created a thriving year-round business. By
9, our store was the center of the universe for the neighbor-
d children. That fall, a crowd that rivaled our grand-open-
mob gathered around the store as a "real doll"—Mattel's
bie—burst onto the scene.

Mattel was born in 1942 when Ruth Handler, the youngest
en children of Polish immigrants, and her husband, Elliot,

in her parish, and who always acted sur
box of erasers, chalk, or pencils was add
cost. There were wives of mill workers fro
Inland Steel, and Wisconsin Steel plants
presents until Christmas, knowing that th
would be gift-wrapped and labeled as pr
pensive toy.

Our neighborhood was diverse, made
merchants, athletes, entertainers, even
"Greasy Thumb" Gusik, the Mafia's acco
"the Camel" Humphreys.

Building Relationshi

Mom and Dad knew many people through
the 79th Street Business Men's Associatior
of the street's storeowners. Together their sh
Shore's necessities, and they all patronized
nesses. They weren't wealthy, but as storeov
in their community.

Mom and Dad became fast friends with
Bill and Harriet Grady, who owned Circus N
ther east on 79th Street. Known and loved by
and "Aunt Harriet," they were our biggest st
had worked in our store for a while before sh
the school. They spent hours with my paren
latest toys and the challenges of being in bus
Dad helped Bill furnish the school for their
When folksinger Wynn Stracke visited the Gra
brought props for the event. When they had
visit from the fire department, Dad brought
used his station wagon to help Dad deliver toy

"Belle and Manny were the alpha and the omega o
were there when we opened Circus Nursery and
fourteen years later. In between, they were the gre
Manny meant a lot to the 79th Street Business Mer
He was always the first to volunteer suggestions for f

Wee Folks was official Barbie headquarters in Chicago.

started making toys with industrial designer Harold "Matt" Masterson. In the late 1950s, while Elliot was developing a new talking doll that later became Chatty Cathy, Ruth came up with an idea of her own. She had noticed that when their young daughter played with paper dolls, she would imagine them in grownup roles. Ruth dreamed of a lifelike doll, one that would inspire girls to think about what they wanted to be when they grew up. She created Barbie the Teen-age Fashion Doll, named after the Handlers' daughter, with slender hips and a real waist.

My parents were present at the 1959 New York Toy Fair when Mattel unveiled Barbie. (It was at the Toy Fair that my parents judged the play value of the toys they purchased.) Earlier that summer, while meeting with the top brass at Mattel in California, Mom and Dad had been given the option to buy stock in the company. They had never bought stock but they did now: they had a new store to pay for, but they were sure this company was worth the investment. While other toy stores passed on the opportunity to carry the Barbie line, not knowing whether the doll would succeed, Wee Folks bought every Barbie product Mattel made.

Mattel spent more than $500,000 to advertise Barbie in commercials that aired during the "Mickey Mouse Club Show" in 1959. She debuted at $3 apiece, and sales topped 350,000 dolls the first year, making her a cultural icon as well as a merchandising phenomenon.

Wee Folks became Chicago's official Barbie headquarters, and hundreds of eager girls came to buy the latest, hottest Barbie outfit. Our association with the doll more than made up for our first years when we couldn't open an account with Mattel. The store devoted the entire middle aisle to all things Barbie. Ongoing promotions like "Bring in your old Barbie doll and get a new one" sent girls into a frenzy. Their excitement was further fueled by the Barbie Fan Club, which Mattel launched as a national organization that helped girls create chapters in their own areas. Free membership entitled girls to an official club card decorated with the Barbie emblem. Barbie clubs conducted playtime activities, staged neighborhood fashion shows, and gathered members to swap dolls, clothes, and accessories.

"What I do remember about your dad's store was a sumptuous display of Barbie dolls near the front of the store. I imagine there was a big puddle of drool under that display from all the little girls who were dying to have a new outfit to dress Barbie up in. In kid terms, 'news' didn't mean turning on the radio or TV. You were hip only if you were up on the latest Barbie couture. By keeping us all aware of the momentous changes in kid culture, your dad made an invaluable contribution to civilization."—Bee Hanson

"As far as I know, Wee Folks was the only toy store in the area, way before the superstores like Toys 'R' Us. When we were kids, if we got a good report card, my dad would take us to Wee Folks to pick out our own prize. We'd take all night to walk up and down every single row of toys. My favorite aisle was the one with the Barbie doll clothes. My platinum-haired, bubble blond Barbie wore gold lamé cocktail dresses and pink negligees with high heels, way before Barbie thought to become a doctor or astronaut."—Marcia Sacks

"I worked at Wee Folks from 1961 thru 1963. I still think about your parents and the way they ran the store and treated the kids (and me). I remember your dad extended the kids 'credit privileges' at a very young age. I used to help 'design' the front window, and we received complaints when I put Barbie and Ken and the bedroom set in the same window."—Nancy B. Levun

Barbie eventually sold in more than 150 countries and was showcased in the Smithsonian Institution. Ken, named after the Handlers' son, appeared as a companion to Barbie in 1961.

Christmastime

In late October 1959, Dad received a prized delivery at the back door. He lugged two huge boxes off the delivery truck and placed them in the back room.

"What's in there, Dad?" I remember asking.

"You'll know soon," he said with a wink. "It'll make Christmas even more special this year."

On the first Friday night after Halloween, near closing time, Dad and I pulled the heavy boxes to the front of the store. He

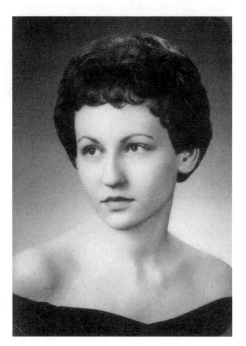

*Caryn Lazar, South Shore High
School, class of 1959.*

scored each seam with his razor-blade cutting tool and the cardboard fell away to reveal a giant Santa Claus, whiskers, red suit, and all. We tugged the jolly old elf into place in the larger display window. Dad fiddled with wires, hiding them under layers of cotton snow, and plugged him in. It was spellbinding. Santa bowed, rose up, put a finger to the side of his nose, and nodded. He bowed again and came up grinning and waving his arms in welcome. Inside the second box was a lifelike Rudolph. After we plugged him in, Rudolph bobbed his head as Santa nodded and smiled. It was the first mechanical window display on 79th Street, and it was amazing. Word must have spread because the next day, Saturday, kids stood outside the window for an hour before the store opened to see what Mr. Wee Folks had done this time. Santa and Rudolph celebrated many holiday seasons with us, but the first was the most special.

The month of December was what we in the toy business waited for all year. More than 75 percent of our total year's income was made in that month. By November the storeroom shelves that were set aside for layaways were packed. Thank goodness Dad had been wise enough to rent space for the season on the vacant second floor above the store, plus a smaller store next door. He lugged hundreds of people's Christmas presents on his back up the creepy stairs to that dreary second floor using a thick mover's strap.

The one-drawer layaway file cabinet below the cash register had grown to a two-drawer cabinet stuffed with brown envelopes. Each envelope housed details of a family's layaway in anticipation of a magical Christmas Eve delivery by Mr. Wee Folks—or was that really Santa? Many layaways were held for an entire season on a twenty-five-cent deposit and delivered even if the account was still unpaid.

People getting paid just before Christmas would come in to make their layaway payments, mostly in cash. When the cash drawer overflowed, Dad stashed the money in an old refrigerator next door. At the end of the day, he would walk the "cold" cash over to the bank accompanied by Mike, the area beat cop.

"I have fond memories of Christmas time and your folks. I worked at Wee Folks for two Christmases and what a madhouse it was. Your dad was easygoing and fun to work with and your mom was a delightful lady who was more businesslike and with definite plans for everyone in the store."—Eileen Silberman-Crasko

Every morning in December we brought in fresh bakery goods from Dressel's Bakery down the street and set them up in the back room. Starting at eight o'clock, the scent of cinnamon and sugar and the aroma of fresh-brewed coffee wafted through the store. Many customers came in with their entire gift lists and sat at the counter while we fetched the coveted items and Mom wrapped them. Sometimes mothers brought their children with them. If they grew tired of the playroom, Mom would give each child a sweet roll in the back room. It was my job to follow the little critters to remove all their sticky fingerprints from the merchandise. Whenever there was a lull, there were shelves to stock and merchandise to bring up from the basement or out of the stockroom.

"We had a little Christmas ritual. Each child would write a list of what he wanted Santa to bring him or her. A few days before Christmas, my wife and I would march over to Wee Folks and confront your parents. Up and down the aisles we'd go, your mom with my wife and the girls and your dad and I with my sons. Your parents always told us what toys were worth the money. What really impressed us was how with every order for every child your parents would add a book at their expense. They were caring people. After the first Christmas, they would welcome us at the door with 'Here are the Cronins.'"—Mr. and Mrs. Mark Cronin

Starting at nine o'clock every Christmas Eve, we entertained customers who waited until the last minute to shop. One fellow who was uncle to twelve nieces and nephews would take until midnight to make his selections. I helped him choose the appropriate toys, Mom wrapped and labeled them, and Dad lugged them to his car. Last-minute visitors were sometimes large families who had no place to hide surprises from inquiring eyes.

"There were five of us. I was the oldest, with the youngest eleven years my junior. . . . Mom did not go to Wee Folks to finish her Christmas shopping; she went there to do her Christmas shopping. I'm sure that she must have bought gifts elsewhere for adults on her list, but her kids were the main shopping list. She knew that at Wee Folks she could take care of her entire list literally at the eleventh hour. Wee Folks did not stay open just for Mom, but we were always the last to leave. I considered it a great excursion, and always tempered my helping mom with a lot of playing with this, that, and the other.

"I don't know how many years my mother, Alice Michaels, made the annual Christmas Eve foray to Wee Folks, but when I was old enough to help I would tag along. Because we were also in the retail business, we would not arrive at Wee Folks till after 8:00 p.m. on Christmas Eve. We never left before midnight, but they were always glad to see us. Of course, we always left with a station wagon full of toys."—Tim Lewis

"Once I saw Manny on Christmas Eve sneaking into my garage. I heard my dad say, 'Put it in the garage.' It was 2:00 a.m. We had six kids in the family and he delivered to us all."—John Melaniphy II

During the week before Christmas and on Christmas Eve after the customers had left, we delivered to our customers' homes. On one Christmas trip we encountered a youngster in the driveway pleading for help. "Please help me get that aerial off the chimney before Santa gets here!" he implored.

Now we used Dad's 1958 Chevy Nomad station wagon, which was piled high with toys. Often with fresh snow on the ground, we loaded up the wagon for our first run of the evening. We started at the Monoghans, then went to the O'Tooles, and on to Chatham to see the Brown family. Jane Brown and her family had been customers for years. They were one of our earliest black customers and just a few minutes by "sleigh" from the store for the Wee Folks Santa.

> *"My husband had met a young man on the West Side who wanted to go to school and needed money for tuition. Together, we made the decision to support his schooling and put back part of our planned Christmas toys. I came in early on Christmas Eve and told Manny. He was very gracious about it, returning them to stock. I paid for the rest of the items and left the store. At 11:00 that night, the doorbell rang. There stood Manny with the toys that we had put back. This included the life-sized three-year-old boy doll that my son was coveting. I said, 'Manny we can't afford to pay for that.' He said, 'It is our gift to you.' We both stood there crying."*
>
> —Dr. Jane Brown

The longer we were in business, the more trips we made. We went back to the store to reload and continue our rounds, delivering orders for the Flynns, the O'Rourkes, and, if Chanukah fell close to Christmas that year, the Goodmans.

Often we had to sneak toys into a garage, a storage shed, or a separate bedroom where the younger kids wouldn't find them. We enlisted the help of the family's older children who no longer believed in Santa Claus. Often the parents met us at the door, sometimes with a cup of hot cocoa and, occasionally, a wrapped gift for Mom. Decorations lit up the homes, some windows displaying Christmas trees decorated with ornaments. Many of these families had been our customers for years and would continue to stick by us as competitors nipped at our heels.

Until I was twelve, I really thought my dad was Santa. After all, he wrapped and stored toys all year and delivered them on Christmas Eve. Yet Christmas was the most difficult time of year for our family. Our lives revolved around the store, the personalities of the customers, their kids, and their troubles. The love and affection my parents showered on customers for twelve hours a day, almost seven days a week, left little for me and my sister. We couldn't celebrate Chanukah earlier in the month because the store was too busy. By Christmas Day, my parents were too exhausted after playing Santa to hundreds of other children to do it for us (except for Dad playing with those trains). While my sister and I unwrapped our gifts, our parents were often asleep in their chairs.

I can't say I remember any particular Christmas gift, but I do remember being surprised at what I received and wondering how my folks knew what I wanted. I wasn't a doll person. I loved westerns and had almost every set of fancy guns and holsters made. Until I was twelve, I played guns and holsters with the boys in the neighborhood. I also had the fanciest bike and lots of arts and crafts. My rock tumbler, wood-burning set, tool kits, and Gilbert chemistry set were my favorites. My folks encouraged my interest in chemistry until I nearly blew up the basement. Perhaps this led to my early interest in medicine and, later, to my job in a research lab. Hundreds of former customers have told me they credit a childhood toy with their interests, hobbies, or profession in later years.

I don't recall that being Jewish was a deterrent to opening our toys on Christmas Day. Being Jewish was like being American to my parents. They never thought about which holiday a family celebrated. The holiday season was special to them because they loved being a part of so many people's lives in such a meaningful way. They also loved it because they celebrated their wedding anniversary on Christmas Day. They didn't think of Christmas as just a day for gifts. They made sure every customer's family was rewarded with their best memories as well. Later, when I had children of my own, I wondered if my parents envied the abundance of time some people had with their families at this time of year.

My parents weren't physically demonstrative people, so there wasn't much hugging and kissing in our family. But I never felt deprived and I don't recall being resentful. I always knew I was loved. And I knew that they loved each other. I saw that marriage is a real partnership, one of give and take, where the woman often steps aside to let her husband shine. Mom played Tonto to Dad's Lone Ranger. She was the brains of the outfit, but his larger-than-life personality made him the darling of our customers. She was content to remain the woman behind the man.

> *"Behind every successful man is a brilliant woman. Belle had the unglamorous part of the business. She kept the books, did the ordering, sent out birthday cards to over 5,000 children every year by hand, handled the customers, and was a wife and mother. Belle and Manny's relationship was a true partnership. They were a team, and their success in business was because of Belle's willingness to be the unseen partner."—Harriet Grady*

Only when I was older did I realize how famous my parents were. One Christmas they gave a discount to a family whose father had been out of work for a long time. There were five children at home. My parents received a note:

> *"Once more I am disregarding your kindness and sending you a check for the full amount of my Christmas order. While I am grateful for your kindness, I am mindful of the care you took wrapping each gift and the kindness you always show my family. I look forward to another Christmas, because it seems the one occasion which definitely brings me into contact with you, who, I am happy to say, make life worthwhile."*

For years to come our mailbox was stuffed with Christmas cards from our customers, many including a family photo. Some customers wrote to Mom for half a century. She always wrote back, even well into her eighties. She treasured these cards and photos for the rest of her life. She especially loved the big Irish families. She kept a file on each family, and in her old age she loved to take out the photos to see how the children had changed through the years. Often she passed along her letters from young writers to their parents.

> *"This evening I was once again telling the stories about Wee Folks and the Lazars and how good you were to me by extending credit when you knew how poor I was. My children are grown and are all doing well. I did not fail you—I raised them well—thanks in part to you and Mr. Lazar."—Name withheld by request*

Wee Folks had become more of an institution than a store. For twelve years, my folks had supported the community. In the years to come, especially those following the grand opening, the community would step up to support my parents with more than their dollars.

A New Home

Right after the grand opening, Mom received an urgent call from Joliet. The doctor treating her stepfather, David Hyman, had decided that he could no longer live alone. Grampy was in his eighties and had had a series of heart attacks. Mom and Dad decided that he needed to live with us, but how? There was no room in our third-floor walk-up above the old store. That's when we experienced a *bashert*—a fated or predestined moment.

The day after the doctor's call, Catherine Smith came in to the store. She was a long-time customer whose children had grown up playing with us, and she loved my parents. She and Mom talked endlessly over the counter. Catherine lived at 78th and East End, one block from the new store, in a tidy three-bedroom house. Her husband, a contractor, had built their home—one of three alike, each on a small lot—but now her growing family needed more space.

Catherine had heard of Mom's dilemma with her step-father. Getting right to the point, she said, "Belle, I want you to buy my house."

"But we've opened a new store that's twice the size, Catherine. We just can't afford it."

"Don't worry about the money," Catherine replied. "Just come to the house next week and bring your lawyer."

Mom talked with David. "Belle, let's buy the house together," he proposed, "and I will pay my own way." He offered the down payment, Catherine persuaded her husband to substantially lower the price, and the deal was made.

We all loved Grampy. For a rabbinical scholar, he sure had a wicked sense of humor. He always had a joke or a little treat to sneak you before dinner. He would walk to 79th Street, take in the sights, and come home to read the Jewish papers. He was an introspective man who read and slept a lot. Mom made dinner more often to keep him eating. Grampy lived with us for a year-and-a-half before health forced him into a nursing home. He died in 1963.

Our new home and the two others on our side of the street butted up to a three-flat on the north, so we had no alley like most of Chicago's houses. Alleys were so prevalent, in fact, that the city employed alley inspectors, awarding the well-paying jobs to the mayor's cronies. Our house was on a corner lot and the sidewalk came right up to our front door. A grassy easement on East End Avenue ran alongside to the east, which Dad mowed when he cut the front and back lawn every week. A chain-link fence separated our house from that of our neighbors, Hy and Rose Kaplan. The Kaplans owned the Jewish deli on 79th Street, so we saw them a lot. I often played touch football with their son, Bobby, passing the ball back and forth over the fence.

Dad began to tackle major projects around the new house, especially in the basement where Grampy lived. Dad wanted to create a comfortable space for him. He paneled the basement and made a built-in wall unit for a television as well as a full-size aquarium. This was no fishbowl; it was a sixty-gallon tank built into the knotty-pine walls. He dropped the ceiling to put in acoustical tiles. He put a false floor over the concrete so it would be warmer. With the dropped ceiling and the raised floor, you had to be five-foot-eight or shorter to stand up straight. All of us were short, but Grampy David stood more than six feet tall. Yet he never complained. Dad also built a secret room under the stairs where my sister played with her dolls.

When it rained and the sewers in South Shore flooded, our basement sewer would back up. Thinking ahead, Dad screwed a metal standpipe into the floor drain to hold water if the sewer backed up in the future. We would have flooded out many times without it. Yet despite his efforts, a torrential rain in the early 1960s flooded the basement. The rushing water forced its way out the top of the standpipe, and the whole basement, along with family photos and mementos, was ruined in a pool of sewer water.

In 1959, Dad fell off the store's balcony while retrieving a buggy for a customer. He was taken by ambulance to Jackson Park Hospital, where he stayed for a week, recuperating from ruptured discs in his back. From that time forward, he had to wear a white wrap-around corset with heavy support bones.

While Dad was hospitalized, Mom, Burton Picard-Richardson, and two full-time employees ran the store. To keep him busy during his recovery, Mom brought Dad sheets of ceramic tiles and bags of grout mix from the craft section. He tiled everything he could lay his hands on. Ashtrays, coasters, dinner trays—nothing was safe and everything was fair game.

His tiling fetish didn't stop there. Dad had built an immense barbecue pit in our backyard—about six feet long and three feet high—and I guess the structure looked barren to him. After being discharged, he took sheets of half-inch-square multicolored ceramic tiles and covered the entire thing. Thousands of tiles later, we had the spiffiest barbecue in South Shore. It seemed to make everything taste better. Dad must have liked what he did with the barbecue because he proceeded to tile the kitchen table, trivets, and other things around the house.

After we bought the house on 78th Street, Dad's widowed mother and his bachelor brother Phil, a World War II vet and avid stamp collector, left Douglas Park and moved into our third-floor walkup above the old store. Grandma Lazar and Uncle Phil lived there for many years. We all got together during the holidays, and I still recall going to their apartment for Passover seders. Grandma Lazar constantly amazed the neighbors, who would call us to report that she was sitting outside on the window ledge washing her windows. She was over ninety at the time. After Uncle Phil died, Grandma Lazar moved to Milwaukee to live with her daughter Ethel. We made the long pre-expressway trip to Milwaukee as often as we could. It gave us a chance to be closer to Dad's family, and it was especially good to see my favorite cousin, Karen, and for her younger brother, Mark, to see my dad, whom he loved dearly. No one knows for sure how old Grandma Lazar was when she died, but rumor has it she was 104.

Like many middle-class white families in the area at that time, we had a wonderful "colored" maid. Maude came once a week after we moved to the house. She was one of the few people of color I had known well up to that time. While we did have a few black customers then, I didn't have the close relationship with them that I had with Maude. I saw other black women leaving houses all over the area every day. They waited for the bus outside our store at the East End stop. I can still sing the songs Maude taught me, like "Bringing in the Sheaves." Her songs always seemed so sad, always about life's travails. I didn't realize at the time just how bad the lives of black people had been or would become.

The first black family moved into South Shore in 1957, one of the first to be displaced by housing shortages in the city. In a way, that year marked the beginning of the end for South Shore. That was the year the Illinois NAACP named Chicago schools the most segregated of any major northern city. The organization charged that new schools were being built in white areas with empty classrooms, while South Side black schools were so overcrowded that children were attending in shifts. Education became the unifying force that began to tear our neighborhood apart.

Snapshots of boys and girls hoping to win Wee Folks' cutest-preschooler photo contest were on display at the Avalon Theater so patrons could vote for the winner.

CHAPTER 6

The Scary Sixties

Urban Renewal

CHICAGO'S NEIGHBORHOODS BEGAN CHANGING RAPIDLY in 1960 after the completion of the Dan Ryan Expressway, which ran north-south through the city and carved a wide swath through black and white communities. By 1962, many dislocated black families had moved into the newly built Robert Taylor Homes public housing project, which stretched for two miles along State Street both north and south of 47th Street. Robert Taylor was just north of Hyde Park, the neighborhood my family lived in before moving to South Shore. At that time, Robert Taylor was considered the largest public housing development in the world, containing more than 4,300 housing units in twenty-eight buildings, each sixteen stories high. Mayor Richard J. Daley proudly dedicated the projects as a safe place to live and raise families. It turned out that he was wrong. Crime flourished in these buildings for many years.

The changes in Hyde Park and other Chicago neighborhoods in the early 1960s could be traced to urban renewal efforts in the 1950s. In 1953, the Urban Community Conservation Act extended eminent domain rights to neighborhoods threatened with economic decline. Those neighborhoods included the north end of Hyde Park, which faced increasing delinquency and a growing collection of ragtag buildings. The University of Chicago, located at the south end of Hyde Park between 50th and 59th Streets, backed the Conservation Act and began razing buildings, replacing them with retail shops, houses, and high-rises. The university also expanded its campus with several new buildings.

The Woodlawn neighborhood, which extends south of Hyde Park to 67th Street, was similarly affected by the Conservation Act. In 1950, 17 percent of Woodlawn's population was black. By 1960, the percentage had risen to 89 percent. Unemployment rose in unskilled occupations while housing and average family incomes deteriorated. The population of this area became the most transient in Chicago. The growth of powerful street gangs, caused by the alienation of young blacks, also contributed to Woodlawn's deterioration.

By the 1960s, the construction of the Robert Taylor Homes, the urban renewal projects in Hyde Park, and the deterioration of Woodlawn began a wave of relocations that affected South Shore. Our neighborhood was about three miles south and east of Hyde Park, and adjacent to the southern border of Woodlawn. The new South Shore residents were primarily black, less educated than the previous residents, and generally blue collar.

Although their acute need was housing, black families also saw better educational opportunities for their children in South Shore. Throughout the city, education had become a unifying force for black Chicagoans, especially since 1961, when several black families brought suit against the Chicago Board of Education, accusing it of segregation in the schools.

Webb v. the Board of Education of the City of Chicago ended with an out-of-court settlement after the school board agreed that a panel of five experts, chaired by Philip Hauser, would conduct a study of segregation in Chicago public schools. In

March 1964, the Hauser Study found that the schools were indeed segregated and that the quality of education in black schools was inferior to that in white schools. Between April and November 1964, the school board adopted the recommendations of the Hauser Study, at least in principle. The board opened enrollment on a citywide basis for all trade and vocational schools and issued the statement that "we will continue to be guided by, and comply with, state and federal laws in the spirit of the 1954 Supreme Court decision on desegregation."

The new families moving into our community wanted what we did: a decent place to raise their kids, good schools, and good neighbors. They wanted to walk safely to the grocery store and sit on their front porches, watching their homes appreciate in value. Unfortunately for South Shore merchants, the new families had fewer dollars to spend, but they were good people who enhanced our neighborhood's ethnic and religious diversity.

Yet many white kids in South Shore became leery of blacks. I remember the day at South Shore High in 1958, when the first black teacher entered our school. These snooty kids, these *pishers* (Yiddish for a squirt, a nobody), plastered themselves against the lockers in mock horror to give him a wide berth. I felt ashamed. I can only imagine how he felt.

By the summer of 1961, race relations were strained. On July 9, the *Chicago Tribune* reported on a "Freedom" march to Rainbow Beach on 79th Street, about two miles east of Wee Folks: "Two hundred police officers were called to quash an attempted 'wade in' at the [Rainbow] Beach when over 200 black youth attempted to wade into the water of this once all white area. Twelve whites were arrested for refusing to disperse." Later the same month, however, blacks and whites swam together at the same beach without causing a disturbance.

By the summer of 1963, white homeowners who had lived in South Shore for many years, some all of their lives, were being pushed out of the neighborhood by greedy real estate agents embroiled in panic selling. They wanted white homeowners to sell now and sell cheap—a strategy that generated sales and made a killing for the realtors, the only ones who profited from the racism and fear.

The realtors represented South Shore as a potential slum, predicting a nonstop influx of blacks. The agents told white residents that blacks would bring more crime and impose their "lower standards" on South Shore. They goaded white homeowners with threats of home devaluation. To fan the flames that "colored" people were coming, they hired blacks to walk up and down the streets. They steered targeted black families to specific all-white areas, helping them register their kids in schools.

After a few months, the fear was palpable. The agents purchased homes from panicked whites and rented them to black families on all-white streets. "For Sale" signs never appeared on lawns. People just left in the middle of the night. Many whites moved to Chicago's southern suburbs, such as Glenwood and Homewood, or to northern suburbs like Northbrook and Deerfield. Some changed jobs and moved to other parts of the country. Synagogues began to close. Apartment buildings were sold. We went from Camelot to "we care not" in a few short years.

What was so wrong with living next door to a black person anyway? What was so scary about them? Why were we willing to believe the worst of them when we accepted so many other ethnic groups already in our midst? Didn't we Jews learn after the Holocaust that we can't let people push us around?

We weren't a group of Caucasians itching to be racists. Most whites in South Shore didn't hate black people. We just wanted to live our accustomed lives and earn a decent living, raise our families, and get along with everyone. But our beautiful, ethnically diverse neighborhood lay wounded at the hands of greedy realtors. We were gullible and they were relentless. We were cowards and they grew rich.

The Summer of '63

By the summer of 1963, I had married, moved out of my family's house on 78th Street into a basement apartment in the neighborhood, and was expecting my first child. Wee Folks was still a place where people went for happy reasons like birthdays, Christmas, and parties. But the store had also become a bastion of sanity for the area. Through the confessional of the counter, customers began to confide their fears and worries rather than their hopes and dreams. They expressed dissatisfaction with their lot in life and anxieties about being hurt or killed. They

I share a moment with Grandma Lazar at my 1961 wedding at the Drake Hotel. Dad's sister Ethel is in the background.

were worried about how their children would fare in the new world that was South Shore. Parents still sought advice on child rearing from Mom, and kids still had fun trying to beat Dad to the draw with the latest toy six-shooter. But Mom thought that customers were coming in now more to vent their frustrations than to make a purchase. Either option seemed all right to her. All around us was chaos, but my parents seemed unchanged, steady, treating the new residents with the same respect they had shown the old. The only change I noticed was that Wee Folks started carrying more black dolls.

"Everyone loved Manny. He was a real character, a mensch *[a special person who can be respected]. He treated me like family, including sharing his thoughts on just about everything. I loved him and learned much from him. When the neighborhood was changing, he gave me his philosophy about race relations. He always treated*

people as individuals, not as stereotypes. He hired some black guys to help around the store. He treated everybody who walked through the door the same. Belle and Manny are more a part of my past, my growing up, than just about any teacher or friend other than my immediate family."—Burton Pickard-Richardson

That summer, Mom and my sister had gone on vacation, leaving Dad and a couple of employees in the store. Dad invited his nephew, Mark Sharpe, his sister Ethel's son, to come from Milwaukee to help for a few days. At age eleven, Mark had his share of problems. Ethel had mouth cancer and his dad, Sidney, was sick and in and out of the Veterans Administration Hospital. Dad treated Mark like the son he never had. Mark still remembers that year as the best of his life.

They went fishing in Lake Geneva, Wisconsin, spending hours in a rowboat as Dad taught Mark to bait his hook. Dad showed him wrestling holds, something he couldn't do with his girls. At his father's shoe repair and dry cleaning shop in Milwaukee, Mark had frequently seen wrestlers Dick the Bruiser and Crusher Lisowski pick up their clothing. In Chicago, Dad took Mark to the Medinah Temple just north of downtown to see Verne Gagne, the only man to win the American Wrestling Association's Championship ten times, and Bo Bo Brazil, famous for inventing the "coconut headbutt." I have no idea how or if Dad knew all these celebrity wrestlers, but he managed to get Mark backstage to meet them.

Dad seemed to have passes for everything. He took Mark to cool places like circuses, Riverview amusement park on Chicago's North Side, and the Lake County Fair, where he put Mark into the spinning bucket ride and laughed as he stood watching near the gate. Mark still recalls trips to Chicago's Kungsholm Restaurant, which staged operas with large puppets.

When our family went to Milwaukee to visit the Sharpes, it was like Christmas. Dad brought box kites and model airplanes for Mark and dolls for Karen, his sister. Dad wanted Mark to have a gas-powered plane, but Ethel was afraid of them, so Dad taught him how to make kites from cut balsa wood yardsticks and newspaper.

We drove to Milwaukee often, especially after Grandma Lazar moved there. We loved the big seders at her house—lots of people, food, and noise. She and Aunt Ethel cooked for days before the event. Grandma made those terrific Jewish delicacies, the artery-clogging *gribines* (fried and salted chicken skin, fat, and onions). Just recalling their taste gives me heartburn.

Before one trip, Dad bought Mark a chronograph watch, a fancy one with lots of dials and numbers. On our trip to Milwaukee, Dad wound the watch over and over. He wound it so much that it broke. When we arrived, Dad gave Mark the usual headlock greeting and then sadly put the watch in Mark's hand. He felt bad about breaking the watch, he said, and even worse about not knowing how to fix it. Up until then, everyone thought Dad could fix anything. His reputation was blown. "Maybe you could take it apart and see what makes it go," he said. Taking things apart was something at which Mark excelled.

When Mark was ten, Dad gave him his first regulation-size baseball glove. It was black leather and way too large. Dad taught him how to oil it, wrap it over a ball, and tie it with string to conform to the shape of the baseball.

Dad also introduced Mark to Lionel trains, bringing him new add-on components on every Milwaukee trip: engines, grass, trees, switches, gates, people, animals, and transformers. Mark's parents bought a huge table for the train set, which took up most of their basement.

Sometimes the Sharpe family came to Chicago and Dad would crank up the tile-covered barbecue. He was the only one allowed to light it, cook on it, or even stand around it. It was his guy thing in a house full of women.

During the summer of 1963, Mark worked in the store to earn a few bucks. It was then that he discovered the new "addition" to the store's basement.

> *"To get to the basement, you went down a flight of old wooden stairs to a storeroom underneath the store, piled to the ceiling with every toy in the world. This wasn't the first time I had gone into the basement, but it wasn't small anymore."—Mark Sharpe*

"Hey, Mark, how do you like my new storeroom?" Dad asked, grabbing him around the neck and dragging him, wrestler-style, into the store's basement. "I made it myself."

"How did you do it?" Mark asked.

"Well, first I drilled a hole into the south wall, put a stick of dynamite into it, and blasted a hole. Behind the wall was another room that hadn't been used for years, not since Prohibition."

"But aren't we under 79th Street?" Mark asked, hearing cars whizzing by overhead.

"I got my hands on some old city plans. That's how I knew how deep and how far to go. If you put your ear to the wall, you can hear the movies playing at the Avalon Theater."

"I thought my Uncle Manny was a king. To an eleven-year-old it seemed like making tunnels under the street was part of the fun. Knowing my Uncle Manny, you never knew. Maybe he was planning to build a giant underground Lionel Railroad. When he told me how he blasted across the street I was amazed. I always loved going down there after that just to see if Uncle Manny got more creative with his expansion."—Mark Sharpe

In the summer of 1963, Manny and Belle were going to visit Mattel in California.

"Instead of closing the store, Manny just handed me the keys and let me run the store. That felt good, both having been trusted with the responsibility and helping Manny get away without having to close the store. The biggest thrill was working through the annual bedlam of Christmas. I probably worked harder then than at any time in my life—and loved it."—Burton Pickard-Richardson

On August 28, near the end of that restless summer of 1963, the Reverend Martin Luther King Jr. shared his dream of racial equality with more than two million people on the Mall in Washington, D.C. In South Shore, we were unaware of how dramatically our world would soon be changing in the wake of that speech.

Then, on November 22, our world and the world outside Chicago fell apart. I was in the hospital having my first child, Kim, when the obstetrician told me that President Kennedy had been killed in Dallas. I thought he was kidding.

The assassination of Kennedy by Lee Harvey Oswald, and then of Oswald by Jack Ruby, played out on TV, the nation reliving the gunshots over and over. In Chicago as elsewhere, people cried uncontrollably in the streets. Impromptu shrines appeared on street corners, and many stores closed early. The nation was in mourning, and now being run by Kennedy's fifty-five-year-old vice president from Texas.

Lyndon Johnson's priorities were civil rights and a "war on poverty." After his landslide election in 1964, Johnson introduced "the Great Society," geared toward improving the health, education, and nutrition of poor Americans. The Civil Rights Act of 1964 outlawed racial discrimination in public accommodations, and the Voting Rights Act of 1965 ensured everyone the right to vote. In 1966, Johnson appointed Robert Weaver, the first black cabinet member, to serve as secretary of the newly created Department of Housing and Urban Development. Johnson named Thurgood Marshall the first black Supreme Court justice in 1967.

The war on poverty was being waged throughout the nation's racially divided neighborhoods, including South Shore. In the 1940s and 1950s, our all-white neighborhood had been about 40 percent Jewish, 20 percent Protestant, and 40 percent Catholic. South Shore's population went from almost all white to almost all black between 1963 and 1967. The new residents were mostly black families with children, often replacing residents with no children or grown children. Many of these new families struggled financially.

"In 1964, there were three other black families on 78th and East End. In 1965, there were twelve. By 1967, the block was almost entirely black. I had been to only black households prior to moving to South Shore and I thought that all white people were in the KKK. I was invited over to a white friend's house for a play date. He caught me searching his closet and asked me what I was doing. I told him I was looking for his Klan robe, as I'd also seen pictures of children in the Klan. He laughed and told his mother, who gently told me they were Jewish. She told me her people were just as hated by the Klan as my people were. I learned later about the term 'white

*flight' and felt bad, as I had made some really good friends. I felt
things change in a few short years."—Andre Nickerson*

Before change came to the neighborhood, South Shore
had a "system" in place with churches, synagogues, and youth
groups. Many of these facilities catered to whites. But in some
cases Jews were restricted. As black families started moving
in, they too, in many cases, were not allowed to participate.
They were often less educated and more rough-mannered
than the existing groups.

Several community groups saw the need to combat discrimination by creating programming to which the newcomers
could relate. Dr. Jane Brown recalls that the Young Men's
Jewish Council and the Jewish Community Center included
blacks in all of their new and expanding programs. These programs were not designed strictly for blacks, but welcomed the
participation of all community residents. Membership dues
were drastically reduced to accommodate more people, resulting in a strong gain in membership. Programs like arts
and crafts, dancing, tutoring, music lessons, and sports were
scheduled both before and after school. From June through
August, there was summer camp and overnight camp. Most
of the black people moving into the community were drawn
to these wonderful programs.

The Youth Committee of the South Shore Commission coordinated many public and private programs at local "tot lots"
and field houses. Several programs were aimed at troubled
youth. The commission revitalized its Youth Guidance Program
for first-time offenders, cooperating with the police in following up on anti-social youth activities.

Gang Warfare

Despite the efforts of community organizations, new sounds
began filling our neighborhood, especially with the appearance
of gangs. Sitting on their porches on a summer night, residents
could hear teens fighting, windows breaking, sirens screaming,

and, sometimes, gunshots firing. You couldn't ride a bike through the area at night without being afraid of running into members of the Rangers or Disciples gangs who were beginning to terrorize the neighborhood. More armed cops were walking the beat.

Artificial barriers cut South Shore into boundaries that blacks could not safely cross: to the west, the dividing line was South Chicago Avenue, then Stony Island Avenue. To the north, 79th Street seemed to be the dividing line within the neighborhood. Black and white gangs clashed at these boundaries.

The gangs started enforcing geographic color barriers. If you were black, you crossed Stony Island Avenue at your own risk, going no farther than the Stony Island viaduct. The sparse lights under the viaduct had been shot out despite their protective wire mesh coverings. Garbage in the viaduct's windswept corners contained remnants of the melting pot, from Sears flyers and used oil filters to human excrement. The smell of urine and feces could knock you out from a block away. Graffiti on the walls boasted the signs and mottoes of gangs that made this putrid area their stomping grounds. New signs sprung up weekly. Black and Hispanic gangs both claimed it as their turf, and wars were fought to decide who was right. God protect you if this was your only way home.

Black families displaced from Hyde Park and Woodlawn, and those emigrating from southern states, kept moving into South Shore. Racial prejudice ran amok. Small civic organizations formed with the credo "Keep them out." Some white homeowners created restrictive covenants that ensured their homes would be sold only to other whites.

> *"I was working as a stock boy in the drugstore, but was in school when it happened. It had started getting rough on the street. I'd become the manager at the drugstore and had been robbed at gunpoint three times. I'll never forget it as long as I live. The guy put the pistol in my belly and taunted me. I left the area then.*
>
> *"There was never a formal effort to protect the schoolchildren. If you were lucky, you had a parent escort you back and forth to school. Police were in the school but they either couldn't or wouldn't suppress the gang activity."—Andre Nickerson*

After a particularly bad rash of gang vandalism, our insurance company threatened to drop coverage if we didn't put rolling iron gates over our doors and windows. Dad refused. "I won't insult my customers by doing that," he said. "I'll just find another insurance company." He did, but he paid more than double the old premium.

My parents made other business decisions that reflected the changing times. We had never sold fireworks, but after a customer's kid lost a hand to a cherry bomb, Dad stopped selling even sparklers and snakes. Later, as television and the movies featured caped crusaders like the Green Hornet and Batman, Wee Folks celebrated these heroes who fought crime and preserved justice and the American way by selling lunch boxes, games, and toys.

Through it all, my parents continued to show kindness and respect to all neighbors and customers, and continued to live and work in South Shore, even after a barber was shot in his shop just down 79th Street in 1963. It was the first shooting on the street that I remember.

"I am African American and my family moved into the neighborhood in early 1964. Your father sold all the Beatles stuff when they stormed the country. Beatlemania was upon us. A hand-painted poster of the Beatles' heads was draped across the store, advertising BEATLE WIGS! I remember how all the kids thought it was real cool to see the Beatles stuff in the window. I'll never forget going into the store when no one else was there to buy a Beatle wig. Your father asked me why I wanted to buy it. He could see that I was trying to fit in. There were not a lot of other African Americans in the neighborhood yet. He told me to be proud of who I was, and even if I bought the wig, it would not change who I was. I bought it anyway but never forgot what your dad had said to me. I felt a bond with him afterward that grew as the years went by."—Andre Nickerson

"1964 was a very stressful year for me. We had just moved from Cabrini Green into the South Side. Wee Folks was my greatest discovery of the new neighborhood. I was a skinny black kid of nine, yet I recall how the display windows served as a therapeutic device for me. What was between that window and me erased how painful things were in and around me. I remember the Aurora model mon-

Send Your Letters To Santa Claus

Emanuel and Belle Lazar's annual "Letters to Santa Claus" contest, in which $100 in toys is awarded area boys and girls, enters its last three days of judging tomorrow.

Deadline for all letters is 6 p.m. Wednesday. Winners will be notified by phone Christmas Eve.

To enter, a boy or girl under the age of 12 must write a letter to Santa Claus stating what he or she would like for Christmas. Requests must be within reason.

Letters are then deposited in the Playskool postal station at the Wee Folks store at 1708-10 E. 79th st., owned and operated by Mr. and Mrs. Lazar.

The contest is free and entries are not required to buy at Wee Folks. In its fourth year, the contest will award gifts to more than 20 youngsters.

Wee Folks offers shoppers toys not commonly found in Chicago.

Mom and Dad read many touching stories in the letters to Santa they received.

ster contest. I don't recall the prize, but I do remember all the gory displays of the Hollywood monsters. The very first time I ventured into Wee Folks I was politely informed that I'd have to have a parent accompany me to be in the store. I didn't have any money, but I just fell in love with the place. I remember the Danny O'Day doll and a toy drum set that I was trying to save my little bit of lunch money for. To this day, I know what a real toy store smells like. To me, Wee Folks was Toyland. Thank God for its existence and the opportunity to express my fond memories of that place and time."

—Gregory McDonald

"One Christmas, my three-and-a-half-year-old son wanted a Bat-mobile Dashboard. It was the number-one thing on his list and I had searched everywhere for one but they were sold out. I had moved out of the area, but I went back to Wee Folks about two days before Christmas. One was available for about $10. I was so thrilled to find one, but when I heard the price my face must have really fallen! We had very little money in those days and that was a small fortune to spend on one toy. Your mother looked at me with sympathy and gently said to your dad, 'Maybe we could let her have it for $7.' That was about all I had left and I was so grateful that Santa did not fail that year."—Diane Helstern

On January 26, 1967, Chicago's "snowfall of the century" dumped twenty-three inches in twenty-four hours. More than seventy-five million tons of snow were loaded into railroad cars and sent as a belated Christmas present to kids in Florida. Cars and buses were at a standstill. Commuters from Chicago sub-urbs spent the night in hotels. But my dad kept moving, com-ing to my rescue. I was a single parent with two young children. That day I was out of baby food and most groceries, and my car wouldn't start. Dad put a car battery, jumper cables, and food on a sled and trudged more than a mile up the middle of 79th Street to my apartment. It took him four hours. Then he trudged back. He was fifty-eight years old.

Dad was beginning to look his age—back bent, fingers gnarled with arthritis—as he spent weekdays working in the store and sunny summer Sundays planting flowers and trimming the tall hedges around the house. But when he drove his prized yel-low two-door '62 Pontiac Grand Prix with the black leather in-terior, he turned into the kid he never had the time to be. Just like the boys in the store, he had customized his "toy" with real wal-nut interior, including the dashboard and console. He added a dual chrome exhaust. Dad always went for the horsepower.

Seventy-ninth Street was aging too. Empty storefronts stood like old men in a row, the doors gaping like toothless mouths and the windows of the apartments above staring like vacant eyes. Every day more old men joined the march.

On a larger scale, President Johnson had wearied of his battles, and in March 1968 announced he would not run for reelection.

The following month, the Reverend Martin Luther King Jr. was killed by James Earl Ray. The black community had lost its leadership. Enraged, many blacks reacted to his assassination with looting, burning, and shooting. Whites and blacks felt unsafe in their own homes.

"I remember when Dr. King was assassinated and there was looting. I was working at a store on the street and I remember my boss saying that if something happened, we would need to help Mr. Lazar as he said Mr. Lazar would do the same for us if the situation was different."—Andre Nickerson

The West Side of Chicago burned in a frenzy of rioting, looting, and killing that spilled into South Shore. Rioters torched the fledgling businesses that had tried to survive in the midst of gang warfare. Bodyguards flanked ministers as they fended off threats from gang members to destroy their churches. Heavy stone and metal garbage cans were hurled into store windows all over 79th Street. Wee Folks' large double windows were shattered and our new insurance policy was terminated. In all, nine people died in the riots. More than 1,000 were left homeless and 2,500 were arrested.

Mobs clashed with police all over the city. The Illinois National Guard patrolled areas of high crime, looting, and violence, like Stony Island and 87th Street near Chicago Vocational High School. Students had been released early from school, but it only set rebellious kids free to do their worst. White teens raged against pent-up black hatred while black teens raged against the murder of their leader. Blacks and whites ran through bumper-to-bumper rush-hour traffic, smashing car windows and throwing rocks at their drivers.

In the emerging age of television realism, we witnessed roaming foot patrols of fearful, angry whites threatening to stop the rioting and looting by force. We saw cars of combatants ready to overthrow black gangs that they perceived would now be coming to their neighborhood. Mayor Daley put out a "shoot to maim" order for looters and a "shoot to kill" order for anyone holding a Molotov cocktail.

The next day, April 5, many schools closed just before lunchtime, thrusting even the youngest kids onto the street. They were told to go straight home, but many had working parents and could not go home. Some parents chose to stay home and not send their kids to school at all that day.

Two months later, Senator Robert F. Kennedy, having just won the California primary, was killed by a Palestinian Arab named Sirhan Sirhan.

In August, the 1968 Democratic National Convention in downtown Chicago provided a platform for an antiwar protest playing out on the city's streets. It was a made-for-TV event, featuring hundreds of armed troopers and National Guardsmen and more than 2,500 young people chanting and running wild as they protested the war in Vietnam. Through the immediacy of live television, we saw many graphic scenes of terror: heads cracked with billy clubs, throats choked with mace, bodies hit by chunks of cement, police officers injured as they muscled demonstrators into paddy wagons. The City of Chicago's official report stated:

> Large amounts of hair spray were sold in the Old Town area stores during the time of the Convention. The expulsion of hair spray from a can when set fire to works as a homemade flame-thrower. Royal Blue Food Store at 744 Fullerton Avenue reported large groups of Yippies (the name given to the demonstrators) purchasing large quantities of hair spray. It is common knowledge that Yippies have no use for hair spray or other cosmetics for personal use.

The Conrad Hilton Hotel on Michigan Avenue in the heart of Chicago's downtown lakefront was convention headquarters. In front of the hotel, Grant Park served both as a beautiful centerpiece of the area and a gathering spot for demonstrators. Now the park was dark except for the glow of bonfires. Blood ran in the gutters. An armored van sported giant searchlights.

The CNN Time Web site reports:

> Outside the official convention proceedings, anti-war demonstrators clashed with 11,900 Chicago police, 7,500 Army

troops, 7,500 Illinois National Guardsmen and 1,000 Secret Service agents over 5 days. The violence centered on two things: the Chicago police forcing protesters out of areas where they were not permitted to be; and protesters clashing with police, and their reinforcements, as they tried to march to the convention site.

City ordinance required that parks be cleared by 11:00 P.M., but this was rarely enforced. Mayor Daley now felt the parks should not be left for the demonstrators' activities at night and enforced the ordinance. Every night the order was barked into a bullhorn: "This is your final warning! Clear the park—disperse, you have five minutes to disperse. You have five minutes to get out of this park!" A chant rose from the crowd of rioters: "The whole world is watching, the whole world is watching. . . ."

The whole world *was* watching, but no one watched more closely than the Black P Stone Nation. This large and dangerous gang existed for conflict and became more powerful through chaos. It had taken the BPSN less than a decade to transform itself from an aimless group of twelve poor teens hanging on a corner a few miles north of South Shore into a well-funded, 4,000-member-strong machine of terror. Fear, in fact, was the gang's main weapon, and by the end of the 1960s, the Black P Stone Nation—formerly known as the Blackstone Rangers—had South Shore choking on fear for its life.

*Mom and Dad at their new
Glenwood home, late 1969.*

CHAPTER 7

The Birth of Two Nations

The Blackstone Rangers—1960

IN THE SUMMER OF 1960, five miles northwest of Wee Folks on a street corner in Chicago's Woodlawn neighborhood, twelve kids in their early teens were hanging out. Several were recent Audi Home (Cook County Detention Center) and St. Charles (Illinois Juvenile Corrections Facility) parolees and already hardened criminals.

These teens—who called themselves the Blackstone Rangers—felt just as imprisoned on the street as behind bars, trapped by poverty and prejudice. "As they came out of St. Charles, they were convinced of the idea that America (i.e., the America they knew) is a jail in pretty much the same way St. Charles is a jail," wrote the Reverend John Fry in *Locked-Out Americans.* "They had gone from one jail, Woodlawn, to another jail, St. Charles, then returned to the Woodlawn jail."[1]

"You can have it all" was the message blared on television, and they interpreted it as "You ain't nothin'" without fine clothes and a good car. Without these trappings, they "wouldn't 'mount to nothin'." They needed money. They needed to belong. Eventually, membership in the Blackstone Rangers gave them both.

According to an Illinois Department of Corrections gang-training document, the gang's name originated in 1959 at 6536 South Blackstone Avenue, the home of their "main man," a street tough and high-school dropout named Jeff Fort. He and his followers hung out at the corner of 64th and Blackstone.[2]

In fact, many of these original Blackstone Rangers, who came from single-parent families, lived at Fort's house. The Rangers later referred to these early years as the period of creation. They dodged school, ashamed of their ragged clothes and gym shoes soled with cardboard. They frequented soup kitchens, hungry for a hot meal. They shoplifted and vandalized. They discovered drugs and prostitution among the vacant stores and abandoned cars of the streets.[3, 4]

Somewhere in Woodlawn, a youngster named Thomas Gunn, the youngest of four children, was also hitting the streets. His parents often worked two jobs so their family could have food and clothes. It was a strict home, but a loving one. But no matter what goodness lay inside their apartment, this boy was drawn to the Rangers' fast life. He loved the excitement, the thrill, and the comradeship.

In *The Blackstone Rangers: A Reporter's Account of Time Spent with the Street Gang on Chicago's South Side*, R.T. Sale describes how alliances with smaller gangs allowed the Rangers to grow into the largest, most menacing force in Chicago. Fort controlled the turf known as Jackson Park, just east of Woodlawn. A small rival gang roamed 70th Street. When the two gangs finally realized neither could defeat the other, they merged.[5] In those early years, the Rangers' leadership consisted of Fort and his right-hand man, Eugene "Bull" Hairston.[6, 7]

From the start, the Blackstone Rangers were different from other gangs. For one thing, Fort called the Rangers an organization or a nation, not a gang. And as the two other major black Chicago street gangs of the early 1960s—the Vice Lords and Black Disciples—became involved in politics, the Rangers allied themselves with the Black Power movement.[8] Being a Ranger meant you were black and didn't take crap from anyone. Black people don't take it—that's what *negroes* do. Black people *resist*.[9, 10]

This was the same message preached by the Nation of Islam in the 1960s throughout U.S. prisons. While NOI followers believed in Allah, the Holy Koran, and the resurrection of the righteous, they also believed in mental resurrection. The "so-called Negroes," they said, were most in need of mental resurrection.

Social scientist Charles Eric Lincoln coined the term "Black Muslim" in 1961 to distinguish NOI followers from Orthodox Muslims, whom he called Moslems.[11]

This radical version of Islam—"the black man's true religion," as the NOI called it—blossomed inside jailhouses, where angry young black men found its anti-white, anti-America message appealing.[12] Those particularly susceptible to NOI teachings were poor, lower class, formerly Christian young black males. These disillusioned youth refused to follow the religion of their white oppressors. Membership in the NOI gave blacks in general and gang members in particular an empowering sense of pride.

The Nation of Islam had considerable influence on Jeff Fort and the Blackstone Rangers, who fed off the concept of black separatism. Portions of the NOI doctrine were added to the Rangers' laws. It was almost predictable that, with the increase of gang members in prison and the NOI's reach into those prisons, a sort of homegrown enemy would emerge: black ex-prisoners with a warped misunderstanding of Islam, harboring hatred of whites and the government. Fort used this hatred to further his own goals.

Mom hadn't heard about the Nation of Islam before it first came to call on Wee Folks one hot summer afternoon in 1962, when three black boys dressed in their Sunday best showed up on her doorstep.

"Ma'am, we got a new paper for you—*Muhammad Speaks*," said one boy, thrusting a copy of the new weekly newspaper published by the Honorable Elijah Muhammad into her hand. The boys told her they were from the new Nation of Islam mosque in Hyde Park. The paper's front-page headline proclaimed, "Some of This Earth to Call Our Own," and espoused Elijah Muhammad's message to America's black men and women: that they should be respected by civilized societies as a nation of people.

Not only was the black separatist Nation of Islam growing stronger in our neighborhood that summer, it had actually begun its grip on the Blackstone Rangers and South Shore on a summer day three decades before, when the despair of America's Great Depression was palpable and lynchings, race riots, and terrorism against blacks were commonplace. Blacks were fleeing the South to find opportunities in the North.

Birth of the Nation of Islam—1930

On July 4, 1930, a mysterious yellow-skinned little man disguised as a door-to-door peddler of silks and African wares appeared in a poor, mostly black section of Detroit. Wallace Dodd Fard had just been released from San Quentin, having served three years for selling narcotics. Using aliases and claiming to be a missionary, Fard began conducting meetings in areas where most blacks were Baptist or Methodist.[13]

He preached three main concepts that became the foundation for the Nation of Islam movement: first, that Allah is God; second, that the white man is the devil; and third, that the "so-called Negroes" are the superior race. He told anyone who would listen how Christianity was the white man's religion and being used to enslave the black man's mind.[14]

Fard said that the only hope for blacks in America was to convert to Islam, their natural religion. He believed that until they regained their true religion and language (Islam and Arabic) and formed a separate state, they would never achieve freedom, equality, and justice. He gave glowing accounts of the religion of their brothers and sisters in Africa. The word "negro," he professed, was created by white men and was not the proper name for African Americans. "You are really members of the lost tribe of Shabazz," he resounded. Master Fard Muhammad, as he became known, described the end of days, the Armageddon, which would be fought in North America between blacks and whites.

Detroit police labeled Fard a street peddler, dope-dealer, and fraud. They saw him as a slick salesman for a pseudo-religion that exploited the poverty and weakness of black immigrants. Yet he successfully recruited more than 8,000 followers into his Lost-Found Nation of Islam between 1930 and 1934.[15] People without hope formed his flock, segregated Americans who had no trouble believing in his militant theological doctrine. These newly converted Muslims believed that Allah, the one and only God, had appeared in the person of Master W. Fard Muhammad in Detroit in July 1930, and that he was the long-awaited "Messiah" of the Christians and the "Mahdi" of the Muslims.

Attending one of Fard's meetings in August 1931 was Elijah Poole, an unemployed assembly-line worker. After years of sharecropping in the South, Poole had moved to Detroit with his wife and eight children for better economic opportunity. Captivated by Fard's message, Poole accepted Islam and embraced Fard as God himself, soon becoming his primary Islamic student.

Fard convinced Poole that the difference between Muslims and other black political and religious groups was that black and white people did not come from the same God. The "Hidden Truth" was that blacks were the righteous and divine people and whites were blond, blue-eyed devils. "America is being divinely judged for the evils that white men did to black slaves," Fard said. He cited movements like the Ku Klux Klan and Nazism as examples that the racial myth of white supremacy was wrong. He started restoring converts to their "true" names, history, religion, and ethnicity.

Fard saw in Poole his successor, the next leader of the Lost-Found people, and gave him the true name of Elijah Muhammad. "The name Poole was never my name," Muhammad would later write, "nor was it my father's name. It was the name of the white slave-master of my grandfather after the so-called freedom of my fathers."

Even with a fourth-grade education, Muhammad quickly became an integral part of the Lost-Found community. Fard promoted him to Supreme Minister, charging him with the task of raising the social and moral standards of millions of oppressed blacks and increasing their hope for better lives.

In 1932, Fard was arrested in connection with alleged sacrificial murders. After being released from jail, he named Elijah Muhammad the Minister of Islam. Shortly thereafter, Master Fard Muhammad—the Savior, the Prophet, the Great Mahdi—disappeared, and was never heard from again.

In 1934, Elijah Muhammad moved to Chicago[16] and established a newspaper, *The Final Call to Islam,* the first of many publications he would produce. The Lost-Found community also established religious centers and started businesses that encouraged commerce between and among blacks. Followers called Elijah Muhammad the Messenger of Allah.

While in Washington, D.C., in 1942, Muhammad was arrested for draft evasion. Like many other male members of the Lost-Found, he was imprisoned for four years for being a conscientious objector. He converted many fellow prisoners to Islam.[17] He won his release at the close of the war and returned to Chicago. Now an NOI martyr, Muhammad founded Chicago Temple No. 2 on the South Side, at 5335 Greenwood Avenue in Hyde Park. He was called the leader of the Allah Temple of Islam.[18] He opened other temples in Detroit, Milwaukee, and Washington, D.C.

Elijah Muhammad became the voice for Islam in America, laying the groundwork for the black civil-rights revolution of the 1950s and 1960s, when more than five million southern blacks came to the promised land of the north. Chicago's black population alone exploded from 300,000 in 1940 to 800,000 in 1960. Thousands were attracted by the NOI's nationalist propaganda and became followers. All it took was $10 and a letter to Muhammad and a man could shed his slave name and assume his original identity. High-profile people like Cassius Clay joined the NOI ranks, abandoning his slave name to become Muhammad Ali. Black Chicago musicians like Ahmad Jamal also converted.[19]

Elijah Muhammad's black separatist doctrine taught followers of the NOI to pray for the time when they would receive their own territory in the United States. He awaited the final battle of Armageddon, when Allah would end the era of white supremacy in the West and the black race would reign supreme. This led many to believe that the NOI was not a religion, but a political movement whose purpose was racial empowerment and equality.[20]

The Muslim theology, in fact, was an intricate merger of philosophies, including numerology and variations on Islam, Christianity, Jehovah's Witnesses, and Freemasonry. Eventually, it became a mixture of racism, science fiction, mysticism, and carefully chosen theological doctrine, all pitched to believers in race-war rhetoric. People disenchanted with the slow progress of the civil-rights movement were especially drawn to the NOI, as were disenfranchised black men like Malcolm X.[21]

Malcolm X

Malcolm Little, the son of a Baptist preacher, moved from Lansing, Michigan, to Chicago in 1952. Little had just spent seven years in prison. There, he had studied the Nation of Islam teachings and been strongly affected by Muhammad's "white man is the devil" thesis.[22]

Little had reasons for believing that message. The Ku Klux Klan had burned down his father's house for stirring up trouble with his back-to-Africa preaching. The Klan-like Black Legion had killed his father; his mother went mad and was institutionalized, and Malcolm and his siblings were placed in foster homes. After eighth grade, when he told his favorite teacher he wanted to be a lawyer, she said, "That's no realistic goal for a nigger." He dropped out of school and into a life of crime, working as a small-time numbers runner, often under the influence of marijuana and cocaine. At twenty-one, he was sentenced to seven years in prison for armed robbery.[23, 24, 25, 26, 27]

As he explained years later in his essay titled "Why the Nation of Islam Grows So Quickly in Prisons": "Among all Negroes the black convict is the most perfectly preconditioned to hear the words, 'the white man is the devil.' . . . You let this caged-up black man start realizing, as I did, how from the first landing of the first slave ship, the millions of black men in America have been like sheep in a den of wolves. . . . 'The white man is the devil' is a perfect echo of that black convict's lifelong experience."[28]

Malcolm Little impressed Elijah Muhammad when they met, and the young man studied under Muhammad to become an NOI minister. His Muslim name became El-Hajj Malik El-Shabazz, and he became known as Malcolm X. The "X" denoted "unknown," indicating that the true heritage of African Americans was stolen during the slave trade. [29, 30, 31]

Elijah Muhammad needed more visibility for the Nation of Islam and saw his protégé as the person who could invigorate the NOI. He proposed they work together to increase membership. During the 1950s, Muhammad promoted the now Minister Malcolm X to NOI's post of national spokesman.

Malcolm X was a good orator, full of fire. In 1954, he took over as minister of the New York Temple No. 7. In 1957, he became minister of a temple in Detroit. During that year, he also married Betty Sanders, who became Betty Shabazz. He proved to be a good father to their six children and a loyal husband.[32]

By the late 1950s, the Nation of Islam was flooded with converts, and Malcolm X and Elijah Muhammad were media sensations, making the covers of *Life, Look, Time,* and *Reader's Digest.* On July 13–17, 1959, television sets across America were tuned to a CBS special called "The Hate That Hate Produced." The documentary told of black racism and the growing desire for black supremacy among segments of Americans. It told of the Nation of Islam movement and how it obscured the true intention of the Islamic religion. In the documentary, Malcolm X emerged as one of NOI's most important leaders.[33]

But he grew increasingly resentful as the NOI refused to join the mounting civil-rights struggle under Martin Luther King Jr. In 1962, Malcolm X's faith was shattered after learning that Muhammad was having adulterous affairs, violating Muslim teachings. He had heard rumors for years about the affairs, which caused numerous Muslims to leave Chicago Mosque No. 2. Now Malcolm was convinced of Muhammad's lack of sincerity.[34]

Muhammad, on the other hand, seemed threatened by Malcolm's growing popularity.[35] Elijah Muhammad needed to groom a new, more loyal lieutenant. He found one in Louis Farrakhan.

Louis Farrakhan

In February 1955, Louis Gene Wolcott accepted a friend's invitation to Elijah Muhammad's Chicago temple. The young singer, dancer, and violinist known as "Calypso Gene" had experienced bias against blacks in his predominantly Jewish neighborhood in the Bronx, and he despised both whites and Jews. When Wolcott first heard Muhammad speak, he immediately enrolled in the NOI.[36, 37]

Louis became Louis X in 1955 and proved himself capable and disciplined, quickly rising to the rank of minister. Beginning in 1956, he worked as the minister of Muhammad Temple No. 11 in Boston, building it into one of the NOI's strongest temples. He later adopted the name Abdul Haleem Farrakhan and came to be known as Louis Farrakhan.[38]

Farrakhan moved up the ranks to a leadership position, eventually replacing Malcolm X as the Honorable Elijah Muhammad's national spokesman.[39] In 1963, a rift within the NOI erupted when Malcolm X took charge of the organization's convention in Chicago. The FBI, the media, and other forces contributed to the divisiveness. On March 8, 1963, the *New York Times* announced, "Malcolm X Splits with Muhammad," revealing that he planned to form a new Black Nationalist Party, cooperating with local civil-rights groups to heighten the political consciousness of blacks.

Five months later, on August 28, Martin Luther King Jr. joined other civil-rights leaders in the historic March on Washington and delivered his "I have a dream" speech at the Lincoln Memorial. King received the Nobel Peace Prize in 1964. Too soon, however, many blacks became disappointed with the slow progress of the civil rights movement. Tempers grew short. More and more blacks turned to radical leaders. Among them was Malcolm X.[40]

Malcolm X finally broke all ties with the Nation of Islam on March 18, 1964. The next month, he made a pilgrimage to the holy Islamic city of Mecca. He was amazed to see people of all colors worshipping together and to hear Orthodox Moslems preaching equality of the races. He abandoned the argument that whites are devils.

In his "Ballot or the Bullet" speech of April 3, 1964, Malcolm X reported that he was still a Muslim, but now saw the need for a separation of religion and politics. He formed his own Muslim mosque in 1964, where he espoused a secular, Black Nationalist platform.[41] He formed the Organization of Afro-American Unity and moved increasingly toward socialism. Early the following year, he worked to establish a multiracial Orthodox Islam as an option for African Americans.[42] But on February 21, 1965, while speaking passionately in Harlem on political nonviolence, Malcolm X was gunned down. Many believed his assailants were members of the NOI.[43]

Farrakhan continued to rise within the Nation of Islam. As he conducted rallies across the United States, he conveyed his message of African American separatism and economic rebirth while continuing his attack on whites and Jews.[44] In time, he embraced Jeff Fort and the Blackstone Rangers as his angels of death. According to Lance Williams, a teacher of "The Sociology of Violence" for the Center for Inner City Studies at Northeastern Illinois University, Farrakhan put high-level Rangers in touch with the Libyan government through his international network. The action would have dramatic consequences.[45]

First, however, the Rangers and other gangs would be embraced by President Lyndon Johnson's war on poverty, which sought to prevent America from being irrevocably divided along racial lines.

The Blackstone Rangers—1964

Throughout the early 1960s, much of black society, not just teenaged members of gangs, felt oppressed and desperate to improve their lot. They wanted equality—in housing, in education, in employment. In 1964, having declared his war on poverty, President Johnson established the national Office of Economic Opportunity. The OEO, which continued until 1973 when President Nixon cancelled it, was formed specifically to address the needs of a disadvantaged black society.[46]

In Chicago, a community group known as The Woodlawn Organization believed that the way to fight poverty was to shower ghetto-based political coalitions with money. Empowerment, they reasoned, would defeat poverty. Outside observers wondered why anyone would give large sums of money to poor, uneducated inner-city gang members without also giving them guidance. But promoting the concept of community action became more popular than actually undoing the culture of poverty. One common community-action approach was to train ghetto blacks in federal Job Corps centers, designed to find work for underprivileged kids. The centers often became money-laundering dens of iniquity.[47]

In the early days, the Rangers sought jobs only to be refused when their gang affiliation became known. Occasionally, someone found a job, but it was hard to keep, as these teens had little discipline and didn't respond well to authority, especially to taking orders. Policies, rules, and regulations didn't fit with their brute-force tactics.[48]

By 1964, the Black Disciples and Jeff Fort's Blackstone Rangers were Chicago's reigning gangs. Fort's band of a dozen loners had become an organized, armed 250-member criminal street gang, easily recognized by their red felt berets. There were daily shootings. Their weapon of choice was the zip gun, a cap pistol rigged with an explosive and copper tube in the barrel that shot a .22 shell. Complaints poured in from area residents about nightly gang-banging and open warfare between rival gangs. The Rangers saw themselves victorious and proclaimed themselves the power of the community.

The Rangers had long since been booted out of the Wood-lawn Boys Club because of inappropriate behavior. Because they were so disruptive, gang members weren't welcome inside local settlement houses either. The YMCA of Metropolitan Chicago and the Chicago Youth Development Project subsequently set up programs to guide inner-city gang members toward better lives. Area churches acted as fiscal agents for Operation Bootstrap, whose officers included members of the Chicago Board of Education and the Chicago Police Department. The volunteer workers were courageous, even fearless, but the gang members looked upon these efforts with humor. Once they discovered that having a social worker was a sign of status, they started calling social-service agencies to get one. It was good to be bad enough to need one.[49]

By 1965, high-profile white Chicago philanthropists joined the community-action bandwagon, pumping new money into the inner city. They made loans to start businesses and clean up neighborhoods. They funded educational projects. They sought to create jobs, build a community center for teens, start a newspaper for Ranger members interested in writing, encourage black-owned businesses to expand, create a community police patrol—even start a drum-and-bugle corps. They were out to cure what ailed Chicago. From their executive seats, these men acted as if all the street gang members needed was a good example, a fresh start, and the encouragement that people were willing to take a chance on them.[50]

The Rangers soon gained national recognition because of their support from prominent businessmen, entertainers, and politicians. They formed business ventures with Sammy Davis Jr., among others, and had the support of the late W. Clement Stone, a self-made millionaire who later gave $1 million to the Rangers.[51, 52]

But the faith of such benefactors proved misplaced. Newspapers reported that one of the main Ranger-occupied churches had become a gun arsenal. Bull Hairston, Fort's second-in-command, was jailed for solicitation to commit murder. The philanthropists stopped funding many of the programs as they realized much of the money was used for other purposes.

Yet these good samaritans still believed the Rangers' stories of police brutality and thought their money could overcome police harassment and trumped-up arrests. The philanthropists funneled many thousands of dollars into a fund that became known as the Blackstone Rangers Legal Defense Fund. Over time, with the ample legal support, acquittals increased. But the philanthropists were discouraged to learn that the number of cases remained the same.[53]

While Chicago courts and police tried to squash the gangs, one man believed he could reform them. Reverend John Fry, the leader of the First Presbyterian Church in Woodlawn, turned his church and its resources over to the Rangers, sometimes using the church's money for bailing out gang leaders. By the fall of 1965, Jeff Fort and his gang were holding their city-wide meetings at Reverend Fry's Church.[54]

From his association with Fry, Fort realized that the Rangers' appearance as a religious organization was essential to running a prosperous gang operation. Religion gave them a cloak of legitimacy and social acceptability, allowing them to exploit a free society without being regulated, inspected, monitored, or investigated. The success of the Rangers depended on how effectively they could take advantage of this attitude. Other gangs later copied this approach.[55]

Fort raised funds from do-gooders and the government by promoting the Rangers as a religious, socially conscious self-help organization bent on lifting the community. He received thousands of dollars in grants for inner-city development. He promised to use the taxpayers' money to educate children, aid small-business owners, and improve Chicago's deteriorating Woodlawn community. In reality, only a small amount of money went toward good works. The rest helped finance campaigns for gang recruitment, the purchase and sale of weapons, narcotics sales, and a campaign of terror aimed at the small-business owners striving to maintain Woodlawn's economic existence. The Rangers increased their stranglehold on the neighborhood through battery, drive-by shootings, prostitution, robbery, drug sales, intimidation, extortion, and murder.

Thanks to philanthropists and politicians, the Rangers had become a rich and fearless street army governed by a fearless leader. Jeff Fort was ready to implement even bigger plans for his organization, and had come up with a new name befitting its rapidly increasing population: the Black P Stone Nation.

Birth of the Black P Stone Nation—1966

Jeff Fort had united more than fifty West Side area street gangs into one enormous, insidious operation controlled by a twenty-one-man commission called the Main 21. Leaders of twenty of the largest gangs made up the Main 21, with Fort as the chief.[56]

The newly named Black P Stone Nation, with the "P" standing for peace, adopted a symbol: a pyramid illustrating the followers' relationship to the Main 21. The five-pointed star inside a crescent moon and pyramids had twenty-one stones, each standing for a Main 21 member. Among this group were George "Mad Dog" Rose, Lee "Stone" Jackson (now deceased), Leroy "Mr. Maniac" Hairston, Bernard "the Colonel" Green, and George "Porgy" Martin (now deceased).[57] Fort encouraged other gangs to join what now resembled an organized crime syndicate.[58]

"The 'Nation' has always been more than just a criminal syndicate," said Lance Williams of the University of Illinois–Chicago School of Public Health in a speech about the Black P Stone Nation. "The Rangers benefited from the War on Poverty. In 1966, as a reward for arranging a gang truce with the Eastside Disciples, the Rangers were given a federal grant of more than $900,000 to conduct job training programs and create future leaders of the black community."[59]

Between April and December 1966, with Reverend Fry's support, the BPSN grew from 500 to 1,500 members. During 1967 that number doubled. Graffiti grew on the walls of buildings. The gang's slogan, "Stones Run It," and "BPS" (for Black P Stone) were scrawled on buildings all over Chicago, including South Shore, and struck fear in the hearts of residents.[60]

The gang continued branching out, their recruiting efforts no longer confined to Woodlawn and neighboring areas. As their influence spread, crime increased. It moved from north to south, encompassing the Woodlawn area first and then moving to South Shore and farther south to other neighborhoods. Hyde Park was protected by the University of Chicago, which had a large presence there. Other neighborhoods, like mine, weren't so lucky.

In the early 1950s, the Grand Crossing Police District and the South Chicago Police District just to its south defined the South Shore neighborhood. We lived and worked in the South Chicago District, but Grand Crossing was close by. The population for these districts combined was about 165,000, mostly white.[61]

In the early 1960s, police districts were redefined. The Grand Crossing District was combined with the Woodlawn District just to its north and called the Grand Crossing District. Similarly, the South Chicago District was combined with the East Side District just to its south and called the South Chicago District.[62] In 1952, the occurrence of Class 1 crime, considered to be the most serious (murder, rape, aggravated assault, robbery, burglary, theft, and auto theft), was about 1,000 incidents in Grand Crossing and 4,000 in Woodlawn for a total of 5,000 in the area that became the new Grand Crossing District. The Class 1 crime rate for South Chicago was about 1,200 and for the East Side about 300, for a total of 1,500 for the area that would become the South Chicago District.[63]

By the mid-1960s, crime in these areas had grown substantially. The new Grand Crossing District had more than 7,000 incidents of Class 1 crime (a 40 percent increase) and the new South Chicago District had more than 3,300 incidents (a 220 percent increase). By 1969, the numbers further increased to a little more than 8,200 in Grand Crossing and almost 4,000 in South Chicago. Between the early 1950s and the late 1960s, Class 1 crime had increased 65 percent in Grand Crossing and 270 percent in South Chicago. As South Shore was in the South Chicago District, this drastic increase substantially changed the character of our neighborhood.[64]

"I saw a car full of Rangers stomp a kid once, using the incident as an initiation ritual for a new recruit. It was savage and brazen, right outside the drugstore where I worked in the middle of 79th and East End. Another car pulled up and it was higher-ranking members who saw this. They showed pistols in their belts and said the stomping is what happens to people who refuse to join. The kid suffered three broken ribs and a lacerated kidney. They had to remove his spleen. He also lost three teeth."—Andre Nickerson

BPSN recruitment contributed greatly to the rise in crime. During one bloody recruitment year, 1966, more than forty people were shot, four died, one child was kidnapped, thirty people were beaten in the streets, and Molotov cocktails were hurled through the windows of homes in which the sons had not been allowed to join the gang. Between 1965 and 1969, more than 200 people, many who were not gang members, were slain in gang-related crimes and almost half of those charged were under the age of twenty-one. Nothing was safe from the gangs' influence. Playgrounds and streets ran with the fresh blood of the previous night's gang executions, with innocent children murdered in the crossfire. The gang gave these youths confidence to commit robberies and rapes, conduct protection rackets, and hold recruiting drives. All the while, the BPSN claimed to be a boys club.[65]

The Chicago Gang Crime Intelligence Unit reported that in May and June of 1966, sixteen youths were shot because they were not members of the gang or refused to join. Thirteen more were beaten or stabbed.[66]

The BPSN shot forty-one young people in their 1967 recruitment drive. Four died. One child was kidnapped and beaten. The gang's efforts expanded membership as well as dues. The money went into their treasury and was added to the monies already raised from extortion to be used for bail and guns. Fifty-two complaints of extortion—in which the BPSN demanded money in exchange for protecting businesses—were filed with the police in instances where the accused either identified himself as a BPSN member or was a known member of the gang.[67]

Gangs in South Shore

By the mid-1960s, gangs had begun organizing in Wee Folks' neighborhood, on 79th and 87th Streets. Extortion squads preyed on South Shore merchants. Many businesses on 79th Street had been robbed. Probably due somewhat to the influence of the Nation of Islam, the gangs felt that white Jewish merchants in particular were there to rip them off. The cry of "Mighty Blackstone Rangers" rang in the ears of their victims.

A South Shore resident remembers this time of siege.

"It was the spring of 1967 and heavy gang recruiting was going on at South Shore High School. Ranger recruiters would overwhelm individuals or small groups of boys. My best friend and I heard about this and would use alleys to dodge their advances and keep from being trapped. Usually, one kid was threatened and hit in the face or the chest as a warning to the others. Those tales struck fear in most of my friends. One day, we were unfortunate enough to walk right into a group of five Rangers at the mouth of the alley behind our homes. They pushed us around and threatened us with bodily harm if we didn't join right then and there. Scared to death, we made a run for it, hoping to make it to my friend's backyard. This was our lucky day. His dad, a Chicago fireman, was home. As we drew nearer, we saw he had something behind his back. As we were telling what happened, the Rangers came boldly down the alley between East End and Ridgeland. I was frozen. My friend's dad told them to go away. They replied with a disrespectful obscenity and started to challenge him. From his side, my friend's dad pulled a 12-gauge shotgun. The Rangers told him they had business with us and to step out of the way. He primed the shotgun. The Rangers stopped dead in their tracks. He made the oldest gang member look at my friend and I. 'Remember their faces,' he roared, 'because if any harm comes to them, I'll remember your faces, hunt you down like the rats you are, and blow your faces off with this shotgun.' He made the Rangers tell us their names and warned that if they showed themselves on that block or in that alley, their gang-banging days would be over."—Andre Nickerson

Crowds of BPSN members hung around street corners. Former playgrounds turned into asphalt jungles. Many apartments, buildings, homes, and businesses were painted with gang slogans. While armed Rangers stood guard, others painted the face of the Southmoor Hotel at 6646 Stony Island with "Blackstone" in letters two feet high.[68]

"The pall of the Rangers overtook the efforts of the neighborhood to be a safe place. Most of the boys in the Rangers lived further north in the Kenwood neighborhood, which had undergone an acute phase of urban blight. What was once a mecca shriveled up into decayed buildings and crime became rampant."

—*Andre Nickerson*

In South Shore there were so many calls for help that police couldn't keep up. There was no formal effort by school officials or police to provide protection at schools. While there was a police presence in the schools, they seemed impotent to suppress the gangs. Some black parents escorted their children back and forth. Many of these families had relocated from other neighborhoods to escape this type of crime and intimidation. Now people stayed home, refusing to go out at night. They locked up their teenage boys.

In the 1960s, the priests at Mount Carmel High School on 64th and Dante in Woodlawn communicated with Fort, asking him to declare the school a safe zone. The Rangers seemed afraid of the priests and agreed. (In a touch of irony, two members of the first Mount Carmel graduating class following this agreement became police officers and years later arrested Fort and put him away for life.[69])

Toward the end of 1967, recruitment terror began to recede, partly because of the new tenaciousness of Mayor Richard J. Daley and the Chicago Police Department's concerted efforts. The BPSN became the first street gang to successfully set up chapters in other cities like Milwaukee, Cleveland, and Gary, Indiana. At that time, social agencies and police estimated gang strength between 2,000 and 4,000 members.[70]

In the late 1960s, the Disciples fought a series of bloody turf wars against the BPSN for control of the Woodlawn and Englewood neighborhoods on Chicago's South Side. There is no accurate accounting of how many individuals were killed between 1966 and 1970, but it is fair to say that the gang wars of that period were the bloodiest on city record.

Meanwhile, sometime in 1966, two rival gang members stabbed one of Thomas Gunn's closest friends. Gunn hunted them down and shot them. He was fifteen. He was convicted of attempted murder and served two years in Chicago's juvenile detention facility. When he was released in 1968, the world he returned to was hell.

The Black P Stone Nation—1968

After the assassinations of Martin Luther King Jr. and Senator Robert F. Kennedy in the spring of 1968, the summer that followed was tense for all Americans. Race riots and war demonstrations tarnished the Democratic National Convention in August. Chicago's Mayor Richard J. Daley and Cook County States' Attorney Edward Hanrahan held a news conference announcing a new public policy: war on the criminal gangs of Chicago. The *Chicago American* newspaper quoted Winston P. Moore, warden of the Cook County jail, as saying, "Let's face it, these gangs have turned into the black Mafia of Chicago selling dope, prostitution, and engaging in extortion. Doing anything for a buck." Moore tried to dispel the myth that these were poor, misguided youth. Mayor Daley's policy was successful, with gang members vigorously prosecuted and prisons quickly filled.[71]

In 1968, Jeff Fort invited Larry Hoover, head of the Gangsters street gang, to become part of the Black P Stone Nation. As this would mean a demotion for Hoover, he declined. The Gangsters ranks grew and took in parts of Chicago's far South and West Sides.[72]

In 1968 the gang-banging became so fierce, and so many were killed, that the BPSN—in a gang merger with the Disciples, formerly the Devil's Disciples—reached truce agreements. Each gang had instructed its members not to molest members of the other, and the leadership formed a court of order to deal with violators. The truces were never formally rescinded, but they did eventually disintegrate, as one gang member would attack a rival.[73]

The Black P Stone Nation just got bigger and stronger and richer in the 1960s, thanks in part to the efforts of the Reverend Jesse Jackson and his Operation Breadbasket. In his book *Shakedown,* Kenneth Timmerman, a *New York Times* investigative reporter, retells what he believes is an accurate story of how Jackson turned racial grievances such as job discrimination into a moneymaking machine for himself and his organization[74]—and how Jackson began a business relationship with the Blackstone Rangers that would last for decades.[75]

Timmerman reports how, through Operation Breadbasket, Jackson organized boycotts of national chain stores in black neighborhoods that employed few black workers.[76] Jackson targeted grocery stores like Hi Low and manufacturers like Country Delight, pushing them to hire more black workers and to increase shelf space for products made by black-owned businesses.[77]

Fort and the Rangers provided the muscle Jackson needed to put teeth into his boycotts and roust merchants not interested in paying for protection.[78] According to Timmerman, the friendship between Jackson and Jeff Fort grew as Fort went from store to store, demanding contributions from the owners or "We will burn you down."[79]

Whenever Jackson needed burners, boycotters, or bullies, he could count on his friend Fort for willing bodies. When activist groups launched hunger movements in Illinois in 1968, Jackson put Fort and a group of Rangers on a bus to the Illinois capital of Springfield to pose as victims. When Jackson proclaimed the number of blacks who had gained employment from his efforts, many of them were Rangers.[80]

That was the case in Jackson's Operation Breadbasket boycott of the Red Rooster grocery chain in 1968. The chain had a history of providing poor quality and charging high prices in black communities. The stores already employed blacks, several in upper management positions, but Jackson demanded that the company hire members of the Blackstone Rangers' Main 21. After a protracted fight, the chain gave in. The Main 21 were to be shown on the chain's books as inside store inspectors and security guards.[81]

But the way Jackson ran Operation Breadbasket raised criticism even within the black community. The only products he pushed were made by a handful of black businessmen. They made donations to his organization, but some of the funds were diverted to him personally.[82]

Timmerman describes how Jackson's half-brother, Noah Robinson, contributed to the success of Operation Breadbasket and Operation Push, not to mention the Black P Stone Nation. Robinson had purportedly graduated from the prestigious Wharton School of Business at the University of Pennsylvania in 1969. With Jackson's and Robinson's help, Fort received many Chicago government contracts through minority set-aside programs. Robinson was responsible for Fort and his gang receiving an annual $155,000 grant from the Federal Office of Minority Business Enterprise to train minorities in operating their own businesses.[83, 84]

Timmerman describes how in 1969, Jackson's Breadbasket movement started Black Expo, a trade show for black business owners in Chicago. Jackson cut a protection deal with Fort to guard the gates and keep other gangs from disrupting the high-profile event. For this effort, the Rangers were to get a piece of the gate. But the plan almost failed when Fort and several Rangers with sawed-off shotguns broke in on Jackson while he was counting the proceeds, demanding a third. The standoff lasted for hours and a new deal was made, presumably for a larger piece of the take.[85]

Wee Folks—January 1970

In the nine years between 1960 and 1969, the Black P Stone Nation had expanded its operations from Cottage Grove on the west to Lake Michigan on the east, and from 21st Street on the north to 111th Street on the south. Wee Folks was right in the middle.

Remarkably, throughout the difficult changes of the sixties, the store was holding its own. South Shoreites who had fled the neighborhood still called to place orders. Those residents who had remained were loyal customers. The same personalized attention, the best toy consultations, the prettiest gift-wrapping—all still came with a smile with each toy bought at Wee Folks, and now shipping was added to the list of customer services.

During the sixties, a new black clientele developed, just as refined, just as loyal, just as concerned about the education of their children as were our other customers. For the successful black families who came from Pill Hill, money was no object when it came to gifts from Wee Folks. For those who worked at the steel mills, or as domestics in nearby homes, dollars were scarce and the gifts more modest. Mom and Dad, who never noticed the color of a person, embraced them all—regardless of race, religion, or budget—just as they had embraced every customer over the past quarter-century.

And yet Mom and Dad had finally faced up to the reality that the old neighborhood was getting too dangerous, both as a place to live and a place to work. Last year they had sold their little three-bedroom Georgian at 78th and East End and moved to suburban Glenwood. They had recently signed a lease for a new store location in a shopping center just around the corner from their new home. They were sad to leave South Shore but looking forward to celebrating Wee Folks' twenty-fifth anniversary this summer in a new place.

So many changes had taken place in South Shore and at Wee Folks since that hot summer day in 1962 when Mom bought a copy of *Muhammad Speaks* from those three boys from the Nation of Islam mosque in Hyde Park. She could never have foreseen the transformation of the neighborhood at the hands of Jeff Fort and the Black P Stone Nation. The notion that the teachings of Elijah Muhammad as represented in his newspaper would, directly or indirectly, lead to her husband's murder less than eight years later would have struck her as preposterous.

February 5, 1970

The Black P Stone Nation had a hit man, an enforcer, someone who killed for the gang. He had been arrested many times and was currently out on $5,000 bond for allegedly murdering another gang member. Thursday, February 5, 1970, was the day he was supposed to appear in bond court. He was not a robber, but this was an emergency. His leader, Jeff Fort, was in jail on local and federal charges. To raise bail money, everyone in the organization was ordered to do whatever he needed to. This man was Thomas Gunn.

Friday, February 6, 1970

On February 6, 1970, Clayton Moore, the Lone Ranger, opened his first fast food franchise in Chicago. Abbie Hoffman and the Chicago Seven went on trial for inciting riots at the 1968 Democratic Convention. The first U.S. Cabinet meeting outside the White House was held at Chicago's Field Museum.

And on Friday, February 6, 1970, Thomas Gunn murdered my father, Manny Lazar, the Pied Piper of South Shore.

The same week Gunn killed my father, Jeff Fort was charged with attempted murder, murder, kidnapping, aggravated assault, contempt of Congress, fraud, conspiracy to commit fraud, mob action, and disorderly conduct. You could just as easily add the murder of Manny Lazar to the list. To my mind, Fort was as guilty as Gunn for my dad's death.

A former assistant U.S. attorney once said of the Black P Stone Nation, "If you take 100 people, sophisticated criminals, and give them huge amounts of money, unlimited time, heavy weapons, dozens of ruthless helpers, and the ability to meet on a daily basis, you can create incredible havoc."

And they did.

*An overturned display island in
the aftermath of the murder,
February 6, 1970.*

CHAPTER 8

Trials

Saturday, February 7, 1970—Noon

MIKE O'ROURKE, THE FIRST OFFICER on the scene after Dad had been shot, and his partner, Kevin Murphy, were assigned to the Wee Folks investigation. They called Mom the day after the murder to make an appointment for the detective's interview. They picked her up at her new home in suburban Glenwood, where she and Dad had moved a few months before, and drove her to the police station.

February 7—12:40 P.M.

At the office of the Homicide/Sex Crimes Division at 90th and Cottage Grove, Detective Pablo Valdez took Mom's statement.

Although he was kind during the two-hour interview, Mom was forced to relive every horrendous detail of the previous night.

PABLO VALDEZ: What relation was the deceased to you?

BELLE LAZAR: He was my husband.

VALDEZ: Do you and your husband own a business at 1708–1710 East 79th Street?

LAZAR: Yes.

VALDEZ: Did anything unusual take place in the store yesterday? Can you tell me in your own words?

LAZAR: Yes—my husband was shot—I guess it took place between 2:00 and 2:30 P.M. He and I were alone in the store. My husband was in the stockroom at the rear of the store. When the man came in, he asked me for some toys for his eight-month-old niece. I took him over to the aisle furthest to the west and attempted to assist him in his search for some items. He selected a Roly-Poly toy. I took it to the wrapping counter. He said he wanted something else, so I followed him to another area of the store and he picked up a Gingerbread doll. I suggested he take that because a child of that age would like it. Then I brought the items to the cashier's counter in the center of the store. He had also picked out a stack of blocks that he placed on the counter.

VALDEZ: Did you suspect him at this time?

LAZAR: Well, I was in the cashier's area in the front of the store, leaning up against the east counter where the new security buzzer had been installed. I was observing him walking around the store. I had an uneasy feeling about him from the time he came in, so I was carefully watching where he went. Suddenly, he pulled a gun from inside his jacket. He was facing north. Apparently, my husband had just walked into the main store from the back room. The man yelled, "Don't move or I'll shoot." My husband did not say a word. The man was pointing his gun in Manny's direction. Then the man shot my husband at least three times. Right before the man shot, I managed to press the security alarm button. When I heard the shots, I got scared and hid behind the cashier's counter. Then, I heard a big commotion, and the next thing I knew the man had left. He had been in the store only fifteen minutes and I was never more than fifteen feet away from him. I got up and went to where my husband was lying. I didn't know he was dead. Then a woman came into the store and notified the police and fire departments.

Mom went on to describe the gunman as a slender black male, about six feet tall: "He was a neat dresser, clean shaven, slow of speech, with tight-fitting dark pants and a light brown waist-length jacket. The gun was small and dark." She told the officer that nothing was stolen. She remembered getting her favorite red plaid Pendleton blanket from the back room and covering Dad while she waited for the ambulance.

That same day, detectives interrogated three other witnesses. One, Terrence Robbins, a black bus driver, had been standing near Wee Folks, at the corner of 79th Street and East End Avenue. Robbins reported:

I was waiting for a bus at the stop about 50 feet away from the toy store when I heard at least four shots. They seemed to be coming from the store. I started walking toward the store and was almost in front when the shop door burst open and a tall, young negro man with a gun in his hand staggered out. I was about fifteen feet from him. He turned and slipped on the sidewalk, picked himself up, and ran around the corner to the parking lot. He jumped into a waiting black Cadillac with what looked like Indiana license plates and which had a male negro driver.

The second witness, Christopher Kane, a white off-duty Chicago police officer from the Gang Crime Intelligence Unit, happened to be parked across the street in his police car. He recalled:

> I saw a man slip and drop to the pavement as he ran out of the store. The man looked up and down the street and then ran to a black four-door Cadillac parked in a vacant lot east of the store.

Robbins told of running up to Officer Kane's car and telling him about the shooting. He jumped into Kane's car and the two men tried to pursue the gunman through the eastbound alley. They never got close enough to get a license number, but they did confirm that the car had Indiana plates.

Janet Mosely, a black woman and an occasional Wee Folks customer who was seven months pregnant, was the third witness. She told detectives:

> I had been looking in the display windows and I was just entering the store when I heard a shout and several gunshots. I saw the offender climbing over a toy display next to the cashier area. He ran right past me. Then he just stood in front of the store. He looked up and down the street. He looked right at me. He was only about six feet away. He started running around to the parking lot next to the store and thirty seconds later I saw him get into a black Cadillac that was parked there and drive away through the alley.

The police had heard from their informants that the gunman in the Wee Folks shooting was a member of the Blackstone Rangers' core group, the Main 21. The Rangers had struck such a chord of fear in the neighborhood that most people did their best to avoid them. Crossing them could mean death. Yet other area residents came forward to fill in bits of information about the events following the murder. Over the course of the trial, Mom would be astounded that so many people would risk their lives to give their testimony.

The next few days were a blur. We made funeral arrangements between condolence calls and telegrams from all over the United States. Noted Chicago newspaper columnists like Tom Fitzgerald of the *Chicago Sun-Times* published stories on Dad and the store. A neighbor was quoted as saying that the Lazars had been running the store for as long as anyone could remember: "When the area became predominantly black and other white storeowners moved out, Mr. Lazar stayed because he regarded everyone as his friend."

As Jews, we did not have an official wake. The immediate family was allowed to see Dad and say goodbye in the back room of Piser Memorial Chapel on Stony Island Avenue before the casket was closed. Visitation was on February 10, a cold and gray Tuesday. Floral arrangements and telegrams from former customers, fellow retailers, friends, and relatives filled the room.

Dad wore a gray suit. It seemed strange to me, as I had seen him in a suit only a few times in my life, like at my wedding and when he and Mom went to dinner with the Schoenemans at the Chez Paree. I preferred to see him in a checked flannel shirt and his signature baggy pants. It was unnerving to see him so still and quiet. In life he had been perpetual motion, always on the move with a joke or a wisecrack. As is customary, he wore his *tallis* over his shoulders.

Hundreds of people, black and white, poured into the chapel for the service: aldermen, police officers, community leaders, customers and neighbors, former customers from out of town, mobsters, merchants, reporters, friends—even State Senator Richard Newhouse and his wife, Katherine, longtime customers who paid their respects with tears in their eyes. The distinguished senator would later be the first minority to run for mayor of Chicago.

Dr. Jane Brown, then executive director of the Young Men's Jewish Council, remembers that when the word came out about

Dad's murder, everyone at the "J" just stood there crying, say-ing, "'Why in the world would anyone hurt Mr. Lazar? What are we going to do now? It is too late for this neighborhood now.' You would be surprised how many people felt they had to leave the neighborhood after your dad was shot."

During the days of grieving (shivah) that followed, hun-dreds of customers called with condolences. Everyone expected Mom to fall apart after the funeral, but she didn't. To begin her healing, she set about doing what she knew Dad would have liked: she called Dr. Brown, local schools, churches, nursery schools, and Head Start programs, inviting them to Wee Folks to take whatever they needed from the store at no charge.

Mom rejected my offer to run final sales to raise money she would need for years to come. She feared for my life if I worked in the store. "I have lost one family member," she insisted. "I will not lose another." The remaining inventory was sold for ten cents on the dollar at an auction at the store one month after the murder. I understood why Mom refused to attend. She couldn't bear to see the fruits of their labors sold to the highest bidder. I couldn't bring myself to attend either.

"Everything to be sold to the bare walls!" said the adver-tisements. Merchandise was boxed and ready to go to the high-est bidders, as were the pastel-colored metal displays, the black wrought iron playroom gate that kept kids from straying into the store, and the homemade workbench. An eager but somber audience of toy dealers, jobbers, wholesalers, discounters, and vintage-toy collectors awaited. Did these bidders think they were buying a piece of South Shore history? Were they aware that the box lot of Barbie dolls had to be wiped clean of the owner's blood to make them ready for sale? The proceeds were meager compared to the retail value of the items, and this mod-est sum would have to last Mom for the rest of her life, more than twenty-five years. Dad had life insurance, but since mur-der was not considered accidental death, the double indemnity provisions payable for accidental death didn't apply.

Hours after the auction ended, Wee Folks looked like the va-cant music store my parents had seen when they first looked at the property. Thousands of pieces of merchandise had been ripped from the shelves, the basement emptied to the concrete walls. The metal display racks, once the epitome of retailing excellence, stood bare. Brightly lit display cases that once held the latest Madame Alexander dolls and Steiff animals were dim and pillaged. Without Dad there to change them, the burned-out fluorescent lights overhead remained dark. The shelving showed a layer of dust.

The auctioneers had sold all the goods and displays, but nobody could purchase the soul of my parents' business. The sweat of years of making a hard living in a joyful atmosphere still stained the tiled floor.

Monday, February 9—10:00 A.M.

Three days after Dad's murder, Mom was asked to come to the station to look at mug shots of known offenders on file with the Gang Crime Intelligence Unit. She didn't know at the time that many of them were members of the Blackstone Rangers' Main 21. Mom identified the gunman from hundreds of other photos without hesitation. His face had been seared into her memory like a portrait etched with a wood-burning set. Within four days of the murder, the finger of guilt began to point at the man she identified: Thomas Gunn, a member of the Main 21 and a police informant.

Other witnesses were called in. Kane, the off-duty officer, identified the same photo, adding that another armed robbery had taken place an hour before just down the street, and wondering if there was any connection. Robbins and Mosely identified the same photo. They also picked out a picture of the car they had seen in the parking lot next to the store and its driver, later identified as Manfred Johnson. An all-points bulletin was issued for both Gunn and Johnson.

News of Dad's shooting was all over the street and it was playing out daily in the media. Many people worried about our safety. When a newspaper account accidentally listed my home address, the police had to drive my daughter, Kim, who was six, and my son, Ian, who was three, to and from school. Too young to grasp the significance of a police escort, my children simply thought that riding in a police car was cool.

Tuesday, February 10

Manfred Johnson was apprehended February 10. The car he was driving had been reported stolen a few blocks from the store. Johnson was known to be involved with the Blackstone Rangers. Arresting officers told him he had been seen as late as 2:00 P.M. on February 6 in a Cadillac with Thomas Gunn. Johnson denied any part of the offense, stating he was with friends at the time of the killing. He refused to take a polygraph test. Delving into Johnson's background, the officers discovered he had been associated with Gunn in the past, and that on one of these occasions there was a fatal shooting. After he was picked up and witnesses identified him as having driven the getaway car, Johnson volunteered the following:

> That day Gunn and I were drivin' 'round the 'hood, cruisin' for girls. Thomas wanted to stop for some smokes at the drugstore at the corner, so I pulled the Caddy 'round back in da alley next to the toy store. Didn't want no cop running the plates. It was stolen, ya know. A coupla minutes later he come runnin' out. He say, "Get out of here fast. I had to burn the guy." Then I took him back and dropped him by his house.

Johnson tried to use his information to plea-bargain the felony car-theft charge. No sale! So he changed his story again, attempting to use his girlfriend as an alibi for the day of the shooting. (When she refused to go along with his story, she later said, Johnson tried to kill her. Mad as hell, she volunteered to be questioned and identified the black Cadillac as the one he had been driving.) When his alibi didn't fly, Johnson admitted he had been involved with the Blackstone Rangers in the past and was afraid that what he knew would get him killed. After a couple of days, he was released on bond. His girlfriend refused to testify in court.

Wednesday, February 11

Thomas Gunn was picked up on February 11. Hank Walker, the arresting officer, knew this shooter well as an informant on the Blackstone Rangers. Officer Smitty McDowell was the Gang Crime Intelligence Unit's informant contact and Gunn's police connection. Detectives Valdez and Walker told McDowell about the evidence they had against the shooter and about the broken watch part I had found at the murder scene. McDowell, who had often met Gunn in his apartment, wanted to be there when Gunn was picked up. McDowell called John Prager, the assistant state's attorney, to accompany him to Gunn's home. Prager was assigned to the Special Prosecutions Unit dealing with the criminal activities of street gangs. He also wanted to be present when Gunn was arrested to make sure he was advised of his constitutional rights. He knew Gunn was a police informant. If this guy was guilty, he didn't want him getting off on a technicality.

McDowell and Prager accompanied the two arresting officers to Gunn's apartment. Livia Reynolds, Gunn's grandmother, recognized Mc Dowell and voluntarily let them in. The four men entered Gunn's bedroom, placed him under arrest, and told him they were taking him to the station to be interviewed by homicide detectives. Valdez advised him of his rights. While in the bedroom, McDowell spotted several watches on the dresser, one with a broken crystal. Gunn admitted they belonged to him. McDowell asked to take the broken one and Gunn agreed. Walker placed it in a small evidence bag.

The detectives drove Gunn to the Cook County Criminal Courthouse at 26th and California in Chicago, where they told him he was implicated in the murder of a South Shore shopkeeper. Detective John Morrison and Sergeant Rudy Chambers joined McDowell during the questioning, but Gunn asked if he could speak with McDowell alone. Gunn asked McDowell to call his grandmother to tell her to get rid of some stuff. The stuff, he claimed, consisted of two guns he was hiding for Delroy Parnell, the man he said had committed the murder. Gunn said he was afraid he would be implicated in the shooting because he and Parnell looked so much alike. McDowell agreed and returned to the apartment. Mrs. Reynolds willingly gave up the two guns hidden under the seats of the living room sofa, a .38 special Smith and Wesson revolver and a .357 Magnum. He put both guns in a paper bag and took them to the crime lab. Ballistics later proved that the bullets taken from Dad's body were fired from the .38 special, which was already reloaded when McDowell picked it up.

Detectives in the Gang Crime Intelligence Unit had already identified Gunn as a high-ranking member of the Blackstone Rangers. They said he was one of the chief hit men and had probably attempted the robbery to get bail money for Ranger leader Jeff Fort, in jail facing a federal felony charge. A Rangers spokesman denied that Gunn was an active member and that Fort needed bail money.

Among the five suspects in the lineup held at 4:30 P.M. on February 11 were Delroy Parnell and Thomas Gunn. Each witness was secluded before viewing the lineup so they wouldn't prejudice each other's recollections. One by one, the witnesses were escorted in front of the one-way glass window to look over the lineup. One by one, Terrence Robbins, Christopher Kane, Janet Mosely, and Mom each identified Gunn without hesitation. Nobody identified Parnell.

The gun, the positive identification by all witnesses, and the watch with the cracked crystal that matched the fragment left at the scene were enough to hold Thomas Gunn for trial without bond. Gunn continued to protest his innocence. He and Manfred Johnson were indicted a week later.

Life without Dad

Eighteen months passed between the end of Dad's life and the beginning of the trial. In that time, our family tried to put together the puzzle of our lives. Mom began a daily routine without the man who had been at her side, at work and at home, for thirty-four years. For her, keeping busy was best. She took a job in the toy department at Marshall Field's in the River Oaks Shopping Center in Calumet City, south of Chicago. No bus went there, so she had to drive, which she didn't like. But after a co-worker volunteered to drive her, she looked forward to going to work.

Mom loved working with the public and selling toys. Since many South Shoreites had moved to the southern suburbs, several of her old customers were now her new customers. When people recognized her, they hugged her and cried. While touching, it also was painful. With each renewed acquaintance, Mom had to relive those last days of Wee Folks and Dad's brutal murder. But she was determined to remain in Chicago until the trial was completed. The job helped fill her days.

My children and I moved into a small condominium down the street from Mom's house in Glenwood. It took us out of the city and gave Mom some much-needed company. I registered Kim in Glenwood's elementary school, and dropped her off at Mom's on my way to work. After school, she would stay with Mom until I returned, just as she had done at Wee Folks. There were no nursery schools in the Glenwood area that met Mom's and my strict guidelines, so I placed Ian in a nursery school in Harvey, a thirty-five-minute ride northwest of Glenwood.

The research grant that funded my job at the University of Chicago lab was not renewed. After much searching, I found a great new job as a bacteriologist at Armour-Dial in Chicago. I started my commute every weekday morning at 6:30, dropping Kim at Mom's and then dropping Ian at school in Harvey. Then it was back to the always-crowded Dan Ryan Expressway to get to work by 8:30. Evenings were the same, just reversed. I arrived home about 6:30 P.M., gave the kids dinner and a bath, and put them to bed. It was tough, but we were safer and closer to Mom.

I can't say I was much support to Mom during those months. Between the commuting, my new job, and taking care of the kids, I was barely keeping my own head above water. I did feel less guilty knowing that Mom had wonderful friends and old customers who continued to write, call, and invite her out. Sometimes she accepted. Other times she seemed content to stay home and putter around her garden with her poodle, Princess, keeping her company. To help keep life normal for Ian and Kim, I took them on field trips into Chicago. Sometimes we went to the Field Museum of Natural History, Ian's favorite.

He knew the names of all the dinosaurs by the time he was two. And sometimes we went to the Shedd Aquarium or the Museum of Science and Industry.

One year after the murder, according to Jewish tradition, our family dedicated the headstone on Dad's grave. Looking down at the etched marble marker, I was struck again by how plain and small it seemed for my larger-than-life father. Looking at the stone that bore only his name and the dates of his life, you couldn't tell that he had been beloved by his family and called "Toy Toy" by his adoring grandchildren. You couldn't tell that he had been loved and respected by thousands of children and adults who had affectionately nicknamed him Mr. Wee Folks and the Pied Piper of South Shore.

I remember thinking that this murder had sucked the life out of our family and our once vibrant community, and I wanted to see the killer pay the ultimate price. After several continuances requested by Gunn's defense, the trial began at last on August 9, 1971. I dreaded it but I couldn't wait for it to begin. I wanted justice for Dad.

Jury Selection—August 1971

Since I had never been exposed to the criminal justice system, I thought the process of building a murder prosecution would be as simple as A-B-C for these legal professionals: "A" for autopsy, "B" for ballistics, and "C" for the case. It was much more involved than that.

The jury selection process was arduous. We sat for an entire day while one person after another was interrogated by first the defense lawyer, Blake Simpson, and then the prosecutor, John Prager. The prosecutors, attorneys, and judge all seemed particularly concerned about selecting this jury. The accused was facing the death penalty and the judge and lawyers had to be sure they could obtain an impartial jury in this highly publicized case. Each prospective juror had to fill out a twelve-page questionnaire prepared by both the prosecution and defense teams. To select twelve satisfactory jurors, the attorneys questioned eighty people:

"Have you heard about the case?
"Are you a customer of Wee Folks?"
"Do you live in South Shore?"
"Have you formed an opinion in this case?"
"Would you have any trouble giving someone the death penalty?"

The jury consisted of five women and seven men. Six were blacks, five were whites, and one was Asian.

Trial Day 1—Monday, August 9, 8:30 A.M.

Mom, my sister, and I were told it was best to sit in on every day of the trial to make sure the jury saw us. We arrived early at the Cook County Criminal Courthouse that first day. State's attorney John Prager had advised us to dress demurely. Mom wore an understated beige pantsuit.

The rough-cut granite façade of the imposing courthouse gave the impression that serious business was conducted here. The 1930s-era building had deeply recessed windows and the adjoining Cook County Jail had fifty-foot-high walls, with guard towers at each corner. Lady Justice stood atop the twenty-foot-tall marble arches at the courthouse entrance. I remember wondering if there would be justice for us. It seemed that being in the right didn't always guarantee that.

It was hot outside. As I was herded along by the throng entering the building, the smell of sweat permeated the revolving doors and the lobby inside. I looked around at the sea of humanity. There were moms with babies, well-dressed men and women with briefcases whom I took to be lawyers, and poor people, black and white, who were there for their day of justice too.

We waited a few minutes on the old wood benches outside the courtroom. The bailiff called us into a dark paneled anteroom behind the courtroom where we were to assemble for each day's proceedings. Prager was there, looking official in his black pin-stripe suit. He had been friendly and warm to us in the past, telling us his case was solid, but this morning he wasn't smiling. "I have some bad news," he said. "A couple of the witnesses may not tell the jury what they really saw. I learned they've been approached, possibly bullied or bribed, by the Blackstone Rangers to change their testimony."

Prager was afraid some witnesses would take the offer. A lot of money was on the table and their lives and their family's lives were being threatened.

Because Prager was active with the Gang Crime Intelligence Unit, and because he was at Gunn's home during his arrest, Gunn insisted that Prager was trying to railroad him. Prager told us the Rangers had put out a $10,000 contract to kill him at the start of the trial. Thankfully, there were no attempts, at least none that he told us about.

Trial Day 1—8:55 A.M.

Prager showed us into the enormous courtroom, also paneled in dark wood. The jury was seated. Mom had a spot reserved next to Prager at the prosecution table. My sister and I sat facing a heavy wood railing just behind the table. These would be our assigned seats throughout the trial. A large wood-framed clock with roman numerals on its face hung on the wall. I would spend a lot of time staring at that clock over the next few days.

Just before court was called to order, a door next to the judge's bench opened and Thomas Gunn and two armed guards came out. Gunn was neatly dressed in a gray designer suit, a blue shirt, and subdued tie. "Maybe the Rangers' legal fund has sprung for his duds as well as his defense," I thought. Mom began shaking when she saw him, overwhelmed by vivid memories of Dad's horrific murder. As Gunn walked to the defense table and turned to face the judge's bench, I could see thick metal handcuffs binding his big hands. I wanted to look directly into the eyes of the man accused of killing my father, but he didn't look at us. He stared at the ground or looked at his grandmother, sitting demurely in a print dress, white laced shoes, and white gloves in the second row behind the defendant's table. I nervously peeked at her, wondering what she was thinking. I don't think she caught me looking.

The two lawyers from the Rangers' defense fund who had originally met with Gunn in jail were not representing him. He had probably lost favor with the Rangers for being an informant, a rat. His new attorney, Blake Simpson, was a seasoned public defender with more than thirty-five years of courtroom experience. He was also a well-known gang lawyer and one of the more flamboyant attorneys in the city. As he showed Gunn to his seat, Simpson looked almost gaudy in his expensive black suit, large gold cuff links, and pretentious gold watch.

Gunn was barely twenty years old, but he already had the set jaw of a hardened criminal. I stared at him, wondering about this man and his past. He may not have been educated, but he wasn't stupid. He was a smooth veteran of other killings for which he got little or no time. So why did he shoot? Was it just his nature or was there something else?

As a police informant on the Main 21, maybe Gunn felt despair over being caught between the streets, the system, and the gang. With one foot in hell and the other in the precinct house, did he subconsciously want to escape life on the street? Maybe incarceration and three squares a day looked better than not knowing where his next dollar would come from or where to hide. Did he murder Dad out of ruthlessness or hopelessness?

We learned from Prager that a decent family had raised Gunn. After his mother divorced and remarried, he lived with her and his stepfather. He told his parole officer he had a good relationship with his stepfather and siblings. He attended school until the tenth grade, when he dropped out and the Blackstone Rangers insinuated themselves into his life. He admitted he had no real religious beliefs. The only thing he believed in was the Rangers street gang. He spoke of his job at a Red Rooster grocery store. Had he been used by Jesse Jackson to wear down the ownership to hire more blacks and then rewarded with employment? Or was Gunn paid by Jackson to cause trouble at the store? Did the teachings of the Nation of Islam cause him to hate whites even more? What led him on that cold February afternoon in 1970 to kill South Shore's beloved neighborhood legend? Was it just one less white guy, one less good guy, one less guy to hate blacks? Or was it one more notch in his gun, one more killing, one more Rangers' success on the streets of Chicago?

Trial Day 1—9:00 A.M.

The court clerk ordered everyone to stand as he announced the entrance of Judge Victor Moran. Judge Moran was an older man, graying at the temples. His long, black robes swished as he entered the silent room. He sat, turned a stern face to the jury, and charged them with finding the truth of the case only from the evidence they heard and saw in the courtroom. He admonished them against reading newspaper reports and watching television broadcasts about the case.

After several sidebars, with both attorneys going back and forth to the judge's bench, the opening statements began. Prager rose to give the jury an overview of what he expected to prove to them during the days that followed. He was a big man, about six feet tall. In a deep voice, he spoke deliberately as he moved toward the jury box.

PRAGER: We will show that the defendant, Thomas Gunn, came into Wee Folks on the afternoon of February 6 with the intent to rob the store. While pretending to be a customer, he aroused the suspicion of Mrs. Lazar and she moved to stand near the security buzzer under the front counter. She was never more than fifteen feet away from Gunn. It was daylight outside and there were bright fluorescent lights in the store. She heard him command, "Stop or I'll shoot." She didn't know her husband had come into the store from the back room. We will show how Gunn shot Mr. Lazar five times, using all of the bullets in his gun. Because Gunn tried to escape from a dead-end aisle, he had to climb over five-foot shelving partitions to get out of the store. We expect the evidence to show there was a pregnant woman who heard the shots, and witnessed Gunn climbing over the shelving and leaving the store. In his hurry to escape, he fell down a few feet from her. She had no trouble identifying him as he got into a dark Cadillac and sped away. You will hear from the off-duty police officer who saw a man running out of the store and gave chase in his police car. You will hear from a bus driver who saw Gunn escape and who joined the officer in the car chase. We expect the evidence to show that Gunn was one of thirty informants for the Chicago Police Department. But there is no contention that the Blackstone Rangers had anything to do with this case.

SIMPSON: *Objection!*

Simpson jumped to his feet, identified himself, and began to speak in a slightly high-pitched voice. He was tall, about sixty years old, and his belly showed a slight paunch.

SIMPSON: Mr. Blake Simpson, your honor, attorney for the defendant, Thomas Gunn. I ask you to declare a mistrial immediately. In his opening statement the state's attorney made reference to the Blackstone Rangers and that is highly prejudicial and has brought into this trial matters that have no bearing on the case. He is only trying to capitalize on the bad publicity and the present fears the general public has about Rangers terrorizing people. This armed robbery/ felony murder had nothing to do with Blackstone Ranger activity. This damage is irreparable and can't be erased from the jurors' minds.

PRAGER: The state wants to make it clear that this is a critical issue in the case. Smitty McDowell, an officer of the Gang Crime Unit, who had a special relationship with the defendant as an informer on gang activities, made the arrest of Mr. Gunn.

MORAN: Does the state intend to bring in evidence of alleged gang relationships here?

PRAGER: Only to the point that the defendant confided in the Gang Crime officer as to where the guns were because of his special relationship with him.

MORAN: The statement that no gang relationship is involved in the crime is a sufficient statement and we should proceed.

Simpson immediately started quoting from the *Rubyat of Omar Khayyam:* "Much before the days of you and I . . . the moving finger of fate having writ it cannot be erased." Judge Moran looked at once bored, aggravated, and angry as he sustained Prager's objections to Simpson's recitation. The judge motioned our attorney to continue. This pontificating by the defense attorney would continue throughout the trial.

PRAGER: We will show that Mr. Gunn has changed his story many times. Over the past few months, he has gone from claiming innocence to being an accessory, and from righteousness to being a robber. We will show that the gun found in his home matched the gun used to kill Mr. Lazar. As to the death penalty, we expect to show that if a murder case can be typical, this one is untypical. This was no stabbing or beating. This was not a single-shot firing. Gunn fired five shots point-blank at a totally unarmed toy-store owner. We expect to ask for you to not only find him guilty but to recommend the death penalty.

Simpson then gave his opening statement.

SIMPSON: We have no quarrel with the fact that this man was killed in his store. We intend to show that there was more than one person involved in this felony. We will show that the close relationship that Officer Mc-

Dowell had with the defendant was going sour. Either this overzealous officer became disenchanted with my client or he had a personal vendetta against him and he framed my client. We intend to show that there is reasonable doubt as to his guilt, and as jurors you must therefore find him not guilty. Thank you.

Trial Day 1—10:10 A.M.

Because I had discovered the jagged glass fragment from Gunn's watch crystal under the store's ball rack the afternoon Dad was murdered, I had been added to the witness list. Prager called me to the stand first.

Sitting in the witness box, I shook uncontrollably. I was finally looking into the eyes of my father's killer. I hated this man who had cheated my children out of knowing their grandfather. Gunn leered at me from the defense table. Although he was ten years younger than I, he intimidated me.

After telling of my relationship to the victim, Prager asked me how Dad was the last time I saw him.

CARYN LAZAR: I saw him on February 5 when I picked up my children at the store after work. My dad was the owner of Wee Folks and he was always there. He was there more than he was at home. He loved everything about the store and he was very happy, in a good frame of mind, and very healthy.

PRAGER: When was the next time you saw him?

LAZAR: At Jackson Park Hospital in the morgue.

PRAGER: What was his condition at that time?

LAZAR: He was dead.

PRAGER: When you returned to the Wee Folks store after being at the hospital, what did you do?

LAZAR: While I was waiting for the crime lab people to complete their examination of the store, I was standing near the exit doors at the front next to the ball display. The evening lights from the Wee Folks sign were on and they reflected off of something shiny on the floor.

PRAGER: What was it?

LAZAR: It was a piece of curved jagged glass. I called the crime lab technician over and he put it in a little plastic bag.

Prager introduced the glass fragment into evidence.

PRAGER: Is this the piece of glass you found?

LAZAR: Yes.

PRAGER: What did you learn about that piece of glass later?

LAZAR: The police told us that it was a perfect match to the watch that they found in Mr. Gunn's apartment. There was a piece of glass missing from the crystal of a watch in his bedroom and this fragment fit like a puzzle piece.

PRAGER: Thank you, I have no further questions.

SIMPSON: Sidebar, your honor!

After a few minutes' murmuring at the bench, the attorneys came back to their seat. The judge asked Simpson if he had any questions for me. "No, your honor," he said.

I was excused. The moment I had been dreading was over.

Trial Day 1—10:35 A.M.

Prager called Mom to the stand. As she stood to be sworn, she could hardly be seen over the high wooden bar of the witness box. She looked so small, almost child-size, as she sat in the wooden chair. I glanced at the clock. It was after ten when she started her testimony. After questions about her and the store, Prager's queries reverted to the day of the murder.

PRAGER: Can you describe the customer that came in that day?

BELLE LAZAR: He was a tall, thin, young negro wearing dark trousers and a light jacket. I had never seen him before.

PRAGER: Mrs. Lazar, do you now know the name of the person who entered your toy store that afternoon?

LAZAR: Yes, I now know him to be Thomas Gunn.

PRAGER: Mrs. Lazar, I ask you to look around the courtroom and tell me if you see the individual who entered your toy store that day in 1970.

LAZAR: Yes, it is the young man sitting at the table next to the officer there.

PRAGER: Can I ask you to come over to the defense table and put your hand on the shoulder of the man you saw in your store that day, the man who killed your husband?

Mom left the witness box and slowly crossed the floor to where Gunn was sitting. She placed her hand on his shoulder as Prager asked. Her whole body shuddered. I thought she might faint. But she pulled herself up to her entire four feet, ten inches, and returned to the witness box.

Over the next hour, Prager carefully walked Mom through the entire sequence of the murder: her nervousness with the shooter, his hair-trigger reaction when Dad emerged from the back room, the details of the shooting, the escape.

PRAGER: What did you do after you heard Mr. Gunn leave the store?

LAZAR: I ran to see my husband. He was lying very still and he was making some kind of gurgling noises.

PRAGER: Did a woman enter the store around this time?

LAZAR: Yes.

PRAGER: Did you know her?

LAZAR: Not at that time, but I know her now to be Janet Mosely. She tried to help me and shortly after that the police came.

Prager took Mom through the trip to the hospital, the pronouncement that Dad was dead, and the return to the store.

PRAGER: What did you observe when you returned to Wee Folks?

LAZAR: Well . . . the one wall adjacent to where the young man had been standing was torn down and there were detectives spreading black powder all over everything and taking fingerprints.

PRAGER: Mrs. Lazar, when did you have contact with the police again?

LAZAR: They came to my home the next day and took me to the police station, where they interviewed me and showed me photographs of several men.

PRAGER: Were you able to identify any of the photographs as the individual who shot your husband?

LAZAR: Yes.

PRAGER: Mrs. Lazar, I ask you to look around the courtroom and tell me if you see the individual whose photo you identified as the man who killed your husband, and would you point him out, please.

LAZAR: Yes, he is the man with the blue shirt and the gray jacket.

PRAGER: Your honor, let the record reflect that the witness has again identified Thomas Gunn. How many days after your husband was murdered did you have occasion to return to the police station?

LAZAR: A couple of days later. There was a lineup with five men. I identified number four as the person who killed Manny. He was the same man as in the photograph.

Mom pointed out Gunn again as the man from the lineup. Then Simpson interrogated her, trying to get her to say the store was not well lit, that she had not really seen Gunn well enough to identify him. If she were really fifteen feet from him, he persisted, why didn't she know exactly what color his pants were?

SIMPSON: Did he wear a hat?

LAZAR: I don't remember seeing a hat. You usually look at a person's face when you are waiting on them.

SIMPSON: Well, Mrs. Lazar, I am looking at your face and I can tell you are wearing a beige suit.

Mr. Prager objected. Simpson turned his back on Mom.

SIMPSON: Can you tell me what color tie I am wearing?

LAZAR: No, sir, I didn't look.

PRAGER: It is brown. Let the record reflect that it is brown.

SIMPSON: Well, in any event, she didn't know what color it was.

PRAGER: Strike that, your honor.

Mom was starting to wither. Mercifully, the judge called for a lunch break and we had an hour to help her gather herself. She was getting a migraine, but she took her medication and brushed aside any words of concern. She had to be strong.

Trial Day 1—1:00 P.M.

After the break, the questioning resumed and Mom had to face the surly Simpson again: *Describe the shooter's clothes. How tall was he? Did you describe him to the officer as a negro? Was the store better lit than the courtroom? How could you positively identify him in a dimly lit store?* Mom, who always prided herself on her presence of mind in times of trouble, shored herself up and assured the court that the store was well lit by high-wattage fluorescent bulbs and that she had no trouble whatsoever seeing the defendant.

LAZAR: Even though he was a handsome, clean-cut-looking kid, the hair on the back of my neck bristled when he came into the store. I know people and I had a bad feeling about this boy.

SIMPSON: Wouldn't your recollection of the events of February 6, 1970, be sharper on the 6th of February of 1970 than now in August of 1971?

LAZAR: I suppose so.

SIMPSON: So you have a good memory, do you?

LAZAR: I think so.

SIMPSON: Well, do you remember asking for your attorney to be called when you went to the police station?

LAZAR: He is a family friend and . . .

SIMPSON: Your husband had just been killed, hadn't he?

LAZAR: Yes.

SIMPSON: And you wanted to cooperate with the police, didn't you?

LAZAR: Yes.

SIMPSON: Then why would you need a lawyer to advise you?

PRAGER: *Objection!*

MORAN: Sustained.

SIMPSON: Do you remember telling the arresting officer that it was a blue steel revolver you saw?

LAZAR: I don't remember ever saying that.

SIMPSON: OK, who was in the lineup you saw?

LAZAR: There were five men.

SIMPSON: Can you describe all five men to me?

LAZAR: Well, there were two who were a little shorter and one very tall and kind of slouchy and this young man.

SIMPSON: That's only four. Who was the fifth?

LAZAR: There was an older man.

SIMPSON: What position did my client have in the lineup?

LAZAR: He was the fourth in line.

SIMPSON: Who took you to that lineup?

LAZAR: I couldn't tell you.

SIMPSON: So on the 11th of February in 1970 you identified him in the lineup, right?

PRAGER: *Objection!* Asked and answered.

MORAN: Sustained.

SIMPSON: What was he wearing in the picture they showed you?

LAZAR: I couldn't tell you.

SIMPSON: Well, I'll put it to you, lady, isn't it a fact that the police officer said to you, "THIS IS THE MAN?"

LAZAR: No, sir!

SIMPSON: I notice you are wearing glasses, Mrs. Lazar. Are they prescription?

LAZAR: Yes.

SIMPSON: Can you tell me what the prescription is?

LAZAR: No, sir.

SIMPSON: How long have you been wearing glasses?

LAZAR: For many years.

SIMPSON: Well . . . exactly how many?

LAZAR: Forty.

SIMPSON: You wear them because you can't see properly without them, right?

LAZAR: Yes.

SIMPSON: Are you nearsighted or farsighted?

LAZAR: Farsighted.

SIMPSON: So you can see close but not see right too far?

LAZAR: I have to wear them for close reading.

SIMPSON: Do you wear bifocals?

LAZAR: Yes.

SIMPSON: Then you can't see any distance without bifocals?

LAZAR: Yes, sir, I can.

On and on it went, for twenty-five minutes, on the extent of Mom's sight and implications about how she couldn't possibly have seen the killer clearly. *Do you wear bifocals because you want to wear them? When was the last time you saw the eye doctor? Who is he? Where is his office? What was the exact date? Why did you wait for that date? Is he an eye doctor or an oculist?*

After several objections by Prager, Simpson fabricated a scenario, explaining why Mom had to go back to the store to close up and the intricacies of the alarm system. Demeaning, obtuse questions, intended to rattle her, followed for another forty-five minutes. Simpson never let up, firing one question after another. Mom was strong but getting weary. I could see her shoulders droop and she was resting her arms on the purse in her lap for stability. I knew her migraine was taking its toll as well.

Simpson's line of questioning continued, trying to impeach witnesses and discredit the state's attorney for being allied with the Gang Crime Unit. He asked Mom if she had heard slang names that only street thugs and other officers would have heard to describe some of the officers and the state's attorney. The day was drawing to a close, and I wondered if there ever would be peace for Mom after this. Wasn't it enough that she had witnessed her husband's murder? Wasn't it sufficient that she had to identify that killer, look into his eyes, touch his shoulder? It was like a rape victim being asked to repeat the details of her ordeal. Mom was painted to be the villain rather than the victim under the tongue of this shrill, sharp-shooting lawyer who seemed to work zealously to free the accused.

After many objections from Prager, Simpson finally concluded his questioning. Prager asked one question on redirect.

"Mrs. Lazar, as a result of your husband's death and the subsequent closing of the Wee Folks Toy Store, have you lost your only means of support?"

Mom replied, "Yes, sir."

At 4:48 P.M. court mercifully adjourned for the day.

Trial Day 2—Tuesday, August 10, 8:45 A.M.

Prager met us in the hall and showed us into the anteroom of the courtroom. It was there that he divulged parts of Gunn's life that were never to be heard by the jury. The stories were like a spider's web: where one strand ended, another picked up. These anecdotes were not admissible in court; the prosecutor was not allowed to bring up a defendant's past deeds because it might influence the jury's thoughts on the present crime being tried. I supposed Prager was telling this to us so Mom would realize that Gunn was one bad dude who deserved to be put away or put to death.

The stories began when nine-year-old Thomas Gunn had murdered a playmate by hitting him on the head with a lead pipe. Then there was Gunn at age fourteen, standing on the corner of Blackstone Avenue, joining the Rangers. At fifteen, he served two years for shooting two rival gang members. Each new story was more hideous than the last: the unbelievable poverty, the police harassment, the pressure of the streets, the expectation to stay connected to the gang. At the end of the tangled stories was a nineteen-year-old boy who had done the unspeakable when he picked up a gun and killed my dad. Mom was appalled. I was enraged. How could the criminal justice system fail good and honest people by not incarcerating him for life long ago?

Another day in court meant another dapper outfit for Gunn, who was ushered into the courtroom in a gray pinstriped suit with a pink shirt. The judge made his usual celebrated entrance.

Now it was time for the witnesses to step forward and testify. Bravely and truthfully, they all did. Prager's worries seemed to fade as not one witness wavered. After being promised police protection, the witnesses had refused to succumb to the pressure of the Blackstone Rangers. Mom forever felt that this was an act of true goodness that our customers and neighbors did for us. They wanted to put away the man who had killed the Pied Piper of South Shore just as much as we did.

Bus driver Terrence Robbins testified to seeing Gunn escape the store with revolver in hand and how he and Officer Christopher Kane pursued the defendant's black Cadillac. Kane corroborated Robbins's story. Customer Janet Mosely described how she could not mistake this man because she was so close to him as he made his escape. They all told of identifying Gunn positively in the lineup. Then they again identified him as he sat in the courtroom.

Trial Day 2—Noon

Over the lunch break, Prager briefed my mother, sister, and me on what was to come. "From now on it's going to be even more difficult," he warned. "You'll hear gruesome forensic testimony and ultimately you'll hear from Gunn himself. That may be the toughest part, as he will undoubtedly lie and you'll know it." Prager urged us to be brave and reiterated the importance of being present in the courtroom and remaining composed.

Trial Day 2—1:00 P.M.

Sergeant Rudy Chambers of District Four Homicide took the stand. He said he was a fifteen-year veteran of the force and had been in homicide for the last four years. He had been on duty as the watch commander on the night of February 11.

PRAGER: On that date did you have occasion to view a lineup at the station?

CHAMBERS: Yes, sir.

PRAGER: Did you know the names of any of the individuals who stood in that lineup?

CHAMBERS: For this crime, we were most interested in two—Thomas Gunn and Delroy Parnell.

PRAGER: Following the lineup, what, if anything, occurred as you were walking to the lockup?

CHAMBERS: Gunn was having a conversation with two attorneys who had asked to see him. Once we were back inside the lockup, Gunn turned to me and said, "The old man was comin' at me with his hand in his pocket, so I thought he had a gun and I shot him."

PRAGER: I ask you to look around the courtroom and tell me if you see that individual who you now know by the name of Thomas Gunn who made that statement to you.

CHAMBERS: Yes sir, he is the defendant, the one in the pink shirt.

Then Simpson took a turn at the witness and badgered him repeatedly, trying to get him to change his story, but to no avail.

Trial Day 2—2:00 P.M.

The state next called Dr. William Spiegel, the coroner. After establishing his credentials, Prager proceeded.

PRAGER: Did you do the autopsy on Mr. Emanuel Lazar and what did that examination involve?

SPIEGEL: The individual was moderately obese, showing no sign of medical abnormality. He had six bullet wounds in his body. My internal examination revealed that three of the bullet wounds were irrelevant; they had no relation to the subject's demise.

Irrelevant? The subject? This was not a *subject!* This was my *father* they were talking about. I flashed back to Prager's words of caution and kept my mouth shut.

The coroner continued:

SPIEGEL: One of the bullet wounds caused major organic effect and was related to his demise and three other bullet wounds again had no relation to his death.

One bullet had entered Dad's body in one place and exited in another, leaving six wounds in all.

Using his own body to demonstrate, the doctor indicated where one of the bullets had entered Dad's body, lacerating his heart and his right lung and lodging in his chest cage. Another bullet had entered his abdomen and careened its way around, exiting the lower chest and striking the palm side of Dad's forearm just below the elbow. Bullet by bullet, Spiegel systematically went through the murder.

PRAGER: Doctor, what is your opinion on the cause of death?

SPIEGEL: He died of massive internal bleeding from vital structures, specifically the heart and the right lung.

There was no cross-examination from Simpson.

Jacob Mitchell, a state firearms expert employed by the police department, testified that it was his opinion the bullets that killed Dad were fired from the .38-caliber special Smith and Wesson revolver recovered from the defendant's apartment. A long list of evidence was produced:

> One .38-caliber special Smith and Wesson revolver with bullets
> One .357 Magnum with bullets
> Photos of the black Cadillac
> Maps
> Plats
> Five bullets removed from Dad's body
> The clothing Dad was wearing when he was murdered
> The watch that matched the crystal I had found
> The crystal I had found
> The test-firing report on the Smith and Wesson
> Lineup photos
> Photos of Gunn holding two guns
> Photos of the store exterior after the shooting
> A photo of the display islands knocked over inside the store
> Morgue photos of Dad

Court adjourned for the day at 4:40 P.M.

Trial Day 3—Wednesday, August 11, 9:00 A.M.

This morning, Gunn appeared in court wearing a black suit and shirt. As a dark black man, he seemed to disappear against the backdrop of his clothes. Maybe that's what he wanted to do. This was "police day," involving damaging testimony for Gunn.

First to be called was Detective Darin Morrison, who had interrogated Gunn when the police picked him up.

PRAGER: What did Mr. Gunn tell you in relation to the homicide?

MORRISON: He told me he understood his rights as advised. He said that he had been up on 79th Street east of Stony on February 6th in the company of a man known as Delroy Parnell. They were together in a black Cadillac owned by another man. He stated that they were there to rob a drugstore. But after checking out the drugstore, Gunn talked Parnell out of it because the escape avenues were very poor. He stated they considered holding up the toy store, but Parnell talked him out of it because he was afraid of apprehension. After that, he stated that he and Parnell left the area and split up, and he hasn't seen him since that time. . . . He further testified that he and Parnell looked a lot alike, and in all probability Parnell had returned and held up the store and he, Gunn, had been identified by mistake.

PRAGER: What, if anything, did you say to Gunn about his statements?

MORRISON: I told him I would arrange a lineup with him and Parnell together.

PRAGER: What did he respond to that?

MORRISON: At this point, he told us that what he originally said was not the truth. He had been in the area with Parnell when Parnell, in fact, robbed the toy store and shot the owner. Gunn said he was driving the car. There was an entrance to the alley and he had pulled into the parking lot east of the toy store. At that time, Parnell got out of the car and went inside the toy store himself. He said he didn't know Parnell was going to rob the store. He thought he was just going in to case it. He didn't know Parnell even had a gun on him at that time. He stated that about fifteen minutes later, Parnell came running out of the toy store, jumped into the car, and said, "Let's get out of here, I had to burn the guy." Then he stated he drove away.

Smitty McDowell, the officer with the Gang Crime Intelligence Unit, testified that he had often been in the apartment of Mrs. Livia Reynolds, Gunn's grandmother. Gunn had been an

informant on the Blackstone Rangers for several years, Mc-
Dowell said, and he knew the family well. He had often met the
defendant in Mrs. Reynolds's apartment and she knew him to
be a police officer. When Gunn was suspected in the homicide,
McDowell went to the home to pick him up. At that time, Mc-
Dowell spied the watch with the broken crystal. The defendant
stated that it belonged to him. After getting the defendant's permission, McDowell put it in an evidence bag. He said that upon
his return to the apartment, Mrs. Reynolds voluntarily gave him
two guns at the request of her grandson.

Livia Reynolds was called and she testified that her grandson, Thomas, lived with her. She claimed that when Officer Mc-
Dowell came to retrieve the guns, he did so without her
permission. I couldn't believe my ears.

When court ended for the day at 5:00 P.M., we were all wondering how many more days it would take to end this seemingly
endless process. Our thoughts turned to the jury. What did *they*
believe? Were they being fooled by some or all of the lies? Would
they find Gunn guilty? Would they give him the same death
penalty he had given to my dad?

Trial Day 4—Thursday, August 12, 8:50 A.M.

Thomas Gunn entered the courtroom in the same suit he had
worn on the first day of his trial, only with a different shirt and tie.

As Gunn stepped to the bench to be sworn in, I wondered
whether Prager could get the truth out of him. Gunn had
changed his story so many times over the eighteen months between dad's murder and today that I wondered if he *could* tell
the truth.

Gunn placed his hand on the Bible and swore to tell the
truth, so help him God. Yet we knew through Prager that Gunn
didn't believe in any religion and his only faith was the Rangers.
So how truthful could he be? He had pleaded not guilty.

His lawyer opened the questioning:

SIMPSON: Do you live with your grandmother and is she in the
           courtroom today?

GUNN: Yessir.

SIMPSON: Prior to February 6th of 1970, did you know Officer McDowell and John Prager?

GUNN: Yessir.

SIMPSON: What was your relationship with Officer McDowell?

GUNN: He wanted me to be an informer.

SIMPSON: And did you give him information at times?

GUNN: No. It was one time he tol' me in a way where either I tell him what I know about a case or he would put it on me.

SIMPSON: So you told him?

GUNN: Yessir.

SIMPSON: In January of 1970, did you have occasion to see him again?

GUNN: Yessir, it was at my grandma's house.

SIMPSON: Will you tell the ladies and gentlemen of the jury the conversation as best you can remember?

GUNN: Well, he wanted some information on Jeff Fort and three or four others in the Main 21. I tol' him I had nothing to tell him regarding that. He tol' me I had no choice, either I give him what he wanted or he would tell people out on the street that I was an informer, and I had to let him know he had already did something similar to that because my grandmother's life had been threatened, you know, by persons I know not of.

SIMPSON: You mean your grandmother's life was threatened.

GUNN: Yessir.

SIMPSON: Because you were an informant?

GUNN: Yessir. He tol' me I had nothing to worry about as long as I stayed as his informant, but if I didn't do what he said to, the next time there was any type of homicide in the area, if it fits my description, I would have the case.

SIMPSON: You mean he would place it on you?

GUNN: Right, he would charge me with it.

For the next forty-five minutes Simpson and Gunn verbally danced around whether Gunn was ever on 79th Street and ever in Wee Folks. Did he own a gun? Did he drive a car that day? Was he in the company of Delroy Parnell that day? He denied all these things.

GUNN: When I was picked up and arrested on February 11th was the first time I knowed anything about the murder.

SIMPSON: What were the circumstances? Where were you and who arrested you?

GUNN: I was in bed when Officer McDowell and the state's attorney Mr. Prager came in.

Gunn told of the ride downtown and being interrogated and booked.

GUNN: Officer McDowell took me in a room and tol' me that either I do what he say or I would go to the penitentiary. He wanted me to keep being an informer. I tol' him I couldn't do it because of my grandmother and all, you know, and I didn't want no part of being his informer no more.

SIMPSON: Did you talk to another officer and try to blame the murder on Delroy Parnell?

GUNN: Nossir, I did not.

SIMPSON: Did you tell him you were out driving with Manfred Johnson that day?

GUNN: Nossir, I did not.

Over and over the defense attorney asked Gunn if he was responsible for the crime, if he knew anything about it, if he knew who might have done it or had anything to do with it. Simpson asked and asked and Gunn answered and answered, like a broken record: "Nossir!"

Trial Day 4—Noon

During the lunch break, Prager told us that there was a lot of evidence against Gunn, including eyewitness identification, forensics, gun and bullet matching, and officers' testimony. He told us not to worry, and that some of the afternoon's testimony may be hard for us to hear. He was right.

Trial Day 4—1:00 P.M.

When court resumed, Prager started his examination of Gunn. The defendant stepped into the witness box to testify on his own behalf. He denied knowing Manfred Johnson and couldn't recall what he did the day of the murder or any time that month.

PRAGER: Do you own a gun?

GUNN: Do I own a gun?

PRAGER: Yes, do you own a gun?

GUNN: Nossir.

PRAGER: Have you ever owned a gun?

GUNN: No, I never had no permit for a gun.

PRAGER: Do you own a watch?

GUNN: I have a number of them.

PRAGER: How many?

GUNN: I said I had a number of them so I had a number of them.

PRAGER: You had a gun in your house in February of 1970, didn't you?

GUNN: Nossir.

PRAGER: You do carry a gun, don't you?

GUNN: No, I don't.

PRAGER: In fact, sometimes you carry two guns.

GUNN: No, I don't.

PRAGER: When is the last time you carried two guns?

GUNN: I haven't.

PRAGER: In your whole life?

GUNN: In my life.

PRAGER: Are you sure of that?

Prager produced a photograph of Gunn wearing two guns in his belt. Gunn took one look at the photograph and flinched, then grimaced.

PRAGER: I ask you, who is this man and whose guns are these in his shirt? Take a look at it.

GUNN: Now you say what—who?

PRAGER: Is that your picture?

GUNN: Yessir, it is.

PRAGER: Is that a gun cuffed in your shirt?

GUNN: No. That was taken on Halloween. It's a cap gun.

PRAGER: Is that another gun sticking out on the side here?

GUNN: No, it isn't.

PRAGER: You had a gun in your pocket on Halloween?

GUNN: Gun?

PRAGER: Yes, gun?

GUNN: No.

PRAGER: That revolver is not a gun then?

GUNN: No, it isn't.

PRAGER: You told these ladies and gentlemen that you never had a gun but here is a photo of you with two guns. Right?

GUNN: Right.

PRAGER: You heard the arresting officer testify under oath that he recovered two guns from your grandmother's house. Correct?

GUNN: I guess he said somethin' to that effect.

PRAGER: Have you ever seen this gun before? (Prager marks it into evidence.) Do you know what type of weapon this is?

GUNN: Just a gun.

PRAGER: A bigger gun than the other gun?

GUNN: Pardon me?

PRAGER: Is it bigger than that other gun you saw here in court?

GUNN: Yes.

PRAGER: Is this the gun you have tucked into your pants in the photo?

GUNN: No. Those aren't guns. They are toy guns.

Around and around they went until Gunn admitted that the police, at his direction, took two guns from his grandmother's house after he called her from jail.

PRAGER: Let's talk about Parnell. When you were picked up, you told the officer that Delroy Parnell did it. Parnell was in the lineup with you, wasn't he?

GUNN: Yessir.

PRAGER: Do you remember telling Officer McDowell that you hated Jeff Fort and that you are a strong enough person to take over the Black P Stone Nation, formerly the Blackstone Rangers?

GUNN: No, I did not.

PRAGER: Did you tell him you liked Jeff Fort, but you still wanted to take over the Black P Stone Nation?

GUNN: No.

PRAGER: Well, sir, what is your relationship with Mr. Jeff Fort?

SIMPSON: *Objection!*

PRAGER: You used the term the Main 21. Will you tell me, sir, what you mean by the Main 21?

GUNN: What do I mean?

PRAGER: Yes.

GUNN: I don't understand the question.

PRAGER: What is the Main 21 you, yourself, referred to?

GUNN: I still don't understand what you mean by the Main 21. You know, when you say Main 21, you know, I said it meant something else, but what you mean I don't know.

PRAGER: Well, what do you mean by it, sir?

GUNN: Exactly what I said, the Main 21.

PRAGER: What is it, sir?

GUNN: What do you mean, what is it? What is the name of what?

PRAGER: Are there persons, sir, in the Main 21?

GUNN: Yes.

PRAGER: Is it a ruling body of sorts, sir?

GUNN: It is a ruling body. It has been called that.

PRAGER: Well, what do you call it, sir? Please tell the jury.

GUNN: Main 21.

PRAGER: All right, what does this Main 21 do?

GUNN: I couldn't say what they do.

PRAGER: How long has it been in existence, sir?

SIMPSON: *Objection!* Are we on trial for the murder of Mr. Lazar or are we here for other matters? If this goes to his credibility, you have already used him as an informer, so you gave him credibility.

MORAN: Sustained.

PRAGER: Are you a member of a gang?

GUNN: No.

PRAGER: That cap you are wearing in the photo, what does that represent, sir?

GUNN: Exactly what it looks like, a cap.

PRAGER: Isn't that a Blackstone Rangers insignia on the cap?

SIMPSON: *Objection!*

A sidebar between Simpson, Prager, and Judge Moran ensued. "Your honor," Prager began, "the special relationship the defendant had with Officer McDowell was based on Gunn's providing information about the Blackstone Rangers. That relationship led Gunn to tell McDowell where the guns were in his grandmother's house."

"You are endangering peoples' lives now if you permit this to go on—the lives of innocent people who have nothing to do with the trial, particularly the grandmother," Simpson snapped back. "There are gang members sitting in court right now listening to every single word. I tell you in all honesty, I wouldn't want to be part of finding innocent victims dead after this trial."

"No one knows better than I, your honor, that members of the gang are sitting in the courtroom," Prager barked, alluding to the price on his head. "Whatever Gunn says in the courtroom is not going to jeopardize the lives of his family. They have lived in the area all the time Gunn has been in jail, and his role as an informer has been out there on the street for a long time. We wouldn't have to go any further with this testimony, your honor, if Gunn would just tell us what the Main 21 was. He used the expression."

"He obviously can't, your honor," Simpson retorted. "It is a secret organization. Can you tell me what the Knights of Columbus consists of?"

The judge sustained the objection and Prager moved on to a different line of questioning.

PRAGER: Do you know Mr. Parnell?

GUNN: Yessir.

PRAGER: Do you remember Detective Chambers, sitting here in court today, telling the jury that you told him two different stories about the incident on February 6, 1970?

GUNN: Yes.

PRAGER: The first time you told him you were with Parnell and Parnell must have done it, and the second time you told the story you told him you were in the black Cadillac behind the toy store and Parnell came running back to the car and said he had to burn the guy. Do you remember Detective Chambers saying that?

GUNN: Yes, I remember something like that.

PRAGER: That wasn't true, was it?

GUNN: No, it wasn't.

For more than an hour, Prager asked Gunn about being in the neighborhood where the murder was committed. Gunn kept saying he did not remember that day at all or where he was or whom he was with. Prager asked him about owning a gun. But finally Gunn slipped.

PRAGER: Did you have a gun in your house on February 11ᵗʰ, the day the police came to pick you up?

GUNN: I had one gun because it belonged to my grandmother. It was a .22, I believe, but I'm not positive.

PRAGER: Earlier, you testified that you didn't know the difference between a .22 and any other caliber gun.

GUNN: My uncle bought it for her.

PRAGER: Well, did she have this big gun in the house, this .357 Magnum that I am showing you, that was loaded? Was that in her house?

GUNN: No, I don't believe she had that.

PRAGER: You don't know how many guns your grandmother had?

GUNN: No.

PRAGER: How did you know your grandmother's gun was a .22?

GUNN: I guess I heard her say it at some time.

PRAGER: Did you call your grandmother from jail and tell her to give the officers who were coming by the two guns?

GUNN: I don't recall.

PRAGER: Did you live at your grandmother's house most of the time?

GUNN: It depends on what you mean by most of the time.

PRAGER: Well, did you live with your grandmother the majority of the time?

GUNN: It would depend on what you consider a majority of the time.

PRAGER: Well, let's try days. Now, are you there the majority of days, sir?

GUNN: I never counted the days I spent with her and the days
          I spent with other people.

For more than half an hour, Prager tried to get Gunn to re-
count where he was at various times on February 5 and 6. Gunn
kept dodging and weaving, saying he couldn't recall and he
didn't know what time it was wherever he was. The judge
looked upset as the defense kept objecting to almost every question. This didn't rattle Prager, but it bought Gunn time to make
up yet another lie. At the end of the day, both the defense and
the state concluded their cases.

Trial Day 5—Friday, August 13, 9:00 A.M.

With their closing arguments came the chance for the prosecution and the defense each to convince the jury that his version
was the only possible version. Prager looked confident as he
stepped in front of the jury box. In a voice that rang with sincerity, he retold the whole story, embellishing the grisliest moments.

> I would like to begin by taking this opportunity to thank each
> one of you for your attentiveness during this trial. We believe
> that the evidence presented shows that the defendant did, in
> fact, kill Emanuel Lazar, and for the commission of the
> heinous crime his penalty should be fixed at death. In decid-
> ing the verdict in this case, you are only allowed to consider
> the evidence introduced throughout this trial and that which
> has come from the witnesses who have taken the stand.

Gesturing toward Mom sitting at the table, he continued:

> The evidence shows that Emanuel Lazar was the owner of a
> retail store known as Wee Folks on 79th Street. On February
> 6th of 1970, Mr. Emanuel Lazar, along with his wife, Belle, ar-
> rived at their toy store early that morning as they had done
> for the past twenty-five years. Little did they realize that on
> that particular morning, Emanuel Lazar was to open his busi-
> ness for the last time.

Prager reiterated the story of the robbery for the jury.

As fate would have it, Mr. Emanuel Lazar decided to come out of the back room and he saw Thomas Gunn with a gun in his hand only ten feet from him. Mr. Lazar attempted to flee from the gunman but to no avail. Gunn had seen him. He pointed his weapon in the direction of Emanuel Lazar and yelled out, "Don't move or I'll shoot." Even as the words "Don't move" were echoing through the store, the gun in his hand was blasting away. The gun was carrying its own message, the message of death, as these five bullets ripped into the helpless body of Emanuel Lazar. The first bullet struck him in the back, causing him to spin around in time for two more bullets to go ringing into his chest. After Gunn emptied his revolver into the body of Emanuel Lazar, the only thing left for him to do was escape the scene of this cold-blooded murder.

Prager recounted the escape route leading to the black Cadillac and how witnesses had described him without any doubt.

Mr. Gunn and the driver of that getaway car knew the true identity of the man who had coldly and calmly murdered Emanuel Lazar before the eyes of his horrified wife.

Prager described Mom's interrogation and that of the witnesses and how they all independently identified the same gunman from mug shots and, finally, during a lineup. He told how the police, armed with the description of the gunman, started their search. He told of the visit he and Officer McDowell of the Gang Crime Intelligence Unit made to the home of Gunn's grandmother, how they found Gunn at home, read him his rights, told him he had been positively identified as the killer of Emanuel Lazar, and escorted him to the Criminal Courthouse.

While he was being transported, the mind of this killer began to work like a trapped animal struggling to think of a way out. Gunn had to think, "How can I get out of this?"

How could he throw off the cloud of guilt that was over his head? By the time he arrived at the office of the Special Prosecutions Unit, the devious, cunning, and calculating mind of this killer had figured out a plan, a scheme, a way out. He would put the blame on someone else. When he met with the detectives, he said he wanted to talk to Officer McDowell alone because he had a special relationship with Officer McDowell. The relationship was that of police officer and informant. This man, Gunn, had been giving information regarding the Blackstone Rangers and the Main 21, of which he was a member, and their activities to Officer McDowell for quite some time. It was at this point that Thomas Gunn was going to take advantage of their personal relationship. When they were alone, Gunn asked McDowell to call his grandmother and ask her to get rid of some "stuff." At that point, only Gunn knew the importance of the "stuff" because, in fact, the "stuff" was two guns that were concealed under the couch in his grandmother's living room. One of these guns was the blue steel .38 caliber special Smith and Wesson that he had used to kill Emanuel Lazar.

When Officer McDowell asked what the "stuff" was, Gunn realized he would have to take another step in carrying out his master scheme by placing the blame on someone else. The young killer knew it would only be a matter of time before the police were able to get a search warrant for his grandmother's house and find the guns. So Gunn told McDowell that the "stuff" was two guns, one of which had been used to kill Emanuel Lazar, but these guns were not his. They only happened to be in his grandmother's living room because Delroy Parnell had given Gunn the weapons to hold.

Now we had a name, Delroy Parnell.

Officer McDowell, wanting to make sure he had the right man for the murder, told Gunn he would proceed to his grandmother's house and get the guns. He said he would apprehend Parnell and bring him in for a lineup. If Parnell was identified in the lineup, then the weapons at Gunn's house would be used to prosecute Parnell.

Prager told of McDowell's visit to Livia Reynolds's home, how she voluntarily gave him the blue steel .38 caliber special

Smith and Wesson and a .357 Magnum. Back at the Criminal Courthouse, two detectives advised Gunn of his constitutional rights. He then stated he would tell all he knew about the killing.

His cunning mind created a fictitious story of how he was riding with Delroy Parnell on the date in question in the area of Wee Folks. Parnell suggested they rob the drugstore on the corner of 79ᵗʰ and East End. Gunn said he tried to deter Parnell from the robbery and they had a lot of discussion back and forth. Gunn said he wanted no part of the robbery and had Parnell drop him off. He said he didn't see Parnell again that day.

Gunn, trying to be helpful, went further to suggest that Parnell killed Emanuel Lazar. That, he offered, was the reason he, Gunn, was mistakenly identified as the killer. After all, the two looked so much alike. The detectives didn't buy this version and told Gunn so. Then that mind started working again and Gunn realized he would have to go one step further. He would have to get himself a little deeper into the murder. He would have to account for the fact that witnesses placed him at the scene. At that point, Gunn switched roles. He decided to assume the role of the driver of the getaway car, so he told the two detectives that what he had previously said was untrue. He would now relate the real version. He proceeded to tell them how he and Parnell were riding in the black Cadillac and discussing robbing the drugstore. Gunn discouraged Parnell from doing that because he didn't consider the exit route good enough. He went further to relate how Parnell told him to park in the lot next to the Wee Folks store. " 'Park in the last stall facing east in the alley and keep the motor running,' he tol' me." Then, Parnell went into Wee Folks. As Gunn sat in the car in this new version, Parnell came running from the scene, leaped into the car, and said, "Let's get out of here, man. I had to burn the guy." Then Gunn, in all his sincerity, told the detectives how he sped down the alley and turned north. And how the two returned to a favorite restaurant in their neighborhood where Gunn returned the car keys to Parnell. At this point, Gunn had neglected one little point. He had been the man who came running out of Wee Folks and he was the real killer.

After telling this new version, Gunn was transported to District Four Homicide, where he was given an opportunity to call his lawyer, one Drake French, a noted gang lawyer. He told French he was a suspect in a murder and was going to the Fourth District for a lineup. Meanwhile, Parnell was picked up and he too asked to talk to French. Gunn and Parnell were transported to the Fourth District separately and placed in a lineup. It was here that the master scheme of this cold and calculating killer was once and for all destroyed.

He stood with four men of similar stature and right next to Parnell as each of the witnesses individually identified Gunn as the killer of Emanuel Lazar.

During the lineup, the final link in a long chain of evidence against Gunn was securely fastened into place. One of the weapons recovered from Gunn's grandmother's home, the .38 special Smith and Wesson, had been tested by the crime lab to see if ballistics would show that it matched the bullets recovered from the body of Emanuel Lazar. The bullets and the gun matched. It was the weapon Gunn had used to murder Emanuel Lazar.

Thus, ladies and gentlemen of the jury, through the evidence presented, you can see that Gunn shot Emanuel Lazar. You also can see what he did after the shooting. He even reloaded the gun. You have seen this through physical evidence and the testimony of many witnesses. Consider the testimony of the witnesses and their credibility. You determine credibility of the witnesses based on their opportunity to observe. Mrs. Lazar said she was with the killer in close proximity for fifteen minutes in a well-lit store. She was as close as two feet away from him. She was only six feet away from him when he pulled the trigger, sending bullets ringing into the body of her husband. You will recall how she stated her suspicion of the defendant and how she never took her eyes from him the entire time he was in the store. You heard the testimony from several other very credible witnesses of their close proximity to the killer.

Speaking directly to the jurors, he continued:

Do you think Mrs. Lazar will ever forget the face of the man who shot her husband? Do you think Mrs. Mosely will ever forget the face of the man who ran by her as she huddled against the wall in a pregnant condition? Do you think Mr. Robbins will ever forget the face of the man running from the store with a gun in his hand? The judge will instruct you that memory and the manner in which a witness testified are ways to determine witness credibility. Consider the testimony of Mrs. Lazar as she watched Gunn empty his revolver into her husband. Consider the professionalism of Detective Chambers as he related the complete fairness of the lineup. Think of the years of experience of the coroner and Mr. Mitchell of the Crime Lab and their precise testimony. The last guideline is reasonableness. Recall the testimony of the eyewitnesses as they described the exact same individual and the long time police professionals spent scrupulously recounting all the many stories fabricated by the killer.

When you go back into the jury room, recall carefully the actions of this defendant when you determine whether or not to impose the death penalty. Each of you had an opportunity to examine the tools of Gunn's trade. This instrument is a five-shot revolver, which Gunn coldly and efficiently wielded on that fateful day. Recall the bullets, five of them, that were found in the body of Emanuel Lazar. Consider the remorse this defendant felt after taking the life of another human being. So much remorse that the first thing he did when he returned home was to fully reload the weapon again. He put five more bullets in the weapon. Who do you think the intended victims were for this round of bullets?

Prager's voice rose with emotion.

Remember the testimony of the coroner. Emanuel Lazar could not have been facing Gunn when he was shot. As Gunn stated when he was trying to justify the murder, "The old man was coming at me with his hand in his pocket and I thought he had a gun, so I had to kill him." This could not have been true, because one of the bullets entered the back of Emanuel Lazar as he attempted to flee from the gunman. That bullet whirled him around to allow Gunn to sink four more bullets into his chest and arms.

Now the decision is yours, ladies and gentlemen. Will he pay the supreme penalty for this heinous crime? Or will he be turned loose onto the streets? The decision rests with each and every one of you. The citizenry has done their part with their testimony. The police have gathered their evidence. As you sit in the jury box, you represent the community and the community is sitting in judgment of Thomas Gunn today. The community is crying out for your verdict saying, "No! No, Mr. Gunn, you cannot take the life of another and walk away. You cannot shoot a man like a dog in his place of business and walk away. You cannot empty a loaded revolver into a helpless man while his horrified wife looks on and expect to pay no penalty."

When you sit in the jury box, do not think of Thomas Gunn as he sits before you now, dressed in his fancy suit and tie. Think of how he looked on February 6th in 1970 standing a few feet from Emanuel Lazar with his gun blasting away. And you have one piece of physical evidence to take into the jury room with you. You will take a portrait of a killer. A photograph of Gunn showing him wearing his red Blackstone Rangers beret, with a toothpick sticking out of his mouth, his hands on his hips, and two guns stuck in his belt, an automatic on one side and a revolver on the other. This is Thomas Gunn, the real Thomas Gunn. This is the killer who struck down Emanuel Lazar in cold blood. This is the man you must find guilty and fix his penalty at death.

As Prager returned to his seat, beads of sweat rolled down his face and he seemed thoroughly spent.

Trial Day 5—1:00 P.M.

Court resumed, and it was Blake Simpson's turn to address the jury. In his closing, he gave Gunn's side of the story. Pacing like a caged lion in front of the jury box, Simpson outlined a story of the frame-up of a man who had been the chief informant for the police but had outlived his usefulness.

My heart goes out to the family of the deceased. I don't want you ladies and gentlemen to have the impression that I am representing a paragon of virtue. I am representing a guy who is wise to the streets. He had probably participated in everything, but murder is another matter. A man used by the police as an informer is usually a pussycat. He is a pussycat and not capable of murder.

Is my client to be believed? I don't know. I really don't know. But I know the police and the Gang Crime Unit believed him for a long time. They thought he was honest and truthful. He said he didn't do it. He said he wasn't there. He said he never owned a gun.

Remember, the defendant need not put on a defense at all. It is the prosecutor's job to prove his case beyond a reasonable doubt.

And I say to you now that it is better to let a guilty man go free than to send an innocent man away. Do you believe the police accounts of what Gunn said to them about burning the victim? I believe that Officer McDowell was disenchanted with this boy because he had outlived his usefulness. McDowell saw Gunn as his bread and butter. Gunn was the man who was going to make him "Mr. Big." Because he was receiving a lot of information from my client, he was busting a lot of gang-related cases. When my client told McDowell what he had, there was already a rumble on the streets that he was turning on his friends and his grandmother was going to be hit. My client was willing to take his chances with the gang, but the police wouldn't let him out.

Simpson's voice rose higher and higher.

Imagine these leeches, these officers trying to get information at any cost. These poor, despicable, sick people, going out onto the streets and gathering information so they can crawl into the prosecutor's office with little bits of information. So they can make arrests of unfortunate people. When their usefulness is over and they are no longer getting the "stuff" from these poor people, they are arrested and thrown in jail. The police are trying to frame the poor, unfortunate people who will no longer do their bidding. So what can a defense lawyer do? He looks for the motive. Have you seen a motive? And what about the gun? They used a witness to prove that this gun did the shooting. And I say it did and the witness said it did. But they didn't know where it came from. Did it come from Gunn's friend and not Gunn himself?

The only thing you are called upon to decide today is, did Thomas Gunn kill Mr. Lazar beyond all reasonable doubt? You stated you could do that when I selected you to be on this jury. I asked if you could be fair to both sides. We don't want you to put him away because he may have been a bad boy in the past. My client went to the Gang Intelligence Unit and told them there was going to be a rumble on the street and both he and his grandmother were going to get hit because he had been informing on Jeff Fort. And what did they tell him? They told him he must go along with them. If not, either they would get him or the gang would.

I was seething. Simpson was justifying the killing and patting the killer on the back for being an informant! I watched Gunn as his lawyer pleaded for his life and while the state's attorney demanded it be taken from him. Mom was so strong and seemed so calm. I could barely contain myself. How could anyone justify what this man did? I watched in disbelief as Simpson whined on behalf of his client.

SIMPSON: Where else but in America could a jury composed of twelve reasonable and unbiased jurors decide the fate of a fellow human being? Where else but in America could a poor slob like that have an experienced trial lawyer court appointed to represent him without any hopes of compensation?

PRAGER: *Objection!* Improper!

MORAN: The jury will disregard the last statement.

PRAGER: Do you want to pay me, Counsel?

MORAN: The remarks will be stricken!

For another hour Simpson argued in front of the jury, delivering a monologue on the criminal justice system, how all killings are vicious, the fallibility of the law, the definitions of reasonable doubt. Maybe he didn't have anything else to offer.

Not only do they want you to find my client guilty, but they want you to become murderers too. They want you to go back to the thirteenth and fourteenth centuries. Let's go back instead of going to the moon. Hell, an eye for an eye and a tooth for a tooth. Kill him! Kill the bastard! Let's do the easiest thing. Take the easiest way out. Let's find him guilty of murder without recommending the death penalty. I ask you, ladies and gentlemen, is this not a world of compromise? It may be in international politics or in labor relations, but when you compromise with a man's life, that's serious business. It is difficult to discuss a situation like this with twelve people who have never been subjected, who have never encountered, who have never been indoctrinated with the ways and methods of certain prosecutors and certain policemen, under the guise of representing the people of the state of Illinois, saying, "We can do no wrong." Consider that this group of policemen and scientific men, laymen and civilians, could be wrong, just dead wrong.

In connection with whether my client was telling the truth, on cross-examination he was asked where he was on February 6th, 1970. Now I ask you, folks, where were you two weeks ago Monday? Most of you would scratch your head and say, "I don't remember."

The only ones who remember a specific date and place and time are those people who must create an alibi. I'm not the man. I wasn't there. I was elsewhere and Joe Blow was with me. Did my client tell you that? Mrs. Lazar went and placed her hand on my client's body. My client didn't say to her, "I'm sorry I did this to you." But he told that to an officer? Isn't that ridiculous?

Manufactured, framed. These are the most difficult cases in the world to defend. I hope and trust, ladies and gentlemen, that you are not that naive not to see beyond the wheat and the chaff. You will observe that I have not made a liar out of any of their witnesses because I think they told the truth. Except Officer McDowell. He is a liar, a boldfaced liar! If he weren't a policeman, he might very well be a thief or a murderer. Thank you, ladies and gentlemen.

Finally, Simpson was finished and he sat down. Mom looked exhausted. Having to sit through the entire trial and listen to the defense almost deify Gunn was torture.

Trial Day 5—3:00 P.M.

Prager again stood to address the jury.

Ladies and gentlemen, after listening to the defense argument, I have to say I have never heard so much junk and garbage in my life. If you can swallow what Mr. Simpson said, let's open the prisons and lock up our briefcases. A frame? It is anything but a frame. Mr. Simpson says the case is just too "pat." That bothers me. This is the argument of a skilled defense counsel when the witnesses are not impeached and not contradicted. These are witnesses who are interested in protecting their community. But when they testify against Thomas Gunn, they are criticized for being too "pat." Ladies and gentlemen, he never went over the facts of the case. All he has is his argument. His opening words were, "We're going to show there is a conspiracy." But he never presented one fact, one bit of evidence from the witness stand, that there was any type of conspiracy. The conspiracy comes out of his mouth. That is your only evidence of a conspiracy. He is a skilled defense lawyer who has been practicing for thirty-five years. So don't let his words and actions fool you. He implied that the witnesses, Mrs. Lazar, Mr. Robinson, and Mrs. Mosely, had a seed planted in their head by the police to identify the defendant. Was there one bit of evidence that the police officers had ever spoken to any of the witnesses in their lives? With all the evidence against him, all Mr. Simpson could say was that the police must have framed him.

He asked you why there was no polygraph given to his client. If he were honest with you, he would tell you that a polygraph is not admissible in court. Mr. Simpson asks you, "How many of you remember what you were doing two weeks ago?" Do you believe that Gunn can't remember five days before he was arrested and charged with capital murder? Do you believe he was at home with his grandmother? Can you believe that man when he said he never possessed a gun when I specifically asked him, "Did you have a gun in your belt?" He said "No." And then he saw this photograph and you saw his reaction. You will see the photograph again in the jury room.

There is one gun and the butt of a second clearly visible. Now, do you believe his explanation that they were fake guns? I guess that his friends, his fellow gang members in the photo, also had fake guns. He said it was Halloween. Do you believe that? I submit to you that if Officer McDowell, an officer in the Gang Intelligence Unit, is able to convince several eye-witnesses to the murder of Emanuel Lazar, people he has never seen before, to identify the photo of the defendant and then again in a lineup, I submit that he is more skilled than any of us can imagine.

Let's try to get this straight. First Gunn blames Manfred Johnson. He says he is the real killer. But Officer Morrison showed that he was the driver of the car. Then Gunn blames Parnell, and now Simpson blames Johnson. And then there is Gunn's grandmother. I suggest to you that she is nothing more than a kindly woman who surely wasn't keeping these guns for her own use.

Prager told the jury that Gunn, because of his long-standing relationship with the police and the state's attorney's staff as an informant, knew criminal procedure. He knew that in giving McDowell permission to get the guns, he was giving the officer permission to search the premises where the gun and watch were found.

Now I ask you, regarding the death penalty, to determine as best you can why you should not give Gunn the death penalty in this case. First of all, Thomas Gunn had his own little court-room at 1710 East 79th Street, where he loaded his gun with five bullets and anointed himself judge, jury, and executioner of Mr. Emanuel Lazar. He killed a sixty-year-old man who never owned a gun, who was totally unarmed. He pulled the trigger five times. Anyone who touched this gun knows that this is no hair-trigger. It must be pulled with a degree of force.

Demonstrating the action to the jury Prager continued.

So we know he had to go BOOM, BOOM, BOOM, BOOM, BOOM. One shot hit that little old man in the back. He wasn't facing Gunn, so he couldn't have done him any harm at all.

At this point, Prager spun around and glared at Gunn, who was sitting tall in his chair.

The man is a consummate liar. Look at his face. Do you see even a modicum of sympathy or remorse for what he did? He's so low he has to climb to get to the bottom.

A reflex action caused Gunn to nod his head in seeming agreement.

When you go back to the jury room, you have to determine whether people like Emanuel Lazar are important, whether a toy-store owner on 79th Street merits your consideration. When the weapon was found in Gunn's apartment, it was already reloaded. Gunn tried to blame another man who was placed next to him in a lineup and not identified as the killer. Finally, when all other lies are catching up with him, he tells Officer Rudy Chambers, "Well, I thought the old man was reaching for a gun in his pocket and that's why I killed him."

But since that admission, he has had time to think about this confession, claiming to this court that he is not guilty. I suggest you can make every reasonable inference why he changed his story. These brave witnesses and the evidence show that they are sick of this type of person, the defendant, in the community. A man who not only comes in and robs but he murders when things don't go as he wants them to. I suggest that this man is even more deserving of the death penalty than the man who kills a policeman. What you are dealing with here is a cold-blooded killer. The evidence shows he is a killer.

The evidence shows he should never be allowed on the street again. I suggest to you, ladies and gentlemen, and it is just a suggestion, that he should never be back on the street again. I think it is your turn to stand up to a man like Thomas Gunn. In a few minutes Judge Moran will instruct you as to the law you must follow. My responsibility has ended. Now it becomes your responsibility because it is your community.

At 4:45, the closing arguments were finished. The judge provided the jury their instructions. He indicated they had

three choices: find Gunn innocent, find him guilty with a recommendation of life imprisonment, or find him guilty with a
recommendation of death. It took them only three hours to
reach a verdict.

The Verdict—Monday, August 16, 1971, 1:00 P.M.

We were all there—Mom, my sister, the witnesses, and me. The
witnesses didn't have to be there, but they wanted to be. Gunn
was led in from the anteroom. Judge Victor Moran asked the
bailiff to bring in the jury. The bailiff asked the jury to be seated,
all except the forelady. A middle-aged black woman stood up.

MORAN: Madam Forelady, has the jury reached a verdict?

FORELADY: We have, your honor.

MORAN: Will you please hand the verdict to the clerk, by
giving it to the bailiff, who will transmit it to the
clerk? Mr. Clerk, will you examine the verdict to
see if it is in proper form? Will the defendant rise
and face the jury?

In a loud, strong voice the clerk read the verdict:

We, the jury, find the defendant, Thomas Gunn, guilty of
murder and we fix the penalty at death.

Gunn was shaking his head as if wondering at the injustice of it
all. I felt relieved that it was finally over. I felt as if a torrent of
tears were just waiting for the slightest provocation to be released into an unstoppable flood. Mom looked anguished. She
didn't like the idea of the killer being killed. She always saw
some good in everyone, even the likes of this animal. Being unfamiliar with the criminal justice system, I believed that because
the jury gave Gunn a death sentence, he would be put to death.
Prager told us that the judge made the final decision on the
death sentence, but that he would seriously consider the jury's
recommendation.

At the close of the trial, few people were left in the room. The only one in Gunn's corner was his grandmother, Livia Reynolds, waving a handkerchief. She looked old and tired. I remember thinking, how can she not love him? He's her flesh and blood. But I wondered how she could ever justify what he did. And I wondered where his parents were.

Sentencing—Monday, November 22, 1971, 9:00 A.M.

After some three months, we were back at the Criminal Courthouse for the sentencing. Gunn was at the defendant's table along with Simpson. Mom sat with Prager. As during the trial, my sister and I sat behind the rail behind the table. Judge Moran, speaking in a slow, deliberate monotone, started what I thought would be the sentencing recommended by the jury.

> The Supreme Court of our State of Illinois has gone through the question of capital punishment and has sustained it. The United States Supreme Court has upheld it.
>
> I am now put in the position of meting out the sentence for this man according to the statutory provisions of the law. But I must be mindful of the fact that here in the state of Illinois, the jury's verdict with reference to the death penalty is merely a recommendation, one which the court need not follow if the court feels that another disposition is appropriate. On the other hand, it is a necessary step to get this recommendation.
>
> There were many things that developed in the course of this particular trial with reference to the past conduct of this defendant, his association with the police as an informant, that make this case somewhat different from other cases I have had before me. I have imposed the death penalty here in this courtroom and I take the responsibility of imposing this penalty to be a grave one. There is no question that murder is a most dastardly crime. I am sure all of us have great concern as to the safety of every store owner, whether big store or small.

The judge went on for about an hour, discussing the Supreme Court, and citing specific cases and points of law. He talked about how, in fairness, the jury should have the opportunity to know more about the background of the individual on trial and how the present system didn't allow for it. He discussed his feelings about finding the killer guilty beyond a reasonable doubt and about imposing the death penalty as a deterrent. He gave his opinion about the excessive length of time between the murder and the trial. I was beginning to wonder if they paid judges by the word.

He reiterated the opening and closing remarks of both attorneys.

I have indicated that in my mind the death penalty is still a deterrent to crime, but I think one of the large factors to be considered by this court is the possibility of rehabilitation.

Rehabilitation? Was he serious? Did he think this man who had killed and maimed several times before, even though we could not bring up his past deeds in court, deserved rehabilitation? I was furious.

My remarks in no way mean to reflect adversely upon the findings of the jury. They faced their responsibility with much difficulty and made a just decision. Looking at the record of the defendant and the testimony, the court would be inclined to impose the death penalty because of the clamor of society for the safety of the streets. This court could be satisfied that a sentence of that kind would deter crimes of this nature.

Because of the many problems that the court envisions in a case of this kind, the court is going to give full consideration and mitigation, and at this time pronounce sentence.

The court feels that the finding of guilt in this matter appears to be justified. The court also feels that this is a case in which the defendant has the possibility of rehabilitation.

Weighing all the matters and facts in this case as well as matters in aggravation and mitigation, considering all of the investigative reports, I now pronounce sentence as follows. Will the defendant rise?

Gunn stared at Moran as he read his decision.

I sentence the defendant, Thomas Gunn, to a term of not less than 100 years and not more than 200 years, for which period of time it will be my order to the Department of Corrections that he be incarcerated in the penitentiary pursuant to law and in accordance with the law. The court wishes to make a note on the record at this time that the parole authorities and correction authorities avail themselves of the record of these proceedings in this particular case, and all of the background information that has been made available to this court, and supplement the same with any psychiatric or other diagnostic services that are possible to then determine the proper course of rehabilitation for this defendant. I think that the court imposing a sentence of a minimum of 100 years emphasizes the gravity of this offense. The defendant should not be released until parole authorities are convinced beyond a reasonable doubt that this person can resume a place in society and be a citizen of merit.

I watched Gunn's face as they read the verdict. He was like stone, no expression. I turned to Mom. She seemed relieved and a little sad. I knew she hated the idea of anyone being put to death. She leaned across the railing to me and said, "I really didn't want him to die." I was stunned. I didn't know what to think.

MORAN: At this time, Mr. Gunn, you are advised that if you are indigent and without funds, you are entitled to have a complete record of your entire trial prepared without cost to you for the purpose of appeal. If you are indigent, the court will appoint counsel to represent you. Do you understand these rights, Mr. Gunn?

GUNN: Yes, I understand.

MORAN: Do you have any questions about your right to appeal?

GUNN: No.

Another man, a stranger to all of us, entered the court and stepped inside the rail. Gunn's lawyer jumped to his feet.

SIMPSON: Your honor, excuse me, but another lawyer, Robert Jones, has filed his appearance, apparently as co-counsel, in this case. I would now ask that my name be removed.

MORAN: Mr. Jones, are you undertaking to represent this defendant from this point forward?

ROBERT JONES: Your honor, our office has undertaken to represent Mr. Gunn and I would like to submit the order for the transcription.

MORAN: Mr. Gunn, is this in accordance with your wishes?

GUNN: Right.

MORAN: Do you have the funds with which to provide your further defense?

GUNN: No.

Prager asked to address the court.

PRAGER: I want to point out, your honor, that the new counsel who is filing his appearance has been retained by the petitioner, which would place him in a different category.

MORAN: Mr. Jones, are you privately retained in this matter?

JONES: Your honor, the word "retained" is a semantic one. It depends on what you mean by retained. There are certain funds that have been paid to our offices.

Jones sounded just like Gunn when he didn't want the court to know the truth.

MORAN: Have the funds that have been provided to you been provided by the defendant?

JONES: No, your honor.

MORAN: Are the funds from sources other than the defendant?

JONES: Yes, your honor.

MORAN: Do you intend to file a notice of appeal?

JONES: Yes, your honor.

And so it ended. I figured that the Rangers' Legal Defense Fund must have come to back to the table.

Both the state's attorney and the jury had recommended the death penalty, but Judge Moran gave Gunn a life sentence. Prager told us that it was because Gunn was under twenty-one at the time of the murder. I assumed at the time that this meant he would stay in jail for the rest of his life. I was wrong.

Mom led an active life after she
moved to California.

EPILOGUE

Thomas Gunn

AFTER HE WAS SENTENCED IN 1971 to life imprisonment for my father's murder, Thomas Gunn made numerous appeals. He appealed because he thought his sentence was excessive. It was denied. He appealed because he felt his identification as a Blackstone Ranger prejudiced the jury. It was denied. He appealed because he claimed the jury was improperly instructed. It was denied. He appealed because he said he was never properly advised of his rights. It was denied. Gunn began to educate himself in prison, reading books by Malcolm X and Mao Tse-tung and learning to use the legal system to his advantage, requesting and being heard at subsequent appeals.

After serving eleven years of his 100-to-200-year life sentence, Gunn applied for parole. It was granted in 1983, partly resulting from his accusations of police brutality. My family wasn't notified of his release, but somehow Mom knew, I think. Gunn returned to a life with the Black P Stone Nation, and within a month murdered again. This time he killed a man who, according to police accounts, had stolen narcotics and money from a drug dealer with ties to the Black P Stone Nation, now known as the El Rukns. Gunn was sentenced to life, once more escaping the death penalty. Again he appealed, claiming police lied under oath when they denied torturing him. He cited corrupt judges, racism, and shakedowns by prison officials. Again the appeals were denied.

Like numerous black men in Illinois correctional facilities who said they had suffered similar abuses, Gunn has always claimed he was a victim. The city of Chicago paid cash settlements to him and other such criminals as compensation for improper police behavior without stating whether the allegations were true. To date, Gunn has received several thousand dollars.

Thirty-five years after he murdered my dad, Thomas Gunn still maintains that, as a nineteen-year-old, he got into an argument with a little Jewish man running a policy racket in the back room of a South Shore toy store. When words became heated, he says, they both reached for their weapons. Gunn drew faster and killed the man. Gunn, who is fifty-four years old, is currently serving consecutive life sentences. At this writing, he will not be eligible for parole for many years.[1]

Jeff Fort and the Black P Stone Nation

According to Rod Emery's *History of the Gangster Disciples*, the Blackstone Rangers—aka the Black P Stone Nation—continued to prosper. Under Jeff "Chief Malik" Fort's leadership, the gang eventually became known as the El Rukns.[2] Fort ruled the El Rukns from his cell.[3]

In the early 1970s Fort and several other gang members were convicted of misspending nearly $1 million of funds from federal War on Poverty programs.[4] Reverend John Fry had assisted Fort in obtaining the grants for use by the Black P Stone Nation to improve their neighborhood. But these funds were abundantly abused.[5]

When Fort was released on parole in the mid-1970s from his first incarceration for embezzling federal money in the Reverend Fry "gang program," he looked for a way to overcome the parole restrictions concerning gang association. The BPSN adopted a decidedly Islamic belief system.[6] "In his new Islamic guise, Fort took the name, Malik, and changed the name of the Nation to Moorish Science Temple of America, El Rukn Tribe, to obtain official recognition as a religious organization," reported William Grigg in *The New American*.[7] As Kenneth Timmerman points out in *Shakedown*, "The advantage of official recognition was that they could then hold private 'religious' services in prison without surveillance. One of his most ambitious schemes was to turn El Rukn into an asset of the international terrorist network."[8]

A Chicago mobs Web site reports: "In reality, the El Rukns [Arabic for "the Stones"] were the upper echelon of the Rangers. The Blackstone Rangers still operated to a lesser extent in the city as various loosely connected factions. The El Rukns began to operate at a very sophisticated criminal level, establishing headquarters at 39th & Cottage Grove, known as 'The Fort.' In 1983, Fort was arrested on drug charges. He was convicted, then incarcerated in a Texas federal prison. In 1986, Fort, along with other high-ranking Rukns, was indicted for attempting to purchase high powered weapons from Libya. Jeff Fort was sentenced to an additional 80 years in federal prison, where he currently resides."[9]

It was Louis Farrakhan of the Nation of Islam who put Fort in touch with the Libyan government, according to Lance Williams, who teaches "The Sociology of Violence" at the Center for Inner City Studies at Northeastern Illinois University.[10, 11] After Farrakhan received a no-interest $5 million loan from Libyan leader Muammar Gadhafi, Fort was encouraged that he could get such funds too. Over the course of five years, federal agents taped more than 3,500 hours of conversations between Fort and the Libyans, including one in which Fort cut a deal with Gadhafi for $2.5 million. The deal included plans to bomb U.S. government buildings and commit other terrorist acts against the United States on Gadhafi's behalf.[12]

According to the Chicago mobs Web site, "In the mid-'80s, the federal government began to go after El Rukn leaders. Many top ranking generals were arrested and convicted on various charges, thus crippling the organization. In the late '80s, the name Black P. Stone Nation (BPSN) resurfaced on the streets. Many factions and sub groups emerged, both during the time of Fort's 1st incarceration, and after his 2nd. The 'official' leaders of the BPSN since Fort's transfer to Marion Federal Prison in California have been his sons: 'Prince Akeem' and 'Prince Watkeeta.'"[13]

The Nation of Islam

Elijah Muhammad remained the leader of the Nation of Islam until his death in 1975. At that time he had more than one million followers and seventy-six mosques worldwide, including one at 73rd and Stony Island Avenue, located a few blocks from Wee Folks. NOI Temple No. 2, formerly a Greek Orthodox church, was purchased and remodeled in 1972 by Elijah Muhammad as a mosque, school, and headquarters.[14]

Following Elijah Muhammad's death, his son was installed as Supreme Minister of the Nation of Islam. Imam Wallace D. Muhammad reformulated his father's beliefs and practices, shunning black separatist views and forging alliances with other American Muslim organizations. He called his creation the "World Community of All Islam in the West" in 1976. That same year, he received $16 million from the head of the City of Sharjah in the United Arab Emirates to build a mosque and Moslem school. Each new mosque became an independent entity, but remained affiliated with the Muslim American Society—also known as the Ministry of W. Deen Mohammed—based in Calumet City, Illinois.[15] In 1978, he changed his organization's name to American Muslim Mission.

Wallace D. Muhammad's assumption of leadership within the Nation of Islam was fraught with controversy, as Louis Farrakhan believed he should have been named Elijah Muhammad's successor. Farrakhan openly disagreed with W. D. Muhammad's movement to Sunni Islam, and he and a few NOI members formed a splinter group to resurrect the teachings of Elijah Muhammad. In 1988, Farrakhan purchased NOI Temple No. 2 and renamed it Mosque Maryam after Mary, the mother of Jesus. It is now the Midwest regional headquarters and national center of the NOI.

"Louis Farrakhan has remained true to the older teachings of Elijah Muhammad. Farrakhan's newspaper, The Final Call, still reprints 'What the Muslims Want' and 'What the Muslims Believe' on the back pages of each issue, in the identical text that Elijah Muhammad printed in the 1960's. Reading these statements evokes memories of newspapers printed by the Black Panther Party or by other Black Power groups.[16]

"In these statements, the Nation of Islam wants equal opportunity for people of all color. They want reparations, preferably a large tract of land set apart from the United States and given to black people, plus their former slave masters should be obligated to maintain and supply their needs in this separate territory for the next twenty to twenty-five years. They want the release of all black Muslims convicted of any federal crimes, and the release of all black people convicted of any capital crime requiring the death sentence. The Muslims are against racial integration and interracial marriage. They want every Black man and woman to have the freedom to accept or reject being separated from the slave master's children and establish a land of their own. The Final Call newspaper carries an ever-present emphasis on black supremacy, on white conspiracies, on white people as devils, and on the Jews as a special enemy."[17]

To their credit, the NOI has a doctrine against drugs, prostitution, pimping, violence, and gang involvement. They encourage opening black owned-and-operated businesses and working to raise the standard of living in poor neighborhoods. They speak out against black reliance on the government welfare system, which they feel perpetuates the cycle of poverty. The NOI uses restaurants and the food-service industry for economic growth. They own thousands of acres of Georgia farmland to employ and feed their people, and operate countless restaurants, bakeries, clothing stores, bookstores, hair care shops, and other enterprises. In 1995, the NOI opened the Salaam Restaurant and Bakery on Chicago's South Side. They want their believers to "Do for Self." They provide NOI security teams for housing projects throughout the nation.[18] NOI converts in prisons are told that when they are released, they will have a job waiting in NOI grocery stores, bakeries, and fisheries. These jobs have kept many from returning to prison.[19]

Today as well as thirty years ago, blacks in prison are more likely to convert to the Nation of Islam, and fully one-third of all federal prisoners are Muslim of one variety or another. Thus, the Nation of Islam seems geared to reach the underclass, and its message emphasizes and capitalizes on the racial inequities and disparities between black and white people in America.

I feel sad that the NOI's liturgy of hatred toward whites in general, and hatred of Jews in particular, created a new truth within the impressionable minds of young black men. This doctrine of hatred reverberated through South Shore in the 1960s. If these young people had listened to the teachings of Martin Luther King Jr. instead of the NOI, would South Shore,

Chicago, or the nation be different? I would like to believe that if they had been around Mom and Dad's positive influence, things would have been not only different but better.

Belle Lazar

The trial behind her, Mom moved to Rancho Bernardo, California, in 1976. She was sixty-five and wanted to be nearer to her brother, Maurice. Uncle Mac had become a prominent cardiac and thoracic surgeon in Los Angeles, and he and his family embraced Mom as a significant part of their lives.

Wee Folks died with Dad, but its spirit didn't. Mom volunteered in the Rancho Bernardo community. She joined Women's American ORT (Organization for Rehabilitation through Training), a Jewish women's fundraising organization. For two decades, she helped the 108 members of the San Pasqual chapter raise money to provide programs and build facilities to help underprivileged people achieve self-sufficiency through technical and vocational training and education. Many students received engineering degrees and many technical teachers were certified, thanks to ORT. Mom loved the idea of making youngsters self-sufficient. For a time, she served as president of her chapter and traveled to conventions.

California neighbors and friends remember Mom as a good friend and role model for children. She paid neighbor children a dime to do chores like emptying her garbage and bringing in the newspaper, inviting them in afterward to visit with her over a cup of cocoa.

I met Belle right after we moved from Ohio to California. We moved to the same apartment complex that Belle had lived in for quite a few years. I met her in the laundry room. She was so friendly, and we just talked and became instant friends. I sort of adopted her as my second mother (my mother had passed away). We included her in all of our family gatherings, and all the family just loved her. I remember one Christmas she came to our house (we had moved out of the apartment complex into our new home by this time) and all the family was there. My brother-in-law, Joe, had a Christmas tree lot each year and he hired Mexicans to work in the lot. Well, he brought one fellow with him to our house, and this fellow could not speak English and he could not read or write. Belle talked to him and gave him a book on how to read. I know he could not understand her, but she just talked to him and encouraged him to learn to read and he really listened to her. I hope that he used her book and learned how to read—that would really have pleased Belle.

Belle was her own Welcome Wagon. Everyone that moved anywhere near her she would go to greet them and welcome them. She always took them a roll of Scott towels (they had to be Scott towels— no other kind would do!) and some other food items that she had. She had so many friends and everyone loved her. She loved children, and everywhere we went if she saw a child she had to stop and talk to that child—no matter what age, color, or nationality. Belle loved her family and always talked about them. I watched over Belle for about nine years and God truly blessed me with a true, loving, loyal friend. The one thing that will always stay in my mind that Belle said was: "Be kind to one another." She was always kind to everyone and everyone loved her. I have truly lost a one-of-a-kind friend that I found in Belle. I loved her very much and I shall never forget her. Rest in peace, my dear, loving friend Belle!—Linda Giammarinaro

For many years my sister, Marta, who never married, lived with Mom. My children and I lived in Chicago, far away from the woman they called "Hookie." The nickname surfaced in 1965, when my daughter, Kim, was two. Mom had just returned from Hawaii and we were driving her home from the airport. Mom was in the back seat, trying to keep Kim occupied by showing her the Hawaiian "Hookie Lau" dance, which Mom had recently learned. For the rest of her life, Kim and Ian and even many customers called Mom "Hookie."

My daughter and son married and started their own families in Chicago, so we seldom saw Mom. But my children and grandchildren brought her great joy in the last years of her life. We kept her up-to-date with photos and phone calls, and she loved hearing the stories my children and I told her about our day-to-day lives. She wrote them letters and enclosed small tokens and articles she knew they would enjoy. She had an especially close relationship with my son, Ian. They wrote to each other often for many years.

Mom carries on the family reading tradition with her first great-grandchild, Nicole, in 1987.

As in her younger years, Mom continued to play the piano. Though the nimbleness was gone due to severe arthritis, her playing always sounded great to my children and me. In 1994, when she was eighty-three, Mom read an article by Ozzie Roberts, a columnist for the *San Diego Union Tribune,* about a poor black youngster who aspired to be a pianist but couldn't afford the sheet music. She packed up her classical piano music—her cherished collection of Shermer Music Library sheet music that her stepfather bought for her when she was a girl—and gave it to the boy.

Roberts subsequently interviewed Mom as well as her neighbors. He found that in her eighteen years as a resident of her complex, new generations of kids had come to think of her as part of their extended family. "Children are the hope of the world," Mom would always say. "They should know that."

In his article, Roberts asked her how she felt about Thomas Gunn. "I felt sorry for that kid," Mom told him. "If he had been raised in a good family and had one nice thing happen to him, he would have turned around. I could never hate that young man. He was a terribly troubled youngster and no one ever showed him they cared. If he had grown up around me, he'd never have done such a terrible thing."

She told Roberts how she and Dad were really at home in the store and she wanted people to remember her most for being herself.

"I truly believe that the good things that people do live forever," she said. "It was never about the money. It was all about the people. We made a living by the grace of God and we made thousands of friends."

Mom corresponded with hundreds of former customers for many years. She also stayed in touch with people she knew from her days in Joliet, including her protégé, Dorothy Mavrich. Mom had inspired Dorothy to teach piano to hundreds of students, a career that lasted fifty years. Dorothy also wrote a children's book titled *Why Not? A Journey through Music Land!*

Dorothy taught at the Joliet Conservatory, across the street from the Rubens Rialto Square Theatre, built in 1926. With its marble arches, Corinthian-column rotunda, crystal chandelier, and grand pipe organ, the domed theater was dubbed by many the most beautiful in the nation. In the 1970s the Rialto was showing its age. Dorothy decided to preserve the theater as a performing-arts center for future generations. She started a grass-roots movement, attracting $500,000 in state appropriations to purchase the theater.

With Dorothy at the helm as president of the Rialto Square Arts Association, the Rialto reopened in 1981. The $6 million restoration revealed the theater's former architectural splendor—so much so that when Liberace performed at a benefit the following year, he remarked to Dorothy, "Now here's a theater to match my clothes!"

Dorothy's friendship with Mom continued throughout their lives. There was always a bond between them, much greater than that between teacher and student. I renewed my relationship with Dorothy before Mom died, and we have become great pals during the writing of this book.

As time went on, Mom's memory began to fail. Her stories about the store became confused with family stories. Yet she clearly remembered the wonderful customers, their names, how they looked, even what they had purchased. She remembered children's names and the good times she and Dad created for them at Wee Folks.

But she could never forget the horror of my father's murder. On the night of February 6, 1970, and every night thereafter, Mom went to bed with the light on and, without Dad by her side, never slept lying down. When she died in March 1999, at the age of eighty-seven, she was laid to rest right where she belonged, next to Dad at Chicago's Westlawn Jewish Cemetery.

Caryn Lazar Amster

I never had a chance to say goodbye to Dad. I never had a chance to thank him for the little Matchbox cars he gave my son and for fixing my plumbing and for always being there for me. I didn't cry when he was killed. I didn't cry for an entire year. Then one day I was assembling a trike for my son. It wasn't going well. Where was Daddy? I sat on the floor and bawled for hours.

After Dad's death, I had quite a few jobs. My first, as a bacteriologist for Armour Dial, was followed by several more: as an assistant in a firm that developed a bacteriological testing method for hospitals; as a marketing specialist for Chicago's Mount Sinai Hospital; as a professional development officer for Happiday Centers for developmentally disabled adults; as a syndicated columnist for Star Newspapers in south suburban Chicago; as a shopping center manager and marketing director for real estate developers; and, for the past several years, as owner and CEO of a marketing, planning, and consulting firm. I have become a professional speaker and trainer on marketing, public relations, and trade show issues and the author of nationally published feature articles in trade magazines.

I remarried in 1982 and continue to live in the Chicago area near my children, Kim and Ian, and my grandchildren, Allison, Matthew, and Nicole. I am also close to my husband's children, Ellen and Michael. I am proud of them all.

Wee Folks

Wee Folks closed twenty-five years after it opened. I have not gone back to 79th Street. Others who have returned describe it

An abandoned Wee Folks, 1972.

as a desolate place with many vacant stores. The Wee Folks building is closed and tired-looking. That's fitting, I think. What could replace Wee Folks? These days, new residents are slowly rejuvenating the area, infusing it with new money in hopes of restoring South Shore's past glory. I hope it continues, but in my heart I know the neighborhood will never be the same.

Wee Folks was the celebration of everything that was good about South Shore and the 1950s and 1960s in America: honesty, sincerity, a willingness to work hard, a love of all types of people. Thousands of children, now adults in their fifties and sixties, still remember Mr. and Mrs. Wee Folks, the charm of the store, and those special toys they once loved. "In some small way I hope I can give back a little something for all your parents gave to the children of South Shore," a former customer said recently. "The day Mr. Wee Folks was shot was, for many of us, the day that South Shore died."

Jewish tradition says that people are not dead as long as someone remembers them. Well, I will always remember my mom and my dad. Mom gave me and my children and most anyone else who touched her life the benefit of her years and world experience. To everyone else, Dad may have been the Pied Piper of South Shore, but to me, he was the guy who set up our train on Christmas morning, the guy with the bad back who gave my children piggyback rides. I dearly wish my grandchildren could have known "Toy Toy," the name their parents gave Dad.

My parents set a huge example for me, one I didn't emulate very well in my early years. I think I'm doing much better now. Mom thought so too. It meant so much to me when she took me aside before she died to tell me how proud she was of me and what a star I had become. I know Dad would have been proud of me too.

I will always remember my parents as people who worked hard and tried to make a difference. As I remember those years, I will always see Mom in her schoolteacher's smock with the big pockets and her white nurse's oxfords, scurrying down an aisle to help a customer find just the right toy or standing steady at the counter to console, encourage, and inspire a new generation of youngsters. I will always see Dad, a baggy-pants Santa, stuffing boxes with toys on Christmas Eve for delivery all over South Shore. I can still see his crooked smile and his twinkling brown eyes when he would say excitedly to a little boy or girl, "Want to see what just came in?"

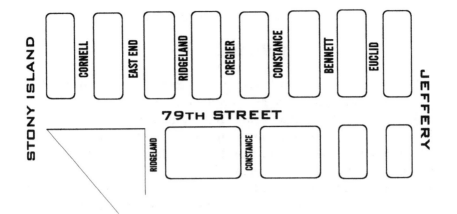

APPENDIX I

Remembering 79th Street

IN WRITING THIS BOOK, I was asked by so many former South Shore customers and neighbors to compile a who's who of 79th Street people and places that I felt compelled to oblige. What follows are my best efforts to re-create 79th Street between Jeffery Boulevard and Stony Island Avenue from 1945 to 1970. The information comes from my library research about South Shore, and your memories and mine of the neighborhood. Tracking accurate and complete information was challenging. During those decades, dozens of stores closed and others moved in. If I have incorrectly listed names, addresses, or dates, or left out the name of your favorite store or storeowner, it wasn't my intention. I invite you to visit my Web site (www.chicagospiedpiper.com) and leave me corrections or additions under "Contact Us."

On the following pages, I hope you'll find some mention of your school, place of worship, favorite stores, and, most important, memories of those great days. This trip down memory lane is for you, former South Shoreites. For those of you who lived outside our neighborhood, our city, or our state, welcome to our world.

GROWING UP

When I was a kid, my world started and ended on 79th Street. That stretch between Stony Island Avenue and Jeffery Boulevard was a safe place to ride my bike, walk from Constance to Horace Mann Elementary at lunchtime, and stop for a sandwich at the bowling alley. I remember the school patrol boys on Jeffery who watched out for us as cars going south made the right turn from Jeffery onto 79th. For a while, I received twenty-five cents a week for walking Art O'Connor to school. Later, I walked from East End to South Shore High School.

In 1950, the population of South Shore was more than 79,000, almost exclusively whites of Russian, German, Swedish, and English descent. The neighborhood belonged to the 8th Ward, and Einar Johnson was our alderman. By 1967, the population was 90,000, including many nonwhites, with more than 8,700 children attending area schools. By 1970, the street had changed dramatically and so had the stores. During the turbulent 1960s, many white owners moved out, but many, like my parents, stayed. For a long time, 79th and Stony Island was the black/white boundary, and Jeffery was near the synagogues and Jewish Community Center.

In those days, most people lived in three-flat or six-flat buildings. Some apartment buildings had retail stores on the ground level and store owners often lived above their businesses. Larger complexes had twenty-five to thirty units or more. All the buildings were brick. If you weren't an apartment dweller, you may have lived in a brick bungalow or a Lake Shore Drive high-rise. Occasionally you'd see a merchant or a family tending a Victory Garden in a vacant lot next to a store or a small lawn around back. I was often caught picking flowers for my mom on the same block as our first Wee Folks store on Constance. Even as a kid, I was impressed by the area's manicured grass and flowerbeds. In later years, those lovely gardens became parking lots.

During those years, Officer Troy Yates protected the merchants. He was promoted from our beat, but kept his hand on the pulse of the neighborhood and tried to keep it from decaying. I'm sure he was well aware of the infamous folks who lived in the big houses in our neighborhood. Jake "Greasy Thumb" Gusik, the alleged financial expert behind Al Capone, lived on Luella. Murray "the Camel" Humphreys had a house on Bennett.

Seventy-ninth Street had everything. In one trip, we could have our car serviced and gassed, drop off our shoes for repair, get our hair cut or curled, pick up groceries, order a Sunday roast at the butcher's, make a deposit at the bank, and add to our Christmas Club at the savings and loan. If we needed a break or the kids got cranky, we could eat a Danish at the bakery, sip a Green River at the soda fountain, or nosh a pastrami on rye at the deli. Everything could be repaired, replaced, and cleaned on 79th—radios, toasters, shoes, hearing aids, furniture, and clothes. Every part or tool for every handyman chore was available at the hardware store.

If we were on a budget, we went to Woolworth's five-and-dime. If we were strapped for cash, we visited the pawnshop. If we were flush, upscale stores beckoned with fine clothing, shoes, and sporting goods. Florists made our homes look more beautiful and so did home interiors shops, which carried furniture, drapes, lamps, paint, and wallpaper. We could have our film developed at the camera shop or pick up the latest color yarn at the embroidery shop. To satisfy kids' cravings, candy stores and small food marts sold a dizzying array of sweets.

Women loved visiting the millinery shops and corsetieres. If they were too tired to cook, there was always Chinese takeout or Italian pizza. Men could stop on the way home from work at one of the local taverns and pick up the evening paper at newsstands on 79th at Jeffery or Stony Island. Dancing schools and civic organizations, as well as the South Shore Country Club, offered activities and recreation. In the 1950s and 1960s, members enjoyed swimming, riding, parties, and special events in the club's grand ballroom and peaceful solarium. The stately lakefront club, now on the National Register of Historic Places, became the South Shore Cultural Center in 1973. Jews weren't welcome in my day, so I never went in, but now everyone can enjoy its golf course and beach as well as plays, concerts, art gallery, dance and piano lessons, and celebrations such as Kwanzaa, African American Heritage Month, and Hispanic Heritage Month.

The neighborhood's doctors, dentists, podiatrists, and pharmacists all kept us well. You could go from cradle to grave on 79th Street. Our Lady of Peace Catholic Church, Protestant churches, and Jewish temples were nearby. So were the funeral homes.

And if you were moving out of the neighborhood, there was a trailer rental and lots of helpful realtors, at least until the latter part of the 1960s, when their intentions changed.

SCHOOLS

Grammar/Elementary Schools
Akiba Jewish Day School–6740 South Shore Drive
Bradwell Elementary–77th and Burnham
Bryn Mawr Elementary–73rd and Jeffery
Faulkner School for Girls–7112 Coles
Horace Mann Elementary–8050 Chappel
O'Keefe Elementary–69th and Merrill
Our Lady of Peace Elementary–7850 Chappel
Parkside Elementary–69th and East End
St. Bride's Elementary–7765 Coles
St. Constantine's and Helen School–73rd and Stony Island
St. Michael's Elementary–8215 South Shore Drive
St. Phillip Neri Elementary–2110 East 72nd
Thomas Hoyne Public Elementary School–89th and Crandon

High Schools
Aquinas Dominican High School–2100 East 72nd
Bowen High School–2710 East 89th Street
Hyde Park High School–6220 Stony Island
South Shore High School–7627 Constance

PLACES OF WORSHIP

Synagogues and Temples
Congregation Agudath Achim–7933 Yates
Congregation Anshe Kanesses Israel–2357 East 75th Street
Congregation B'nai Bezalel–7649 Phillips
Congregation B'nai Yehudah–8201 Jeffery
Congregation Beth Am–the People's Synagogue–7133 Coles
Congregation Beth Joseph–1508 East 70th Street
Congregation Habonim–7550 Phillips
South Shore Temple–7215 Jeffery
South Side Hebrew Congregation–7359 Chappel
Torah Synagogue–75th and Yates (temporary location)

Churches
Bethany Lutheran Church–92nd and Jeffery
Bryn Mawr Community Church–7000 South Jeffery
Calvary Baptist–2309 East 80th
Eighteenth Church–Christian Science–7262 Coles

Our Lady of Peace Church–7851 South Jeffery
Reformation Lutheran Church–80th and Jeffery
St. Bride's–7809 South Coles
St. Constantine and Helen's–7351 Stony Island (later became NOI mosque)
St. John's Methodist–7350 Jeffery
St. Luke's Lutheran–1843 East 77th
St. Margaret's–2555 East 73rd
St. Phillip Neri–2132 East 72nd
Southfield Methodist–1750 East 78th Street
South Shore Bible Church–7159 Cornell
South Shore Community–7401 Yates
South Shore Presbyterian–2824 East 76th
Windsor Park Lutheran–2619 East 76th
Zion Lutheran Church–85th and Stony Island

CIVIC/COMMUNITY ORGANIZATIONS

American Jewish Congress, Stephen Wise Chapter
Arche Club
B'nai B'rith, Henry Horner Lodge #1585
B'nai B'rith, Richard E. Gudstadt, Lodge #1214
Book of the Hour Club
Boy Scouts
Bryn Mawr Women's Club
Chelten-Yates Association
D.A.R. Henry Purcell Chapter
Daughters of Isabell, South Shore Circle #76
Garden Club of South Shore
Girl Scouts
Grand Crossing Improvement Association
Henry Hart Jewish Community Center
Junior Achievement
Kiwanis Club of Southeast Area
Knights of Columbus, St. Phillip Neri, #1846 Council
League of Women Voters
National Council of Jewish Women, South Shore chapter
79th Street Business Men's Association
Southfield Merchants Association
Southmoor Community Council
South Shore Center of Infant Welfare Society
South Shore Chamber of Commerce
South Shore Commission–7921 South Exchange

South Shore County Club
South Shore Hadassah
South Shore Historical Society
South Shore Improvement Association
South Shore Lions Club
South Shore Women's ORT
South Side Catholic Women's Club
Swedish Club, South Side
United Order of True Sisters
Young Men's Jewish Council–76th and Phillips

GETTING THERE!

Chicago Surface Lines

The Chicago Surface Lines ran the East 79th Street streetcars starting in 1908. They were red-and-cream-colored electric railcars made mostly of wood; a clanging bell signaled their approach. One trolley pole rode under an electric wire carrying 600 volts; several are still in place along 79th Street. The rails are buried beneath the pavement. Route East 79 ran from 79th and Western to 79th and Brandon.

Until the Great Depression, the motormen and the conductors who collected fares wore heavy double-breasted blue uniforms with black silk railroad caps and white shirts with black tie. The Surface Line uniform became the standard uniform of the Chicago Transit Authority, which now manages the city's bus and train systems. The CTA added its own buttons and badges, plus a light blue stripe down the leg. The CTA blue uniform became gray in 1968 and wasn't changed until 1986. The East 79th Street line was converted to bus in the early 1950s.

In 1958, city planners saw that a link to the south was a vital component. City officials thought they had the authority to build a toll road, only to find that wasn't true. But they could build a toll bridge. The resulting **Chicago Skyway** is a 7.8-mile elevated expressway classified as a half-mile toll bridge with approaches totaling 7.3 miles in length. Today, the Chicago Skyway connects to the Dan Ryan Expressway (the primary north/south expressway on the South Side of Chicago) on the west and the Indiana Tollway (Interstate 80) on the east. The Skyway had a 79th Street entrance, and the intersection of 79th and Stony Island was to become one of the busiest traffic spots in Chicago in the late 1950s.

The Illinois Central Railroad

The Illinois Central Railroad connected us all. The IC started as a branch built in the 1800s. It was electrified in 1926 as part of the improvements to the entire IC suburban operation. Some of today's station platforms date back to 1900. The seats on the one-floor train cars were made of rattan, a cane weave glued to canvas. The old stations had coal stoves in the warming houses. Incandescent bulbs with white glass shades lighted the car. A two-car train had a conductor and engineer. A four-car train had a conductor, engineer, and flagman. Uniforms for conductors and collectors had gold trim; for flagmen, silver trim. All had IC initials on their coat collars. Crew sizes were reduced in 1966 with the inauguration of automatic fare collection. The uniforms were changed in 1971. My father, Robert Markovitz, an artist, did the illustration that appeared on the cover of the old IC timetables.

The South Shore area stops from the beginning have been: Stony Island, Bryn Mawr (Jeffery), South Shore, Windsor Park (75th), Cheltenham (79th), 83rd, 87th, and South Chicago. During the rush hour, trains ran every seven minutes. During the off-hours, they ran every half-hour until 1963 and, after that, every twenty minutes. Due to decreasing demand, the service was reduced in the 1970s to hourly.

The stations fell into disrepair in 1967 when automated fare collection replaced agents. Around 1970, the stations were painted and the roofs were replaced in the 1990s.—*Mitch Markovitz*

TOY STORES

Visits to Wee Folks often came on the heels of a show at the Avalon Theater or a visit to the Pete's Karmelkorn and Sweet Shop. But our store wasn't the only toy shop in the area in the 1950s and 1960s. The competition was friendly, with stores often assisting each other in fulfilling a customer's special request.

Acme Cycle & Hobby (2520 East 79th Street) sold bikes, trikes, and other wheeled goods and had a large hobby selection.
Bo-Peep Juvenile Furniture–2549 East 75th
Foot Toy Store–6843 South Stony Island
King Cole–2535 East 79th
Lullaby Lane Furniture (2223 West 95th) specialized in children's furniture.

Nadler's Kiddyland–1370 East 53rd
Tiny Tots Juvenile Furniture–2045 East 71st

South Shore Spots off 79th Street

While much of what we needed could be had from Stony Island to Jeffery on 79th, other great experiences were close by.

Alice's Dry Goods (79th and Clyde) was open in the 1950s.

Alpert's Deli (79th and Essex) was across the street from Baron's Shoe Store.

Bidwell Stadium on East 79th was the place for sporting events.

Blinski U Haul Rental Trucks and Trailers (7358 South Stony Island) is where you went when you were moving in or out or friends were getting or giving you their old furniture.

Burny Brothers Bakery (2007 East 71st Street) was my employer briefly when I was sixteen.

Cadet Monogram and Card Shop (2103 East 79th) monogrammed high school letter sweaters. In those days girls put their first name's initial on their cardigans.

Carl's Red Hots (Stony Island and South Chicago Avenues) was the place where "everything on it" meant just that: onions, chili, sauerkraut, pickle relish, ketchup, mustard, you name it. In the 1960s a quarter bought you a hot dog with fries. The same family still operates Carl's.

Cash Erler's Photo Shop (1540 East 83rd) sold cameras and film and printed a lot of the photos of yesteryear. Several people became professional photographers because of their early experiences at Erler's. Curt Erler, who lived with his parents and seven siblings above the store, recalls the old brass National Cash Register.

Celander's Photography (2541 East 79th) closed in 1970, but for twenty years before, Hugh and Marian Celander documented South Shore from their small studio, which was a member of the South Shore Camera Club. Their son, Charles, has brought back memories of the past in his book *Chicago's South Shore*. That book inspired me to write this book.

Chicago Public Library (73rd and Exchange) boasted lovely Tudor architecture and was the biggest and best library in the area.

Circus Nursery (2059 East 79th) was a special favorite of my folks, who were best of friends with owners Bill and Harriet Grady.

Coral Furniture–2042 East 79th

Cunis Ice Cream (2500 East 79th at Kingston) was *the* place for a hot fudge sundae, homemade candy, and caramel apples.

Dick's Home Furnishings–2105 East 79th

Essex Jewelers (2448 East 79th) was destroyed by the same fire that burned down Baron's Shoes in 1957.

Fire departments included **Engine Company #126** (7313 Kingston Avenue) and **Hook and Ladder Company #49, Engine Company #72, and Squad #5** (7980 South Chicago Avenue).

General merchandise stores like **Sears Roebuck & Company** (1334 East 79th) and **Chicago's Last Department Store** (10468 South Indianapolis Boulevard) started springing up in the 1950s.

Gordon's Pet Shop (2538 East 79th) carried small pets, from hamsters to kittens, but the real attraction was the mammoth snake in the window. Mr. Gordon would put a drape over the snake's cage at feeding time because the sight freaked out the moms.

Guarantee National Bank (6760 South Stony Island) and **South Shore National** (7054 South Jeffery) each had walkup and driveup windows.

Hackl's Bakery–South Chicago Avenue

Hazel Dry Goods–2015 East 79th

Hi-Low Food Store–76th and Stony Island

Jackson Park Hospital–7531 South Stony Island

Jewel Food Store–75th and Crandon (in the 1960s)

Kiddieland (on 95th) was a favorite spot for many kids in the fifites.

Lazar Drug Store (Dad's cousins) was the place to rent cold steam vaporizers and have your purchases delivered. After a fire in 1957 the pharmacy became **Rosenbloom's Drug Store.**

Lillian Apparel Shop (2610 East 79th) carried women's clothing and **Estelle's Lingerie** (2516 East 79th) sold purses, hosiery, blouses, and skirts.

Mall Tool (79th at Stony Island and South Chicago Avenues) was the industrial addition to our street.

Mel Turner & Son Auto Repair–1441 East 79th

Mitchell's Ice Cream Shop made great chocolate malts.

Nate's Leather Shop (2506 East 79th) was owned by Nate Chernoff.

National Tea Company Grocery Store–1312 East 79th

Patricia's Dress Shop

Leslie M. Price Realtor–6826 Stony Island

The Overflow (79th and Lake Michigan) was as far east as you went on 79th. From this lake overlook you could see the white-hot flames as they poured slag at U.S Steel's South Works. Mostly it was a make-out spot. More teens hung out there than at the drive-in.

Police departments included **10th District Grand Crossing Station** (834 East 75th) and **8th District South Chicago Station** (2938 East 89th).

Republic Steel–South Chicago Avenue

Shoe Stores

Baron's Shoe Store (2458 East 79th Street) is the place I got my new Tom McAnn "Snap Jacks" and where I thought Buster Brown lived with his dog, Tide. Baron's had big fluoroscope machines to accurately measure feet. A fire destroyed the store in 1957. Other shoe stores were **Sam Devine Shoes** (509 East 79th Street) for Jumping Jacks, **Newman's Bootery** (6720 South Stony Island) for Pied Piper shoes, and **Schoen Boot Shop** (7903 South Cottage Grove) for Red Cross nurse's shoes for women.

The Southmoor Hotel (67th and Stony Island) was the place for proms, parties, and other special events in the 1950s and 1960s.

South Shore YMCA (1833 East 71st), built in 1955, housed a pool, day camp, recreational activities, and the High School Hi-Y and Tri-Hi-Y groups.

St. Constantine's and Helen Greek Orthodox Church (73rd and Stony Island), built in 1953, was a gorgeous building whose stained-glass windows and altar were memorable for their grandure and vivid colors. I attended occasional services there with Greek friends. In 1972 the church became the **Nation of Islam's Temple No. 2.**

The **Thunderbird Motel** (75th and South Shore Drive) had an unforgettable wing-like marquee.

United States Post Office–2207 East 75th

Van's Cycle & Model Shop–2216 East 75th

WGN Flag Company (7984 South Chicago Avenue) made American flags in all sizes, including ones that flew over the White House. Carl Porter Jr. now runs the company with semiretired owner Carl Porter Sr.

White Castle (79th and Essex) was nicknamed the Porcelain Palace.

EATING OUT

We had the best eating places either in South Shore or just a short ride away.

Sit-Down Restaurants
The Alamo Restaurant–2137 East 71st

Alexander Steak House (3010 East 79th–79th and the Lake) served my favorite garlic salad dressing (I've found nothing better), which they dabbed on toasted bread ovals topped with a halved shrimp and an anchovy. Those hors d'oeuvres went well with cocktails but didn't fill you up. Urban legend has it that the Brandy Alexander was invented here. Peter and Anastasia Alexander owned the restaurant from 1959 to 1978. Their daughter Danae remembers visits to the restaurant when she was very young, sneaking behind the long walnut bar and munching on maraschino cherries.

Bon Ton Restaurant–79th and Colfax

The Martinique (2500 West 94th) in Evergreen Park was perfect for special occasions.

Mickleberry's Log Cabin (2300 West 95th) served chicken dinners that Dad liked.

My Little Margie's Café–1351 East 79th (opposite Sears)

The Pancake House (79th and Cornell), across the street from the Avalon Theater, served Silver Dollar Pancakes. The Pancake House also owned **Rex's Restaurant** (79th and Exchange) and eventually opened the **Golden West Pancake House** in Evergreen Park.

The Patio–1951 East 71st

The Sabre Room–in Oak Lawn

Phil Schmidt's (1205 Calumet, Whiting, Indiana) was worth the drive for the all-you-can-eat fried chicken and lake perch. Dad loved their frog legs. A relish tray of cottage cheese, beets, potato salad, and celery and carrot sticks started off each meal. The place was huge, with several connected dining rooms. The decor was quintessential gaudy fifties. We waited in endless lines to get in, even with reservations. If your party was large, you could get a private dining room.

Frank Sylvano's Restaurant–9156 South Stony Island

Timberland–7843 South Cottage Grove

Tropical Hut (1320 East 57th) was a frequent stop after visits to the Museum of Science and Industry.

The Walnut Room at Marshall Field's (State and Madison Streets in downtown Chicago) was a special place to head after Thanksgiving. All dressed up, Mom and I would ride the IC, walk past the store's grand Christmas tree in the atrium, and take the elevator to the restaurant, where carolers sang. The kids' menu offered chicken croquettes, with cloves for "eyes" and mashed potatoes covered with yellow chicken gravy.

Delis

Rib Hill (9129 South Jeffery) was the place for a quick burger and fries. After a fire and major remodeling, it became **Mel Markon's,** a great Jewish deli. Mel Markon's had the best matzo ball soup and corned beef sandwiches anywhere. Other delis included **Herman's** (95th and Jeffery), the **Shoreland** (2238 East 71st), and the **Kingston** (2523 East 79th). **Tula and Gus's Deli,** a non-kosher deli, wrapped its meat in double wax paper.

Drive-In Restaurants and Soda Shops

Art's Drive-In (86th and Stony), with its carhops on roller skates, was a big hangout place for the high-school set. Folks also drove into **Art's, Bob & Jack's, The Pit,** and **Carl's** for real food, grease and all. **Jodee's Boomerang Burgers** (on 95th) had burgers in the shape of a boomerang. **Moishe Pippic's** is fondly remembered.

Melody Lane (1425 West 87th), a large sweet shop, was famous for its Rocket Sundaes. **Topps** made a sundae so big it was called the "Mile-High." If you could eat the whole thing, it was free! **Gaety's** (Commercial Avenue & 92nd) offered mouth-watering candies and ice cream as well as chocolate phosphates.

Pizza

Avalon Park Pizzeria (1324 East 79th), **Giovanni's Pizza** (79th and Phillips), across from Mickey D's, **The Tom-Tom,** which later became the **Roman Holiday Pizza** (77th and Exchange), and **Joe's Pizza** (79th and Exchange), next to the Cheltenham theater, were favorite Friday-night hangouts. In addition to pizza, **Bob and Jack's** (87th and Bennett) served Italian beef sandwiches with lots of green peppers. There were also **Geno's Pizza** (on 87th) and **Pasquale's** (South Chicago).

Takeout

Chicken Delite (75th and Saginaw) had a motto: "Don't cook tonight, call Chicken Delite." Other restaurants include **Hil-Jo's Swedish Restaurant** (79th and Manistee), which had a great Sunday smorgasbord.

Hot Dog Pit (95th and Jeffery) had The Scotty, The Boxer, and other hot dogs named after various breeds. Cheez Whiz topped all the cheeseburgers.

Bars and Liquor Stores

The Ambassador Club–2526 East 79th
Avalon Tap–8055 South Cottage Grove
Chelton Liquors–2900 East 79th
O'Toole's Tom Tap–2411 East 79th

ENTERTAINMENT

The **Rhodes Theater** (538–44 East 79th), along with the **Hamilton Theater** (2150 East 71st) and the **Avalon Theater** (on 79th), were South Shore landmarks for movies and making out. The Rhodes and the Hamilton were demolished, and the Regal Theater, formerly the Avalon, has closed its doors. The neighborhood put up a valiant but unsuccessful fight to preserve the Avalon as the cultural center of the area, offering big-name entertainment. The **Starlite Drive-In** (6401 95th Street) in Oak Lawn was another great make-out spot.

SERVICES

Barbershops and Beauty Salons

Armando and Salvador–2447 East 79th
Clyde's Barbershop–2103 ½ East 79th
Grace's Beauty Shop–2309 East 79th

House of Glamour–2447 East 79ᵗʰ

Looking Glass Salon was a favorite place to get your hair done for the prom or other formal dances.

Cleaners
Care Cleaners–2533 East 79ᵗʰ
Charles Furuyama–2705 East 79ᵗʰ
Imperial–2233 East 79ᵗʰ
Kleanerette–2239 East 79ᵗʰ
Oak Cleaners–2101 East 79ᵗʰ

Currency Exchange
Steel City Currency Exchange (2433 East 79ᵗʰ) cashed checks for the thousands of steel workers from the many plants just to our east, including **the U.S. Steel South Works Plant** (79ᵗʰ and Lake Michigan to the Calumet River).

Funeral Homes and Florists
Piser Funeral Home (69ᵗʰ and Stony Island) was one of four places where many South Shoreites were given their last visitation. Others were **Tews** (on 79ᵗʰ), **Donellan** (7651 South Jeffery), whose undertaker held wakes in people's homes, and **Drumm** (2035 East 79ᵗʰ). Each used several area florists: **Weberg's Flowers** (78ᵗʰ and Jeffery), **Keslik** (2106 East 79ᵗʰ), **South Shore Floral** (7600 South Jeffery), and **Johnson Florist** (2702 East 79ᵗʰ), also called **Holiday Florist.**

SOUTH SHORE
(79ᵗʰ Street from Jeffery to Stony Island Avenues)

Some of these spots were around in the 1950s and some in the 1960s, often in the same location.

Jeffery going west to Euclid (1960–1900 East 79ᵗʰ)
Our Lady of Peace Catholic Church (2000 East 79ᵗʰ) burned in the late 1950s, and it is said that several girls died in the blaze. After that, students always wondered if fire drills were worthwhile.

Shapiro's Drug Store (1958 E. 79ᵗʰ) was owned by Morrie (the pharmacist) and Minnie Shapiro. The store had a soda fountain. Their children were Karen and Neal.

79ᵗʰ Street and Jeffery Newsstand (in front of Shapiro's Drug Store) was run by Adeline, a grouchy woman on crutches, and a man named Bill. As the story goes, Adeline was struck by a car and crippled after having pulled a child from its path. Open 365 days a year, the newsstand did big business. They sold copies of *Forward,* a Yiddish newspaper. Who doesn't remember waiting in line on foot or in a car for a paper, especially on Sundays? In cold weather, Adeline and Bill wore fur-lined leather overalls and snowsuits worthy of Admiral Byrd on expedition. You took a paper and dropped the coins in a dish or gave it to Adeline's assistant, when she had one. Rumor has it that Bill, who was probably her brother, was the corner bookie who paid off bets in the basement of the Pla-Mor Bowling Alley across the street. Bill and Adeline owned several apartment buildings on Jeffery, north of 79th.

Hi-Low Grocery Store–79th and Jeffery

Jeffery Coin Operated Dry Cleaners–1957 East 79th (in the 1960s)

David Weber Cleaners (1956 East 79th) boasted "the Man Who Knows," a fellow who specialized in furs and wedding gowns in the 1960s.

The Pleasant Shop (1952 East 79th) was owned by the Ginsberg family.

The Jewel Tea Company grocery store (1946 East 79th) installed an electric eye in the 1960s that automatically opened the doors. You could activate it as you walked by.

Andree's Beauty Salon–1944 East 79th (in the 1960s)

Brandt's Women's Store for Ladies and Children (1942 East 79th, between Jeffery and Euclid) was owned by the Rosenbaum family. One patron remembers that while trying on clothes, the owner said something to the effect that if that was not adorable, her name was not Mrs. Brandt. To Mrs. Rosenbaum's surprise, the woman's youngster piped up, "But your name *isn't* Mrs. Brandt!"

Marie's Millinery Shop (on 79th, west of Shapiro's Drug Store) was next door to a barbershop that did big business on Saturdays. People also recalled a butcher shop and a men's store just west of Jeffery on 79th.

Jeffery Pub–1938 East 79th

Allied Inventory–1916 East 79th

Bennett Hand Laundry–1912 East 79th

Lawrence Interiors (1910 East 79th) had a manager by the name of Bert Cohen.

James Hair Salon–1902 ½ East 79th

Moline's Candy Store was across from Our Lady of Peach Church. They had special deals for Our Lady of Peace students.

Certified Grocery Store (79th and Jeffery), across from Our Lady of Peace Church, was owned by a Mrs. Rooney, who, as legend has it, paid the passage of young girls from Ireland to America. One day, one of these relatively unsophisticated girls staying with Mrs. Rooney was helping with the housework, but was afraid to plug in the vacuum because she never had used electricity before and was afraid it would jump out of the plug and hurt her. I believe Certified later became a **Hi-Low Food Store.**

The Jeffery Restaurant (79th and Jeffery) was great for hamburgers.

Custards Last Stand (at Jeffery and 79th)—or **Tastee Freeze,** depending on whom you ask—built a minimall in 1963 at the southwest corner of 79th and Jeffery.

Spots going west between Euclid and Bennett (1900–1850 East 79th)

Crest Sporting Goods (79th and Euclid) was across from the bowling alley, and may have been owned or operated by the Ruthsteins. Formerly a hunting spot, it was the place where most people bought their South Shore High School gym equipment and gym suits (blue shorts with green stripes for boys, ugly green one-piece suits for girls, which tied in back so you looked even more like a sack). The guys bought their letter sweaters here so they could give them to their best girl. I got my Girl's Chorus letter there.

Feldstein's Deli (1900 East 79th) was the place kids loaded up on Sputnik Bubblegum. The owner was a Jewish immigrant and his wife. Some called it "Max's Bagel and Schmear."

The SuDon Shop (between Euclid and Bennett), owned by Gertrude Smith for several years, sold Necchi and Elna sewing machines and fabrics. She also taught sewing-machine classes. The store's name was derived from a combination of the names of Gertrude's two girls.

Stieffel's Lamp Store (on 79th between Euclid and Bennett) allowed us to exchange burned-out light bulbs for new ones at no charge.

A Chinese laundry was between Bennett and Euclid.

A dry cleaner was on the southeast corner of 79th and Euclid.

Pla-Mor Bowling Alley (79th and Euclid) was reportedly owned by Jerry Skovie and his sons. It attracted a lot of regulars whose means of support remains a mystery. In the adjacent empty lot, the bowling alley's foundation jutted out and was a good place to climb up and down on the way to school.

Mama Mia's Pizzeria–79th and Bennett

Horney's Dime Store–79th near Euclid

Shell's Hair Styling Center (1955 East 79th) did permanent waves and high styling in the 1960s.

Grant's Cleaners–1832 East 79th

South Shore Library Branch (on 79th one block west of Jeffery) was a storefront.

Charl-Ed Beauty Salon–1917 East 79th

Wagner Jewelers–1914 East 79th

Preferred Cleaners and Dyers–1913 East 79th

Skyline Barber Shop–79th and Euclid

Dr. M. Hopkins Dental Office was above the dime store.

Spots going west between Bennett and Constance (1860–1832 East 79th)

Crane Brothers' Pharmacy (1860 East 79th), on the northeast corner of Bennett and 79th, had the best sundaes and chocolate phosphates at their soda fountain. Stanley and Meyer Crane were both pharmacists.

Eric the Barber Barbershop (on Bennett, around the corner from Crane's drugstore) was the place where Dad had his hair cut and where he brought my son for his first haircut.

IGA Grocery Store was run by a Greek family.

Avalon Wallpaper and Paint–1854 East 79th

Parisian Beauty Salon–1853 East 79th

Ernie's Lounge–1850 East 79th

Slutsky's Hardware–Morris Slutsky, one of Dad's great friends, was the original Rube Goldberg and could fix anything.

Ruth's Liquors (1842 East 79th) was owned by Henry and Dave Block. Most of their regulars were older neighborhood people and they were all friends. It was more like a neighborhood club than a gin mill. If it was your birthday, you could expect the Blocks to have a cake for you.

Avalon Cleaners–1840 East 79th

Schaider's Deli (two doors east of the first Wee Folks store) sold juice-filled wax treats (among other candies), a particular favorite. Kids would throw the wax all over the sidewalk in front of our store until it was black. Mr. Schaider was a grandfatherly figure.

Wee Folks (1832 East 79th), our first store between 1945 and 1957, became **Betty's Parkette Restaurant.** It sold hamburgers and hot dogs to students from South Shore High School.

Dr. Charles Andreas DDS (1832 East 79th), our family dentist, had offices on the second floor above our store. Kids came into our store after visiting him.

Nick's Shoe Repair was owned by Nick Fotopolos, whose son's name was Trent.

Stores going west between Bennett and Constance (1850–1832 East 79th Street)

Jeffery Liquors–79th and Bennett

Volk Laundry–mid-block on the south side of Bennett

Aidner's Paint and Wallpaper (1837 East 79th Street) was an interior decorating shop that also sold artist's oil colors and canvas. This doublewide store, run by Bert Cohen, was set into the point where East 79th jogged and the north side of the street did not match up with the south side. The south corner of Constance was shifted about seventy feet west.

Dressel's Bakery (1835 East 79th) was across from our first store and run by the Kulovitz family. They sold real whipped-cream cakes. They made cakes for every occasion and delivered.

Artistic Barbershop–1833 East 79th

Tenhoff's Tap–1829 East 79th

Miss Margery's and Miss Evans' Dance Studio (79th and Constance) was on the second floor above Tenhoff's Tap, across from the first Wee Folks.

Sonotone Hearing Aid Store–between Constance and Bennett

Kulzer Jewelry Store–on 79th between Bennett and Creiger

Loretta Rozak School of Dance–from Constance to Bennett

Auto Parts Store–79th and Constance

Stores going west between Constance and Cregier (1830–1750 East 79th Street)

Pendergast's Drug Store (79th and Cregier) sold chocolate phosphates and Green Rivers, made with hand-blended syrups, for fifteen cents apiece at an old-fashioned soda fountain. A display case featured penny candies, and Mr. Pendergast used to give kids free samples. He also gave them empty cigar boxes for storing collections of baseball cards and such. Teens hung out around the display of magazines and paperback books.

Mark's Tailor Shop was above Pendergast's Drug Store.

Paulson's Radio Repair (next door to Pendergast's) was owned by the Paulsons, whose son Bill was a pilot stationed at Glenview Naval Air Station during WWII. He used to fly over 79th Street and wag his wing as a salute.

Bender's Shoe Repair (next to Paulson's) featured Victory Gardens during WWII in the adjacent vacant lot grown by Al Randel and his family (of Alpert's). Later, Al's dad bought the land and made it a parking lot for his store across the street. Bender's later became **Polsky's Tailor and Furrier.**

The Electric Shop, which was near Pendergast's, was run by a very old man. The dusty display window contained old electric fans, radios, and strange electrical things. You could have batteries for early radios and cars charged there. The shop later became a real estate or law office.

A barbershop at 79th and Cregier was run by a fellow who, for many years, lived there and kept a tidy yard out back. He had a great collection of comic books. Neighborhood kids traded with him so he always had new comic books for his customers.

Kenny's Lounge (1823 East 79th) was the place "Where old friends meet for a Tom Collins." The owners either worked with or ran a deli on site, where you could place short orders for food, but had to finish before the 4:00 a.m. closing time.

The Caravel Club (1816 East 79th) was home to the St. Phillip Neri Council Knights of Columbus. They held spaghetti dinners and other functions. They also rented out the facility for wedding receptions and special events.

Avalon Tap (79th and Cregier) was owned by a father and son and closed in 1964.

Grimm Barbershop–1805 East 79th

The Knights of Columbus (79th and Cregier) built a clubhouse at the intersection in 1952.

Cities Service (Citgo) Station (79th and Cregier) was owned by Carl Peterson, who had two sons, Ken and Chuck, and a daughter, Jan.

Phillip's Shoe Repair was across the street and down the block from Wee Folks.

Stores going west between Cregier and Ridgeland (1800–1750 East 79th Street)

Miner Dunn's Restaurant (79th and Ridgeland) was known for shoestring French fries, flat hamburgers with fried edges, and orange sherbet served in a white paper cup. One former customer remembers going there at closing time with his father and receiving a whole pie for a dime. (The restaurant wasn't allowed to keep pies overnight.) After being closed for a time in the 1940s, Miner Dunn's reopened in the late 1950s. In later years, new operators bought the rights to use the name in Illinois, kept with a fifties theme, and closed about 1998.

Tony's Cleaners was owned by Tony Formosa. He had a son, Peter Formosa, who made the deliveries. It is believed that the same family owns a successful Chinese carryout restaurant on 47th.

Al's Food Mart (1747–49 East 79th, just east of Ridgeland) was a beloved convenience-style store, started in 1939 by Al Randel after his many years peddling fruit and vegetables up and down the alleys of South Shore, probably from a horse-drawn wagon. During WWII he brought grandfather Oscar into the business. At first, Al's was open twenty-four hours a day; in later years the store closed at midnight. The atmosphere was old-fashioned, with meat hanging on hooks, sawdust covering the floor, and icy bottles of soda waiting for release from a rack when you fed it coins. Parents in need of the *Red Streak Daily News*, a gallon of milk, or a pack of cigarettes would send their kids to Al's. You could run a tab with Al, pay him on payday, and he delivered. The owner of the kosher deli on 79th and Essex would sneak down to get ham, his children claim. Al's closed in 1969.

William's Beauty Salon–1721 ½ East 79th

Jesselson's Fish Market (south of 79th on Clyde) sold fish for many years.

Stores going west between Ridgeland and East End (1750–1700 East 79th)

St. Moritz Restaurant (later **Lorentzen's Restaurant**)–1732 East 79th

Hy's Grocery Store/Delicatessen (1728 East 79th) was owned by Hyman and Rose Kaplan, who lived next to us on 78th and East End. Their son

Bobby worked at his parents' store, which was known for its blueberry Popsicles. Hy was a good-natured man with a strong Yiddish accent. He was hyper and a bit of a rogue, making fake passes at some of the ladies. He was beaten up and robbed one day on his way to work.

Leek's Barbershop (1704 East 79th) was owned by Preston Leek.

Monarch Hospital Supply–Monarch Rentals (79th and Ridgeland) was owned and operated by Rex Philpot.

A **barbershop** between East End and Ridgeland featured a large aquarium. It was run by a woman named Myrtle, who kept the door locked at all times.

Wee Folks (1708–10 East 79th) was the address of our second store from 1957 to 1970. In its previous life it had been **Guido Matay's Music Store.**

Dan's Barbershop–1704 East 79th

East End Beauty Shop–1702 East 79th

Chinese takeout place–79th and East End

Gross Electric–79th and East End

Dave's Beauty Shop–1723 East 79th

William's Beauty Salon–1721 ½ East 79th

Spots going west between East End and Cornell (1700–1650 East 79th Street)

Heller's Drug Store (79th and East End) was eventually sold by Mr. Heller to Joseph Harrill and Maurice Hebert, who bought another store at 75th and Stony. Hebert was killed in a private plane crash in late 1974. Harrill sold the business to an employee of the East 79th Street store named Ernest Watkins. Watkins didn't have a pharmacy but called the business Ernest Drug/Sundries.

Vogue Florist, across the street from the Avalon, was owned by Joan Gruber, wife of the president of Gateway National Bank. A former employee tells the tale of his first day on the job, when Joan sent him on a delivery to a hotel on State Street in the Loop (downtown). He had just obtained his driver's license and had driven a stick shift but twice. It was almost seven o'clock before he returned. He thought he would be fired, but he ended up working for her for another six months.

Connolly's Beauty Shop–across from the Avalon

The Pancake House–across the street from the Avalon in later years

Tally-Ho Restaurant, which was across from the Avalon, delivered meals by electric model trains to each table. A fellow named Ed owned the place; his mother-in-law was the cashier.

Sara Lee Bakery–across from Wee Folks

Junker's Butcher Shop (across from the Avalon Theater) was owned by Fred Junker.

A **parking lot** for the Avalon, just east of the theater at 79th and East End, was run by a relative of Pete Paisano, the theater manager.

Equitable Savings and Loan–79th and East End
William Fleck Real Estate–79th and East End
Sun TV (79th and Cornell) was owned by Merle Spinks and later became a
 bakery.
Joe Biggleys Tavern–79th and Cornell
The Avalon Theater (1645 East 79th) was the pride of 79th Street with its
 mysterious Moorish-temple ambiance. Many South Shoreites remember this theater and its 3-D movies, plus the great Wee Folks giveaways.
 There were several secret places, like a downstairs dressing room, where
 ushers would "entertain" their girlfriends while on duty. The main bal-
 cony was closed for years; smaller balconies were open along the second
 level, like boxes in an opera house. The Avalon became Miracle Temple
 in the 1970s when the owners of Johnson Products, who named it the
 Regal Theater, purchased it. It closed in 2003.
Dr. Morton Mills, a physician, had his offices next door to the Avalon and
 up the stairs.
Comb and Shear Barbershop–a couple of doors west of the Avalon
Phillips Real Estate–near the Avalon
Pearson's Grocery Store was owned by Loren Pearson.
Pete's Karmelkorn and Sweet Shop (79th and East End) was owned by
 Pete Berchos, a Greek immigrant who lived around the corner from the
 shop. Pete's was a frequent stop for loading up on popcorn and penny
 candy before going to the movies next door at the Avalon. These goodies had to be smuggled into the theater. Pete would put all your selections into a brightly colored bag and write the cost on the outside after
 making the calculations in his head. His daughter's name was Christina.
Frank Sylvano's Restaurant was just west of the Avalon and in later years
 moved down to 91st and Stony Island.

***Spots going west between Cornell and Stony Island (1650–1600 East
 79th Street)***
Dart Cleaners–1630 East 79th
Gateway Restaurant–1626 East 79th
Chatterbox Restaurant (1622 East 79th) had a 4:00 a.m. license.
Bob the Barber's Barbershop–1620 East 79th
Dr. Otto DDS (79th & Stony Island) ran his office on the second floor above
 the drugstore on this corner.
Gateway National Bank (7853 South Stony Island) was where most of the
 merchants banked. It was later called the **Southmoor Bank.**
Vacuum Repair Shop (on Stony Island) was famed for the owner's dog
 that, it was rumored, could bark its master's name: P-O-R-K-Y!
Walgreens–79th and Stony Island
McFadden Liquors (79th and Stony Island) was frequented by CTA bus
 drivers and police officers directing traffic on Stony Island.

The Kickapoo Inn (7901 South Chicago Avenue) was at the corner of 79ᵗʰ where Stony Island met South Chicago Avenue. Other than Phil Schmidt's in Whiting, Indiana, the Kickapoo was the only restaurant I knew that served frog legs.

Streeter's News Stand (on Stony Island outside of the Kickapoo) was run by Mark and Phil Streeter, who also booked horses. "Crippled Johnny" worked there during the week and Mark and Phil worked it on weekends.

Peanut Store (79ᵗʰ and Stony Island) sold bags of hot, freshly cooked peanuts. We would share some with the pigeons and bring the rest into the Avalon.

The White Cottage Restaurant–79ᵗʰ and Stony Island

Bigley's Restaurant and Bar (79ᵗʰ and Stony Island) later became a currency exchange.

Shore Bakery (79ᵗʰ and East End)

Smitty's Meat Market used ration stamps during the war.

Chatterbox Lounge–between Stony Island and Cornell down from Walgreens.

Miscellany

In addition to a **uniform shop,** an **embroidery store,** and **a record store** where the new Top 20 list would come out each Friday, these are former stores in South Shore for which I could find no specific address:

Acme Cycle was also known as **Tink's Hobby Shop.**

Avalon Bakery

Bill's Supermarket, where the owner would total up your order by running his fingers across the merchandise at the checkout (and, after officially ringing up the bill, was rarely off by more than 10 cents).

Chris & Kay's Restaurant

Fannie May Candies

Lambert Paint and Wallpaper, owned by Joy Lambert.

Marx Tailor Shop, whose owner came from Cuba.

Mary Dee Corsetieres

Regerio's Shoe Repair, or, as it was known on the street, Jimmy the Shoe's.

The Vera Shop

Volk Furniture, on the north side of 79ᵗʰ.

APPENDIX II

Toy Stories

"It's kind of fun to do the impossible."—Walt Disney

Thousands of toys were sold at Wee Folks during our quarter-century in business. What follows are brief summaries of how some of those toys came to be invented. Background information about the toys came from a multitude of Web sites, many of which are listed at the end of the appendix. Especially helpful was the Strong Museum and its National Toy Hall of Fame. Enjoy this blast back to the past!

TOY: jacks
STORY: Jacks is one of the world's oldest games, dating back to ancient Egypt when animal bones and a wooden ball were used as the game pieces.

TOY: marbles
STORY: In ancient Egypt, Greece, and Rome, people played with marbles made of stone or clay. Alabaster marbles were the norm before glass marbles became popular (and affordable) in the nineteenth century.

TOY: balloons
STORY: Balloons made of rubber were first used in 1824 by Michael Faraday, who invented them for his hydrogen experiments at the Royal Institution in London.

TOY: alphabet blocks
STORY: Heeding philosopher John Locke's advice that playthings should be educational, a nineteenth-century museum curator who pioneered the idea of kindergarten introduced wooden alphabet blocks, which looked then as they do today.

TOY: jump rope
STORY: Children jumped rope as early as the seventeenth century. Girls often jumped along to rhyming songs. The activity has become a competitive sport, featuring multiple ropes and rope-spinning techniques.

TOY: bicycles

STORY: Bicycles were considered speedy transportation in the nineteenth century until the automobile came along. Kids' bikes were manufactured after World War I, with Schwinn debuting its Excelsior Cruiser in 1933. Heavy one-speed bikes evolved into sleek multiple-gear racers and dirt bikes, while the stationary fitness bike has been updated for use in spinning classes.

TOY: jigsaw puzzle

STORY: Eighteenth-century cartographer John Spilsbury is credited with mounting a map on hardwood and cutting around the countries to create individual pieces to be reassembled. Puzzles became commercially popular after the Civil War. By the end of the 1800s, cardboard replaced wood in puzzle-making; modern puzzles are die-cut. Early manufacturers included Milton Bradley and Parker Brothers.

TOY: Steiff Bears

STORY: In 1879, Margarette Steiff made toy elephants as gifts, then added poodles, donkeys, and bears to her menagerie. Her Steiff bears became popular in 1903 after their debut at a German toy show. The bears, which feature jointed arms and legs and a trademark ear button, decorated the tables at the wedding of Teddy Roosevelt's daughter, Alice.

TOY: roller skates/Rollerblades

STORY: Skates featured James Plimpton's easy-turning wheels in 1863, followed by skates that clamped onto shoes. Although most towns in the 1870s had skating rinks, baby boomers made roller-skating a popular pastime. In 1979, hockey player Scott Olsen designed the Rollerblade, with wheels placed in a straight line under hard boots.

TOY: teddy bear

STORY: On a 1902 hunting trip, President Theodore Roosevelt's staff captured a black bear cub for him to shoot. Roosevelt set it free, which gave New Yorker Morris Michton a marketing idea. After getting the president's permission to use his name, Michton hand-sewed his "Teddy" bears, displayed them in his toy store window, and founded the Ideal Toy Company.

TOY: Raggedy Ann

STORY: Johnny Gruelle made a rag doll for his daughter, Marcella. He named the doll Raggedy Ann in honor of two James Whitcomb Riley poems, "The Raggedy Man" and "Little Orphan Annie." Gruelle handcrafted and sold the dolls in 1918 and featured her in a children's book.

Raggedy Andy followed in 1920. Today, Simon and Schuster owns the Raggedy Ann story, and Hasbro sells the floppy dolls with red yarn hair and striped cloth pants.

TOY: Crayola Crayons
STORY: In 1903 the Binney & Smith Company added colored pigments to paraffin wax to create a coloring crayon. The company began selling a set of eight Crayola Crayons for a nickel. The line now includes crayons, markers, colored pencils, paints, and modeling compounds.

TOY: Monopoly
STORY: Invented by Elizabeth Magie in 1904, "The Landlord's Game" developed into a game whose objective was to amass as much cash and property as possible. It flopped. In 1933, engineer Charles Darrow created a spin-off of the game on oilcloth and sold handmade sets of Monopoly for $4. Parker Brothers bought the rights in 1935.

TOY: Lincoln Logs
STORY: John Lloyd Wright, son of architect Frank Lloyd Wright, invented a toy for making log houses in 1916 on a visit to Tokyo. His inspiration? The construction of the earthquake-proof Imperial Hotel his father had designed. The invention, now made by Playskool, is named for Abraham Lincoln, who grew up in a log cabin.

TOY: Magic Slate
STORY: In the early 1920s, a fellow approached Illinois printer R. A. Watkins to sell him the rights to a new toy. The toy was made of waxed cardboard topped by a piece of tissue upon which a message was written. When the tissue was lifted, the message was erased. Watkins said he'd think about it. The fellow called the next day from jail, saying that if Watkins bailed him out, he could have the device. Watkins's Magic Slate was born, now manufactured by Golden Books Publishing.

TOY: Slinky
STORY: Marine engineer Richard James decided he could make a toy out of a torsion spring he tested as an antivibration device for World War II ship meters. Steel alloy allowed his spring to flip end over end as if walking. James debuted the toy, which his wife named Slinky, at Gimbles Department Store in 1945, selling more than 400 in ninety minutes.

TOY: Erector Set
STORY: A. C. Gilbert, a physician, Olympic medallist, and toy inventor, came up with the idea of the Erector Set while watching skyscrapers

being built. Gilbert introduced the toy in 1913 and subsequently served as the first president of the Toy Manufacturers Association.

TOY: LEGO
STORY: Danish carpenter Ole Christiansen created a set of interlocking blocks and named them LEGO (*leg godt* means "play well" in Danish). In 1958, the LEGO Company patented the blocks, which make thousands of configurations when kids add LEGO cars, street maps, trains, and more into their play.

TOY: View-Master
STORY: This updated version of the nineteenth-century stereoscope was the brainchild of Harold Graves, president of Sawyer's Photographic Services, and photographer William Gruber. The View-Master first offered 3-D images of scenery. In 1951, after buying out Tru-Vue and its stereo rights to Disney characters, View-Master made slide reels of Disneyland attractions, Disney movies, and Disney TV programs, as well as other popular children's movies and TV shows.

TOY: Tonka Trucks
STORY: When their efforts to make and sell garden tools failed, a group of Minnesota teachers made toy trucks with the leftover materials. In 1947, they named them Tonka Trucks, after a Sioux word. The durable metal trucks were a hit in the post-rationing years after WWII. Hasbro manufactures the toys, recognized by their bright yellow paint.

TOY: Tootsietoys
STORY: Die-cast toy cars debuted in 1906 when the Dowst Brothers Company of Chicago made a miniature Model T Ford. They called the cars Tootsietoys, named after "Toots," one of the brothers' granddaughters. Strombecker manufactures Tootsietoys.

TOY: Cootie
STORY: Cootie debuted in 1948, the invention of a postman who originally carved an insect's body and removable legs out of wood. Milton Bradley acquired Cootie in 1987.

TOY: Silly Putty
STORY: During WWII, when rubber was rationed, alternatives were experimented with. One substitute was considered a failure because it bounced. The material ended up in a New Haven toy shop, where it became Silly Putty in 1950. Binney & Smith is the manufacturer.

TOY: Mr. Potato Head

STORY: New Yorker Charles Lerner invented Mr. Funny Face, a set of pins shaped like eyes, feet, hands, and noses that kids pushed into a potato or other vegetables to make silly faces. In 1952, his idea debuted as Mr. Potato Head by Hasbro. The popular toy was the first to be advertised on television.

TOY: Yahtzee

STORY: In 1956, a Canadian couple introduced friends to a dice game aboard their yacht. They approached Bingo millionaire Edwin S. Lowe to print up a few games as gifts. Lowe bought the rights and changed the game's name to Yahtzee. Milton Bradley has manufactured the game since 1973.

TOY: Play-Doh

STORY: Joe McVicker made a pliable, nontoxic modeling compound for a nursery-school teacher, and her pupils loved it. McVicker showcased his product at the 1955 National Education Conference and by 1956 Play-Doh was on the market, manufactured by Hasbro. The multicolored compound evolved into glitter and glow-in-the-dark varieties.

TOY: Robbie the Robot

STORY: Robbie the Robot was the real star of *Forbidden Planet,* the 1954 sci-fi classic featuring Leslie Nielsen. Kids coveted the thirteen-inch battery-operated toy version of Robbie when it debuted soon after the movie's release.

TOY: Hula Hoop

STORY: Modeled after a toy from ancient Egypt, Greece, and Rome and fourteenth-century England, the Hula Hoop was first manufactured by Wham-O in 1958. The brightly colored plastic hoop was originally made of wood and intended for use by Australian health nuts.

TOY: Matchbox Cars

STORY: Jack Odell created the original Matchbox Cars in 1952 by casting a tiny brass prototype of a Road Roller and putting it into a matchbox-size container. As popular now as they were then, various models of the miniature cars—made by Mattel—still sell for less than a dollar.

TOY: Frisbee

STORY: Back in the late 1800s, Yale University students tossed pie tins around campus for recreation, yelling "Frisbee" to warn bystanders to duck as the tins—made by the Frisbee Baking Company—flew by. Two inventors started selling the discs at county fairs in 1948, and in 1958 Wham-O bought the rights to the toy and named it the Frisbee. After Mattel bought Wham-O in the early 1960s, the company made professional Frisbees.

TOY: Etch-a-Sketch

STORY: Invented by a French garage mechanic in 1960 and made by Ohio Art, this special screen sports two knobs that turn to make line drawings. The picture is erased by shaking the toy upside down.

TOY: Colorforms

STORY: Colorforms was born in 1951 when art students Harry and Patricia Kislevitz found a way to decorate their apartment walls inexpensively and temporarily. They experimented with vinyl shapes that would stick to walls in colorful geometric patterns until they wanted to pull them off. Budding artists use Colorforms the same way to create art.

TOY: Tinkertoys

STORY: Inspired by watching children poke sticks into spools of thread, stonemason Charles Pajeau started his Toy Tinker's Company in 1914 in Evanston, Illinois, to make building toys. More than one million sets sold the first year. By the 1950s, Tinkertoys boasted colored sticks.

TOY: Radio Flyer

STORY: By day Italian immigrant Antonio Pasin worked as a manual laborer in Chicago. By night, he built wooden red wagons to sell on the side. In 1923 he founded the Liberty Coaster Company, named for the New York harbor statue, and in 1930 began mass-producing the wagons out of stamped metal. The name Radio Flyer reflects the era's fascination with radio and flight. Radio High Sides, for carting kids, were added in the 1950s.

TOY: Yo-Yos

STORY: Although its roots go back to ancient Greece, Americans first heard the word "yo-yo" in the 1920s when Filipino bellhop Pedro Flores was spotted playing with the toy on his lunch hour. ("Yo-yo" means "come back" in the Tagalog language of the Philippines.) Flores mass-produced Yo-Yos until 1928 when he was bought out by Donald Duncan, father of the Good Humor Company. Sales boomed in the 1950s and 1960s with promotional contests. Duncan's looped slip-string model led to tricks like "Shoot the Moon" and "Walk the Dog." Other companies have manufactured the toy, but Duncan was the most successful.

TOY: Little Golden Books

STORY: Little Golden Books cost a quarter apiece when Random House launched the series in 1942. Although the publisher faced a WWII paper shortage, the low-cost, high-quality books became an instant success with titles written by Margaret Wise Brown (author of *Goodnight Moon*) and Richard Scarry and illustrated by Garth Williams of *Charlotte's Web* fame. Little Golden Books have also featured kids' cultural icons such as Lassie, Roy Rogers and Dale Evans, and Smokey the Bear.

TOY: Twister

STORY: While developing a design promotion for Johnson's shoe polish, Reyn Guyer saw a way to use the polka dot paper mat he created as a game in which humans used their bodies as playing pieces. Milton Bradley debuted the game in 1966.

TOY: Lionel trains

STORY: When seven-year-old Joshua Lionel Cowen whittled a miniature wood locomotive and fitted it with a steam engine, it exploded. Years later, when he fitted a small motor under a model railroad flatcar, the electric train was born. Using his middle name, he called it the Lionel train, and in 1901 he assembled a train set with a flatcar and thirty feet of track. Cattle cars, passenger trains, stations, tunnels, and coal cars soon followed. By 1910, electric trains were big business.

TOY: Scrabble

STORY: In 1931, architect and crossword puzzle fan Alfred Butts created an anagram game called Criss Cross that he gave away as gifts. James Brunot received one of those gifts and decided in 1948 to produce them in his Connecticut home. He stamped letters onto wooden tiles, added boards and boxes, and by 1952 was deluged with orders for his Scrabble game. Hasbro manufactures the game today.

TOY: Mousegetar

STORY: Mattel introduced a child-size guitar called a Mousegetar in 1955, the same year the company bought a year's worth of TV advertising on the new "Mickey Mouse Club" show. The fourteen-inch model made in 1957 played the Mickey Mouse Mouseketeer song when the crank was turned.

TOY: SuperBall

STORY: California chemist Norman Stingley compressed a synthetic rubber material to create an exceptionally resilient ball. In 1965, Wham-O manufactured Stingley's ball as the SuperBall, which bounced over rooftops and ricocheted between walls after hitting the ground just once.

TOY: Nerf Ball

STORY: When an inventor brought his idea for an indoor volleyball game to Parker Brothers in 1969, the company simplified the concept and created the Nerf Ball, a soft polyurethane toy, for indoor play.

TOY: Tammy Doll

STORY: The Ideal Toy Corporation introduced the blond teenaged Tammy Doll in 1962. Touted as "the doll you love to dress," she wore a blue playsuit and white tennis shoes, and had a wardrobe that teenaged girls coveted for themselves. She stood twelve inches high, had poseable limbs, and was one of the few dolls available in an African American version. Her family included Mom, Dad, brothers Ted and Pete, sister Pepper, friends Patti, Dodi, and Salty, boyfriend Bud, and pal Misty. Grown Up Tammy debuted in 1965. Oprah Winfrey has said this was one of her favorite dolls.

TOY: Thingmaker

STORY: Mattel created the Thingmaker series in the 1960s, starting with Creepy Crawlers. Thingmaker sets included a molding machine, several molds and bottles of Plastigoop, and various ornaments. Mini-Dragons, Zoofie Goofies, Fun Flowers, Creeple Peeple, and other Thingmaker sets are designed to form bigger toys out of completed pieces.

TOY: Hot Wheels

STORY: In 1967, Mattel cofounder Elliot Handler added axles and low-friction Styrofoam wheels to a standard die-cast model car. By its thirtieth anniversary, the Hot Wheels series had produced two billion cars, more than Detroit's Big Three combined.

TOY: G.I. Joe

STORY: Stanley Weston created a doll for boys in 1965 based on a new TV show called "The Lieutenant." Hasbro's G.I. Joe outlasted the series. The female G.I. Joe was introduced years later, but was a bust.

FAMOUS TOY MAKERS

Mattel

In 1945, Harold Matson and Elliot Handler founded the Mattel Toy Corporation, an enterprise that combined Harold's last name and Elliot's first. They initially made picture frames, but Elliot began a side business of making dollhouse furniture from picture frame scraps. Matson sold out to Elliot and his wife, Ruth Handler, who expanded Mattel's product line into toys exclusively. Hundreds of products later, their recognizable logo appears on such memorable toys as **See 'n Say, Angelina Ballerina, Magic 8 Balls, Masters of the Universe, Little Kiddles, Greenie Stik-M Caps,** and **Fanner 50 guns,** as well as **Hot Wheels** and **Barbie American Girl.**

Marvin Glass Studio

Seventy-five people worked at the downtown Chicago offices of the Marvin Glass Studio, an amazingly prolific company. Marvin Glass's first inventions in 1949 were a **Pocket Theater, Yakity-Yak Teeth,** and a chicken that laid a gumball egg. The Marvin Glass logo on the boxes represented the only toy designer to receive such credit on manufactured items. Some of the toys Marvin Glass designed in the 1960s included **Mr. Machine, Robot Commando, Odd Ogg, Mousetrap, King of the Hill, Rock 'em Sock 'em Robots, Mystery Date, Operation, Clean Sweep, Lite Brite, Bucket of Fun, Sand Lot Slugger, Oh Nuts, Toss Across,** and **Ants in the Pants.**

TOY WEB SITES

www.antiquetoys.com
www.areyougame.com
www.barbiecollectibles.com
www.bigredtoybox.com
www.dazzasbikes.freeserve.co.uk
www.dolls4play.com
www.drtoy.com
www.hasbro.com
www.historychannel.com
www.ideafinder.com
http://inventors.about.com
www.mastercollector.com
www.mattel.com
www.randomhouse.com
www.shareholder.com
www.spookshows.com (Marvin Glass Studio employee recollections)
www.strongmuseum.org

www.the-robotman.com
www.toysngames.com
www.worldhistory.com
www.yo-yo.com

BOOKS

Lucky Meisenheimer, *Lucky's Collectors Guide to 20th Century Yo-Yos: History and Values* (Lucky J S Swim & Surf, 1999).

Notes

CHAPTER 7

1. John R. Fry, *Locked-Out Americans: A Memoir* (New York: Harper & Row, 1973), http://gangresearch.net/Archives/hagedorn/rethinkcrim/chapters/Hagedorn1.htm, April 21, 2004.

2. George W. Knox, "Gang Profile Update: The Black P Stone Nation (BPSN)," www.ngcrc.com/BPSN2003.html, April 22, 2004.

3. Knox, "Gang Profile Update."

4. Lance Williams, "The Almighty Black P Stone Nation: Black Power, Politics, and Gangbanging," lecture given at University of Illinois at Chicago, School of Public Health, transcribed October 18, 2001, revised by Lance Williams, February 12, 2002, www.uic.edu/orgs/kbc/ganghistory/UrbanCrisis/Blackstone/lance.htm, April 12, 2004.

5. R. T. Sale, *The Blackstone Rangers: A Reporter's Account of Time Spent with Blackstone Rangers in Chicago's South Side* (New York: Random House, 1971), pp. 63–64; www.ngcrc.com/BPSN2003.html, April 21, 2004.

6. Knox, "Gang Profile Update."

7. Williams, "The Almighty Black P Stone Nation."

8. Fry, *Locked-Out Americans.*

9. Knox, "Gang Profile Update."

10. Williams, "The Almighty Black P Stone Nation."

11. www.muhammadspeaks.com

12. Fry, *Locked-Out Americans.*

13. "The Chronology of the Life and Activities of Malcolm X," www.brothermalcolm.net/mxtimeline.html, October 30, 2003.

14. The Nation of Islam, Religious Movements, http://religiousmovements.lib.virginia.edu/nrms/Nofislam.html, April 8, 2004.

15. The Nation of Islam, Religious Movements.

16. The Nation of Islam, Religious Movements.

17. Claude A. Clegg III, "Message from the Wilderness of North America: Elijah Muhammad and the Nation of Islam," *Journal*

for Multimedia History 1 (fall 1998), www.albany.edu/jmmh/vol1no1/elijahmuhammad.html, April 24, 2004.

18. Elijah Muhammad, "Message to the Black Man in America," Elijah Muhammad, "Radio talk," WNTA (New York), November 23, 1960, www.albany.edu/jmmh/vol1no1/elijahmuhammad. html, April 23, 2004.

19. Audrey Bottjen, "A Nation Divided," student paper, North Carolina School of Science and Mathematics, November 24, 1997, http://192.154.43.167/history/religion/research/bottjen.html.

20. Bottjen, "A Nation Divided."

21. Bottjen, "A Nation Divided."

22. Stefan Linz, "Martin Luther King and Malcolm X," March 1997, http://stud3.tuwien.ac.at/~e9902644/doc/malcolmx.htm#Malcolm%20X, April 23, 2004.

23. Malcolm X Homepage, www.tcnj.edu/~may3/Malcolm%20X%20Paper, April 23, 2004.

24. Nation of Islam, "Who Are These People and What Do They Believe In?" www.godulike.co.uk/faiths.php?chapter=69&subject=who, October 28, 2002.

25. www.tcnj.edu/~may3/Malcolm%20X%20PaperMalcolm X, April 23, 2004.

26. Malcolm X, www.spartacus.schoolnet.co.uk/USAmalcolmX. htm, April 23, 2004.

27. Linz, "Martin Luther King and Malcolm X."

28. Eric Pement, "Louis Farrakhan, and the Nation of Islam," part 1 of 2, first published in *Cornerstone Magazine,* from *The Autobiography of Malcolm X,* p. 183, www.cornerstonemag.com/archives/iss111.htm, April 20, 2004.

29. www.tcnj.edu/~may3/Malcolm%20X%20PaperMalcolm X, April 23, 2004.

30. Malcolm X, www.spartacus.schoolnet.co.uk/USAmalcolmX. htm, April 23, 2004.

31. Linz, "Martin Luther King and Malcolm X."

32. www.tcnj.edu/~may3/Malcolm%20X%20PaperMalcolm X, April 23, 2004.

33. The Official Web Site of Malcolm X, www.cmgww.com/historic/malcolm/about/bio2.htm, April 25, 2004.

34. www.tcnj.edu/~may3/Malcolm%20X%20PaperMalcolm X, April 23, 2004.

35. www.tcnj.edu/~may3/Malcolm%20X%20PaperMalcolm X, April 23, 2004.

36. Mike Grogan, "The Enemy Within," www.thecallbox.com/mg_art23.htm, April 12, 2004.

37. Jay Rogers, "Louis Farrakhan," www.forerunner.com/forerunner/X0065_Nation_of_Islam.html, April 27, 2004.

38. Profile: "Louis Farrakhan," March 12, 2002, http://news.bbc.co.uk/1/hi/uk/1868328.stm, April 23, 2004.

39. Rogers, "Louis Farrakhan."

40. Martin Luther King, http://stud3.tuwien.ac.at/~e9902644/doc/malcolmx.htm.

41. Malcolm X, "The Ballot or the Bullet," speech delivered April 3, 1964, in Cleveland, Ohio, www.americanrhetoric.com/speeches/malcolmxballot.htm, April 23, 2004.

42. Alex Haley, interview with Malcolm X, *Playboy,* May 1963, www.unix-ag.uni-kl.de/~moritz/Archive/malcolmx/malcolmx.playboy.pdf, April 23, 2004.

43. www.tcnj.edu/~may3/Malcolm%20X%20PaperMalcolm X, April 23, 2004.

44. Rogers, "Louis Farrakhan."

45. "Gangs: Public Enemy Number One: 75 Years of Fighting Crime in Chicagoland," Report of the Chicago Crime Commission, 1995, www.velocity.net/~acekc/CCC%20Gang%20Book%20-%20Main%20Text.htm, April 14. 2004.

46. William Robertson Boggs, "The Late Great American City," June 1991, American Renaissance, www.amren.com/916issue/916issue.html, April 26, 2004.

47. Boggs, "The Late Great American City."

48. Euseni Eugene Perkins, "African American Gangs of the 1940s, Talk to the Chicago Gangs History Project," lecture given February 21, 2002, http://gangresearch.net/ChicagoGangs/gangs&ghetto/Perkins.htm, April 23, 2004.

49. Perkins, "African American Gangs of the 1940s, Talk to the Chicago Gangs History Project."

50. "When Millionaires Funded Gangs," undated article (ca. 1970s?) reprinted by the courtesy of the Chicago Historical Society,

www.uic.edu/orgs/kbc/ganghistory/Millionaires.html, April 27, 2004.

51. Rod Emery, "The History of the Gangster Disciples: In Their Own Words" (Morris Publishers), pp. 10–15, http://gangresearch. net/ChicagoGangs/BGD/bgdnhistory.html, April 17, 2004.

52. Ken Lawrence, "CLR James and the Black Panther Party," www.marxmail.org/archives/June99.htm, April 22, 2004.

53. "When Millionaires Funded Gangs."

54. Knox, "Gang Profile Update."

55. Knox, "Gang Profile Update."

56. Kate N. Grossman and Addon M. Pallasch, "Gang leader's legacy felt in mob beating case," *Chicago Sun-Times*, August 8, 2002, pp. 6–7.

57. Fry, *Locked-Out Americans.*

58. Grossman and Pallasch, "Gang leader's legacy felt in mob beating case."

59. Williams, "The Almighty Black P Stone Nation."

60. Knox, "Gang Profile Update."

61. Chicago Police Department Reports, 1951–1955.

62. Chicago Police Department Reports, 1960–1964.

63. Chicago Police Department Reports, 1951–1955.

64. Chicago Police Department Reports, 1964–1969.

65. http://gangresearch.net/ChicagoGangs/blackstonerangers/Fry/ waralafry.html.

66. Knox, "Gang Profile Update."

67. Knox, "Gang Profile Update."

68. University of Illinois at Chicago, www.uic.edu/orgs/kbc/gang history/UrbanCrisis/WaronGangs.htm, April 21, 2004.

69. Mike Houlihan, "Mt. Carmel hangs tough in Woodlawn," Chicago Sun-Times, June 2, 2002, www.sun-times.com/output/ houlihan/cst-nws-houli02.html, April 21, 2004.

70. University of Illinois at Chicago, www.uic.edu/orgs/kbc/gang history/UrbanCrisis/Blackstone/BRindex.html.

71. http://gangresearch.net/ChicagoGangs/blackstonerangers/Fry/ waralafry.html.

72. http://gangresearch.net/ChicagoGangs/BGD/bgdnhistory.html.

73. Francis Ward, "2 Biggest Youth Gangs Agree On Truce," http://gangresearch.net/ChicagoGangs/lsd/truce.html, April 17, 2004.

74. Kenneth R. Timmerman, *Shakedown: Exposing the Real Jesse Jackson* (Washington, D.C.: Regnery Publishing, Inc., 2002), p. 26.

75. Timmerman, *Shakedown*, pp. 27–29.

76. Timmerman, *Shakedown*, p. 26.

77. Timmerman, *Shakedown*, pp. 24–25.

78. Timmerman, *Shakedown*, pp. 27–28.

79. Timmerman, *Shakedown*, p. 29.

80. Timmerman, *Shakedown*, pp. 27–28.

81. Timmerman, *Shakedown*, pp. 27–29.

82. Timmerman, *Shakedown*, pp. 24–25.

83. Timmerman, *Shakedown*, p. 46.

84. Paul Sperry, "Jesse Jackson's ties to terrorists exposed," March 18, 2002, www.worldnetdaily.com, November 12, 2003.

85. Timmerman, *Shakedown*, pp. 38–39.

CHAPTER 9

1. Thomas Gunn case files, Chicago's Daley Center and Criminal Courts Building.

2. Rod Emery, *The History of the Gangster Disciples: In Their Own Words* (Morris Publishers), pp. 10–15, http://gangresearch.net/ChicagoGangs/BGD/bgdnhistory.html, April 14, 2004.

3. Kate N. Grossman and Addon M. Pallasch, "Gang leader's legacy felt in mob beating case," *Chicago Sun-Times,* August 8, 2002, pp. 6–7.

4. William Robertson Boggs, "The Late Great American City," June 1991, American Renaissance, www.amren.com/916issue/916issue.html, April 26, 2004.

5. "Street Gangs–Chicago Based or Influenced–People Nation and Folk Nation," Florida Department of Corrections, www.dc.state.fl.us/pub/gangs/chicago.html, April 17, 2004.

6. George W. Knox, "Gang Profile Update: The Black P Stone Nation (BPSN)," www.ngcrc.com/BPSN2003.html, April 22, 2004.

7. William Norman Grigg, "Weapons of Mass Insurrection," *The New American* 18 (December 2, 2002), www.thenewamerican.com, November 12, 2003.

8. Kenneth R. Timmerman, *Shakedown: Exposing the Real Jesse Jackson* (Washington, D.C.: Regnery Publishing, Inc., 2002), p. 26.

9. Author unknown, "Black P Stones," Chicago Mobs, www. freewebs.com/chicagomobs/blackpstones.html, April 13, 2004.

10. A. Idris Palmer, "Brutal Legacy," *Nida'ul Islam* (April–May 1998), www.islam.org.au/articles/23/noi2.htm, April 17, 2004.

11. Gangs, "Public Enemy No. 1," www.velocity.net/~acekc/ccc%20 Gang%20Book%20-%20Main%20Text.htm, April 14, 2004.

12. "Bomb and Arson Crimes among American Gang Members: A Behavioral Science Profile," a special report by the National Gang Crime Research Center, www.ngcrc.com/bombarso.html, April 21, 2004.

13. Author unknown, "Black P Stones," Chicago Mobs, www. freewebs.com/chicagomobs/blackpstones.html, April 13, 2004.

14. "Warith Deen Muhammad," adapted from entry submitted to *Encyclopedia of American Religion and Politics,* 2002, http://home. att.net/~spmckee/people_muhammadwd.html, April 17, 2004. (Note: the Muslim American Society mentioned here is not the same group as the Muslim American Society based in Falls Church, Virginia.)

15. "Nation of Islam," Religious Movements, http://religiousmovements. lib.virginia.edu/nrms/Nofislam.html, created by Jan Dodoo with special thanks to Loryn Lawson, who created an earlier version of this page for Soc 452, "Sociology of Religious Movements," Spring Term, 2000, University of Virginia, last modified May 29, 2001.

16. Eric Pement, "Louis Farrakhan and the Nation of Islam," part 1 of 2, first published in *Cornerstone Magazine* 26: 111 (1997), pp. 10–16, 20, www.cornerstonemag.com/features/iss111/islam1. htm, April 17, 2004. *Cornerstone Magazine* is aka Jesus People USA, Evangelical Covenant Church.

17. Eric Pement, "Louis Farrakhan and the Nation of Islam."

18. Eric Pement, "Louis Farrakhan and the Nation of Islam."

19. The Nation of Islam, http://religiousmovements.lib.virginia.edu/ nrms/Nofislam.html, April 8, 2004.

Additional Bibliographic Resources

The following resources were used in addition to those cited in the notes for Chapters 7 and 9. A separate bibliography accompanies Appendix II (Toy Stories).

Bedarida, Francois, and Forster, A. S. (trans.). *A Social History of England: 1851–1975.* London, New York: Methuen & Company, Ltd., 1979.

Berk, Stephen M. *Year of Crisis, Year of Hope: Russian Jewry and the Pogroms of 1881–1882.* Westpoint, Connecticut: Greenwood Press, 1985.

Black, Timuel. "The History of African American Gangs in Chicago." Address at the Undergraduate Research Conference on Gangs, University of Illinois at Chicago, November 9, 2000. www.uic.edu/orgs/kbc/ganghistory/TimuelBlackx.html.

Buckley, Tom. "The Battle of Chicago: From the Yippies' Side." *New York Times Magazine,* September 15, 1968.

Crouch, Stanley. "U.S.'s Own Powder Keg: Convicts and Converts." *Jewish World Review,* June 14, 2002.

Cutler, Irving. *The Jews of Chicago: From Shtetl to Suburb.* Urbana, Illinois: University of Illinois Press, 1996.

Drell, Adrienne, ed. *Twentieth Century Chicago: 100 Years, 100 Voices.* Champaign, Illinois: Sports Publishing Company, 2000.

Fry, John R. *Fire and Blackstone.* Philadelphia: J. B. Lippincott Company, 1969.

Hageman, William. "Ali's Chicago Stories." *Chicago Tribune,* December 21, 2001.

Hamm, Michael F. *Kiev: A Portrait: 1800–1917.* Princeton, New Jersey: Princeton University Press, 1993.

Hanania, Ray. "Midnight Flight: The Story of White Flight in Chicago's Southeast Side." Hanania Enterprises, 2001. www.hanania.com/hanania.htm.

Hauser, Thomas. *Muhammad Ali, His Life and Times.* New York: Simon & Schuster, 1991.

Hirsch, Arnold R. *Making the Second Ghetto: Race and Housing in Chicago 1940–1960*. Chicago: University of Chicago, 1998.

Messinger, Gary S. *Manchester in the Victorian Age: The Half-known City*. Manchester, United Kingdom: Manchester University Press, 1985.

Rosen, Louis. *The South Side: The Racial Transformation of an American Neighborhood*. Chicago: Ivan R. Dee, 1998.

Schlesinger, Arthur M. Jr., and Israel, Fred, eds. *The Russian People in 1914*. Chronicles from *National Geographic*. Philadelphia: Chelsea House Publishers, 2000.

Short, James F. Jr. "Gang Research in Chicago." Presentation at the Chicago Gang History Undergraduate Research Conference, November 9, 2000.

Sterling, Robert E. *Joliet: A Pictorial History*. St. Louis, Missouri: G Bradley Publishing, second publishing, 1988.

Thane, Pat. *Cassell's Companion to Twentieth-Century Britain*. London: Cassell & Company, 2001.

Turner, Richard Brent. *Islam in the African-American Experience*. Bloomington, Indiana: Indiana University Press, 1997.

Web sites

www.ganginformation.com

www.uic.edu/orgs/kbc/ganghistory/UrbanCrisis/Blackstone/BRindex.html

www.uic.edu/orgs/kbc

www.knowgangs.com/gang_resources/black_p_stone/blackpstonenation_001.htm

www.malcolm-x.org/speeches/chickensroost.htm

www.knowgangs.com

www.ngcrc.com/N_4_

www.soulofamerica.com/cityfldr/chicago2.html

Contributors

COVER DESIGNER MITCHELL A. MARKOVITZ was born and raised on Chicago's South Side. He was educated at the American Academy of Art, Chicago, and the Chicago Academy of Fine Art. He is a professional commercial illustrator, art director, and fine artist based in Knox, Indiana, and known for his true-to-life poster campaigns. Among his successes are "Starke Beauty," a poster campaign for the Starke County, Indiana, Tourism Commission; "At the Shore," a series of travel/advertising posters for Atlantic City, New Jersey; and, in 1990, his "Subway Series" in the New York City Transit Museum. He is noted for his "Just Around the Corner" poster series on life in Northwest Indiana, a continuation of the South Shore Line poster series, also on life in Northwest Indiana. Markovitz illustrated and coauthored the book *Moonlight in Duneland,* an anthology of the advertising art of the Chicago South Shore and South Bend Railroad. He served as advertising director and chief illustrator for the South Shore Railroad from 1984 until 2001. His works are featured in the corporate collections of Walt Disney, Nisource, Inc., Lake Erie Land Company, Businessman's Insurance Corporation, BP, Atlantic City Convention and Visitors Authority, and Valparaiso University. Markovitz's art appears on the cover of *The Pied Piper of South Shore,* as do his line drawings in the book.

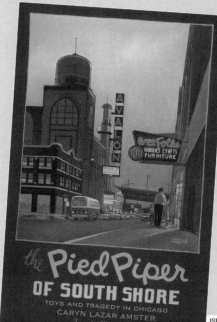

the **Pied Piper**
OF SOUTH SHORE
TOYS AND TRAGEDY IN CHICAGO
CARYN LAZAR AMSTER
Foreword by Mandy Patinkin

This true crime memoir of Chicago toy storeowner, Manny Lazar, known as the Pied Piper of South Shore, is set in Chicago's South Shore neighborhood in the 50's and 60's. It is the story of the life and death of this beloved retailer told in gritty detail by his elder daughter.

The author takes readers from Russian persecution to American freedom, from Hula Hoops to hit men, from murder to trial. It's the story of two children of immigrants, their American dream, and their richly diverse neighborhood in which each fell prey to the brutality of gangs. It is the story of loss and survival, even forgiveness.

A foreword by Mandy Patinkin, a long time customer, thanks Mr. and Mrs. Lazar for providing a place to dream.

Two appendices reveal how the most popular toys of the 50's and 60's got their start and recall the stores along 79th Street in South Shore.

The book cover created by Mitch Markovitz is available for sale as posters and fine art prints. A portion of the book proceeds will be donated to Women's American ORT.

ISBN 0-9758928-0-0
304 Pages

ORDER FORM

the **Pied Piper**
OF SOUTH SHORE
TOYS AND TRAGEDY IN CHICAGO

Books, Posters, Limited Edition Fine Art Prints

Book available September 2004. Posters and Fine Art Prints available NOW!

Order securely online at
www.chicagospiedpiper.com

or mail form with check or credit card information to:
CMA Marketing Group, Inc.,
P.O. Box 366F,
Medinah, Illinois 60157-0366

Call Toll free: 866-50-PIPER (74737)

Name:

Street Address:

City, State, Zip:

Phone Number:

Email Address: (optional)

Visa/Master Card/Discover
(circle one)

Credit Card Number:

Expiration Date:

Description	Qty	Total Price
Pied Piper Books - 304 Pages - $19.95 each plus $5 Shipping/Handling (sent FEDX Ground) - add $1.00 for each add'l book		
Full Color Posters (24" x 33") of the book cover - $29.95 each plus $7.50 S/H for up to 5 posters to the same address. Add $.75 for each additional poster sent to each address. Posters will be shipped from a separate location.		
Special Limited Edition Fine Art Prints (20" x 30") of the book cover without the text - $350.00 each - 150 copies signed and numbered with certificate of authenticity (shipped flat and overnight only – add $45 for S/H)		

See website for our return policy.

Total Merchandise	
8.5% Sales Tax (IL residents only)	
Shipping/Handling	
Amount Total	

This true crime memoir of Chicago toy storeowner, Manny Lazar, known as the Pied Piper of South Shore, is set in Chicago's South Shore neighborhood in the 50's and 60's. It is the story of the life and death of this beloved retailer told in gritty detail by his elder daughter.

The author takes readers from Russian persecution to American freedom, from Hula Hoops to hit men, from murder to trial. It's the story of two children of immigrants, their American dream, and their richly diverse neighborhood in which each fell prey to the brutality of gangs. It is the story of loss and survival, even forgiveness.

A foreword by Mandy Patinkin, a long time customer, thanks Mr. and Mrs. Lazar for providing a place to dream.

Two appendices reveal how the most popular toys of the 50's and 60's got their start and recall the stores along 79th Street in South Shore.

The book cover created by Mitch Markovitz is available for sale as posters and fine art prints. A portion of the book proceeds will be donated to Women's American ORT.

ISBN 0-9758928-0-0
304 Pages